SO-ALI-223

THE END OF THE BEGINNING

BY THE RIGHT HON.
WINSTON S. CHURCHILL

THE UNRELENTING STRUGGLE
THE END OF THE BEGINNING

THE END OF THE
BEGINNING

————— *War Speeches by the* —————

RIGHT HON.
WINSTON S. CHURCHILL
C.H., M.P.

Compiled by CHARLES EADE

TORONTO
McCLELLAND AND STEWART LIMITED
1943

COPYRIGHT 1943, BY WINSTON S. CHURCHILL

ALL RIGHTS RESERVED, INCLUDING THE RIGHT
TO REPRODUCE THIS BOOK OR PORTIONS
THEREOF IN ANY FORM

FIRST EDITION

Published August 1943

PRINTED IN THE UNITED STATES OF AMERICA

"This is not the end. It is not even the beginning of the end. But it is, perhaps, the end of the beginning."

MR. WINSTON S. CHURCHILL AT THE LORD MAYOR'S DAY LUNCHEON AT THE MANSION HOUSE, LONDON. *November 10, 1942.*

Introduction

As the year 1942 dawned on a war-stricken world the Rt. Hon. Winston S. Churchill, Prime Minister of Great Britain, was travelling by train from Ottawa to Washington to resume his conferences with Franklin D. Roosevelt, President of the United States of America. Their deliberations ranged over the four quarters of the globe. The shadow of war had spread across all Continents.

On that New Year's Day, the armies of the Union of Soviet Socialist Republics still persevered in their counter-offensive against the Germans — a recovery which had amazed the world after months of heroic retreat and appalling losses. Great territories of Russia had been recaptured in grim fighting from the Arctic to the Crimea during the previous few weeks. Hitler had recently assumed personal command of the German Army, displacing Von Brauchitsch, but the Soviet troops, inspired and invigorated by success, were pressing on southwest of Kalinin towards Rzhev, threatening Mojaisk in the centre and attacking valiantly in the Crimea. The initiative, for the time, passed to the Red Army.

In Libya the main German Army, under General Rommel, had been forced back from the frontier and was now concentrated south of Benghazi, which had been recaptured by the British. Only isolated detachments of the enemy were left at Bardia and at Halfaya on the Egyptian border.

The Far Eastern scene was gloomy. The Japanese, having struck a massive and treacherous blow at the United States fleet at Pearl Harbour (Hawaii), were reaping rich gains. They had captured Hong Kong, landed big forces in the Philippines, threatened Manila from North and South, and invaded Sarawak and Sumatra. But the gravest peril in the Far East was in Malaya. The peninsula had been overrun from Siam, Penang had been

Introduction

abandoned, and the Japanese were within 190 miles of Singapore itself.

In the five-and-a-half-years-old China War, however, the Japanese were still grappling with the battered, but tireless and inexhaustible armies of Chiang Kai-shek. The invaders had just thrown in 50,000 men in a battle in Northern Hunan. The Japanese had gained many victories in China — but not victory.

Along the Western shores of Europe German troops were ever on the alert for British raiding parties, which had unsettled the garrisons in Norway. Lofoten Island had had another raid and more were expected on the Western coasts of occupied territory.

The only other fighting in occupied Europe was in the mountainous regions of Yugo-Slavia, where Serb guerrillas carried on a desperate struggle against the Germans, who revenged themselves on the helpless half-starved civilian populations.

Throughout occupied Europe, and especially in heroic Poland and Greece, the people were suffering bitter and revengeful repression.

Vichy France, indifferent to the torments of fellow countrymen in the Occupied Zone, pursued a policy of subservience and co-operation with the Germans.

In Britain the people had become accustomed and hardened to the ever-growing demands and restrictions of the war, and compulsion was entering into every phase of life.

The heavy air raids had stopped. In the last month of 1941 only 34 people had been killed by the bombs of the Luftwaffe, the lowest number since intensive bombing began in the autumn of 1940. In December of the previous year the death roll had been 3,829. Civil Defence services had become highly organised, and every arrangement had been made to carry on the life and industry of the country whatever storms might rage.

But still the greatest problem of all was shipping — a vital factor in every aspect of the nation's war effort. Official figures of the losses at sea were no longer published, but there was ground for believing that Britain's fight against the U-boat menace was steadily becoming more effective.

That was the war scene as the New Year dawned and the Prime Minister travelled on his way to the White House.

CHARLES EADE

Contents

Contents

Contents

Contents

xii

Contents

xiii

Contents

THE END OF THE BEGINNING

" Here's to 1942! "

[*January 1, 1942*

Mr. Winston Churchill, travelling from Ottawa to Washington for conferences with President Roosevelt, called his staff and the newspaper correspondents to the dining-car of his train to welcome the New Year. Then, raising his glass to the company, he said: —

H ERE'S to 1942, here's to a year of toil — a year of struggle and peril, and a long step forward towards victory. May we all come through safe and with honour.

"Desert Toils and Triumphs"

A NEW YEAR'S DAY MESSAGE TO THE
FORCES IN THE MIDDLE EAST
JANUARY 1, 1942

[January 1, 1942

F ROM all over the Empire and from the bottom of our hearts we send to the Armies of the Nile and the desert every good wish for the New Year. These armies have behind them a glorious record of victory.

Deserted by their Allies in June, 1940, left only with small and ill-equipped forces, with their communications through the Mediterranean virtually cut, these armies, representing not only the Motherland, but all parts of the Empire, have grown ceaselessly in strength and will still grow with every month that passes They have marched forward steadfastly upon the path of victory and liberation. All defeats and setbacks have been repaired and repaid with interest. Egypt, the Sudan, and East Africa were first of all successfully defended against heavy odds. Abyssinia has been freed and her Emperor restored to his throne and country, from which he had been wrongfully expelled.

British Somaliland has been regained, and Italian Somaliland and Eritrea conquered. Palestine has been defended, Syria freed of German intrigue, Iraq and Persia brought into effective military alliance. Latest of all is the famous victory manifesting itself more plainly every day in Cyrenaica. More than a quarter of a million prisoners have been taken. This proud record of achievement has won the lasting gratitude of the British Nation and Commonwealth of Nations, and takes its place among the memorable campaigns of history.

At one time you had deep anxiety for loved ones at home compelled to endure the bombardment last winter. They have watched your toils and triumphs with glistening eyes. The task is not yet finished. Even greater days may lie ahead. In all these trials, rest assured of the love and honour of those who sent you forth and long for the day of your victorious return.

To the Mediterranean Fleet we send every good wish. The great victories over the Italian Navy, the constant interruption of the enemy's supplies, and the continual flow of supplies to our armies have testified to their magnificent work, and constitute a noble page in naval history.

The R.A.F. have made a vital contribution during all this time. Their determination and devotion to duty have overcome all difficulties, and we have watched with admiration their victorious assaults upon the enemy. We are proud of them and wish them all well.

A Visit to Bermuda

A SPEECH TO THE HOUSE OF ASSEMBLY, AT
THE SESSIONS HOUSE, HAMILTON, BERMUDA
JANUARY 15, 1942

January 2.   *Headed by Mr. Winston Churchill and President Roosevelt, twenty-six States signed a Grand Alliance against the Axis, pledging joint conduct of the war and a fight to the finish.*
      Chinese troops entered Burma to aid British forces.
      In Libya Imperial troops captured Bardia and in Russia Soviet troops recaptured Malo Yaroslavets.

January 3.   *General Wavell made supreme commander of all Allied forces, land, sea and air, in the Pacific.*

January 6.   *President Roosevelt announced to Congress a huge production programme: 60,000 planes in 1942, 125,000 planes in 1943; 45,000 tanks in 1942; 75,000 tanks in 1943. He also stated that United States forces would take up stations in the British Isles.*
      British troops lost Kuantan aerodrome in Malaya.

January 7.   *President Roosevelt presented to Congress the greatest budget in history, expenditure in 1943 to be more than £13,000,000,000.*

January 8.   *R.A.F. raided Bangkok (Siam). British troops made further withdrawals in Malaya.*

January 9.   *Cruiser Galatea sunk in the Mediterranean.*

January 10.   *Officially announced that Mr. Duff Cooper had been recalled from Singapore, where he was Resident Minister.*

A Visit to Bermuda, January 15, 1942

January 11. *Japanese made landings in North-East Borneo and the Celebes.*

January 12. *Imperial troops in Malaya withdrew from Kuala Lumpur.*

January 14. *General Wavell established his headquarters in the Dutch East Indies.*
United States established a unified War Production Board under Mr. Donald Nelson.

IT is a sudden descent which I have made upon you, and I must express my gratitude that so many members of the Assembly should have found it possible at such very short notice — excusable only by wartime conditions — to attend this meeting. Here I come, as leader of the House of Commons, to call upon you in the second oldest Parliament in the world. Here is a representative parliamentary institution with an unbroken continuity almost as long as that of the House of Commons, an institution which began even before the House of Commons attained its full authority. It is a long way back to 1620. Yet these ideas of parliamentary government, of the representation of the people upon franchises, which extend as time goes on, and which in our country have reached the complete limits of universal suffrage, these institutions and principles constitute at this moment one of the great causes which are being fought out in the world. With all their weakness and with all their strength, with all their faults, with all their virtues, with all the criticisms that may be made against them, with their many shortcomings, with lack of foresight, lack of continuity of purpose or pressure only of superficial purpose, they nevertheless assert the right of the common people — the broad masses of the people — to take a conscious and effective share in the government of their country.

That is one of the great causes which are at stake now. We are confronted with embattled powers not based upon the public will, allowing no freedom of discussion, of speech or even of thought, but seeking to subjugate great nations and, if they can succeed, the whole world, on the basis of a party caucus, on the basis of a military hierarchy, on the basis of tyranny, terror and brute force. We are confronted with totalitarian States which deny as a fundamental principle the right of free debate and the expression of popular opinion.

It is against these evil forces that we have been in arms since the third of September, 1939. At one time it seemed that we should be alone. We were for a long time alone. We have stood alone all through the summer and the autumn and the winter of 1940 and 1941. But we did not flinch, we did not weaken. We did not worry because we could not see our way through. We said we will do our duty, we will do our best. The rest we must leave to Providence. And what a reward has come! What a lesson it is never to give in — never to give in when you guard the cause of freedom. What a moral there is to be drawn from that, because now we see great Powers rising that have come to our aid, not wholly because of association with the British Empire but because of association with the cause of which, I will venture to say in no boastful spirit, the British Empire is the oldest custodian, namely, representative government based on the freedom and the rights of the individual.

We have had some great and blessed accessions of help. In the first place we all see now what a service has been rendered to the cause of freedom by the valiant resistance for four and a half years of the Chinese people, fighting the same kinds of tyranny in Asia as have sought to molest us in the Western World. Secondly, we have had the valiant resistance of the Russian armies and peoples to the cruel and unprovoked invasion of their country and the slaughterous attack which has been made upon them — men, women and children alike. And now we see the United States, which under its great President showed its sympathy with our cause at every stage, set upon by those same three villainous Powers, and assaulted with every circumstance of treachery and malice. And so now the situation is widely different from what it was when we for more than a year alone held high the flaming torch of freedom. It is greatly changed. We are now no longer alone. We are marching in a great concourse.

We signed the other day at Washington the agreement of twenty-six countries, including four of the largest masses of population, comprising altogether much more than three-quarters of the entire population of the globe. And we shall march forward together in comradeship until those who have sought to trample upon the rights of individual freedom, the strong principles inculcated in the birth of the English parliamentary system and by the American revolutionary war, by Hampden and by Washington, are beaten down, and until those principles are finally established.

In this vast world struggle, in this convulsion, you in Bermuda happen to be called upon to play a part of especial importance and distinction. Everybody has to do his duty to the cause — first to the British Empire, but above that to the world cause. You had your own life in these Islands. It has run for centuries in a more unbroken course than, perhaps, the life of any civilised community in the world. Suddenly great changes have to be made. I thought it right to ask you, with the full authority of Parliament and of His Majesty the King, to make such alterations in your long-established life as would facilitate the ever closer connection and unity of spirit, and the reciprocity of practical measures for common security, between the British Empire and the United States.

I have got in my pocket the message which I sent you, and on which you decided that you would co-operate heart and hand, that you would put up with many changes and alterations in the balance of your community here for the sake of the old country and the Empire, and of those larger ideas which unite men of all races and all nations and all the creeds.

I said to you: "I have to-day signed a document" — this was on the 25th March, 1941 — "implementing the agreement of September last for the leasing to the United States of bases in Bermuda and elsewhere — and I wish to express to you my strong conviction that these bases are important pillars of the bridge connecting the two great English-speaking democracies. You have cause to be proud that it has fallen to your lot to make this important contribution to a better world."

You have done so. It is not a question whether it is more profitable; this is a question of duty, of world duty, and these Islands on which I have had the honour to set foot this morning have unfailingly and unfalteringly answered the call. Now let me say to you what a reward has come, because we have seen, as

9

The End of the Beginning

events have unfolded, that the whole English-speaking world stands together.

We have other Allies, important and honoured, who are fighting with great valour against the common foe. Still one has the feeling that the English-speaking world have only to march forward together, have only to pool the luck, to guide the forward march of mankind. And for your contribution to these supreme and even, if I may say so, sublime ends, I am very happy to have found myself here to-day to express on behalf of the Motherland and of the British House of Commons our profound gratitude.

Broadcasting of Parliamentary Speeches

A STATEMENT TO THE HOUSE OF COMMONS
JANUARY 20, 1942

[January 20, 1942

In reply to a Member of Parliament who asked whether the Prime Minister would consider making arrangements for the broadcasting of important speeches made in the House of Commons, Mr. Churchill said: —

I HAVE considered this matter long and carefully and also with diffidence, as to some extent at the present time it affects myself. It certainly would be a very great convenience, and would, I believe, be welcomed by the public, if an electrical record of major statements about the war could be made. This record could be used for subsequent broadcasting, which might be deemed an advantage. In my own case I have been constantly asked to repeat the speech I have delivered in the House over the broadcast later. This imposes a very heavy strain and is, moreover, unsatisfactory from the point of view of delivery.

It has been represented to me that in the Dominions and in the United States there are very large numbers of people who would like to listen to a record of the actual speech or parts of it rather than to a news summary, such as is usually compiled — very well compiled — by the British Broadcasting Corporation. Moreover, such a record could be used at the most convenient hours in the various countries concerned, which now encircle the entire globe. I should hope, therefore, that the House might be disposed from time to time to grant me or any successor I may have during the war this indulgence. As an innovation of this kind in our practice should be most carefully watched, I should propose that an experiment should be made in the case of the statement I have been asked to make at an early opportunity upon the present war situation. There must necessarily be in this statement a good deal that is of some interest both in America and Australia as well as in India and South Africa. A Motion will, therefore, be placed on the Paper for discussion, allowing this procedure to be followed on this particular occasion only. As a separate Motion will be required in each individual case, the House would have full control of the practice, and if it were found to be objectionable or invidious or not in the public interest, it could be dropped. Evidently the practice would not be suitable to periods of Party Government.

The record would be the property of this House, and its use, in the event of any controversy arising, would be a matter for decision by the House under Mr. Speaker's guidance. As this is a matter which affects the customs of the House, I shall leave the decision to a free vote.

I am entirely in the hands of the House. If they do not feel they can give me this easement on this occasion as an experiment, I shall not take it amiss in any way, and I will do my best over the broadcast that evening to repeat what I have said.

* * * *

The following Motion stood upon the Order Paper for January 21 in the name of the Prime Minister: "That the statement on the War Situation to be made by the Prime Minister in this House on the First Sitting Day after 25th January be electrically recorded, with a view to being subsequently broadcast." The Prime Minister, however, said: —

As there appears to be so much difference of opinion about this Motion which stands on the Order Paper, I do not intend to press it.

When a Member suggested that a small Committee should be appointed to look more fully into the question, the Prime Minister replied: —

I think we have had enough of it.

12

Tribute to the Duke of Connaught

A SPEECH TO THE HOUSE OF COMMONS
JANUARY 20, 1942

[January 20, 1942

I BEG to move:

"That an humble Address be presented to His Majesty to express the deep concern of this House at the loss which His Majesty has sustained by the death of His Royal Highness Prince Arthur William Patrick Albert, Duke of Connaught and Strathearn, and to condole with His Majesty on this melancholy occasion and to assure His Majesty that this House will ever participate with the most affectionate and dutiful attachment in whatever may concern the feelings and interests of His Majesty."

The late Duke of Connaught lived a life so long that it was not only a link with the tranquil days of the Victorian era, when a large number of people had persuaded themselves that most of the problems of society were solved, but also a link with the life of the Duke of Wellington. During the whole of his career, mainly in the British Army, he was a devoted, faithful officer and servant of the Crown. He held a position of delicacy, not free from difficulty, beset on every side by the possibility of indiscretion when such a position is occupied by one who is a son of a Queen, afterwards a brother of a King, uncle of another Sovereign and the great-uncle of a fourth Ruler. In that position, never did anything occur which did not make the public realize how true the Duke of Connaught was to all the constitutional implications of this position, and all who came into contact with him were impressed by his charm of manner, by his old-world courtesy, and knew that they were in the presence of a great and distinguished representative of our beloved Royal House.

13

The End of the Beginning

I have had many opportunities of meeting His Royal Highness, who was a friend of my family, and I enjoyed his friendship. I served under his command, in 1895, as a young officer at Aldershot, and I know the respect and esteem in which he was held by all the troops and all the ranks in the Forces. For my part, I am very glad to feel that he lived long enough to see the dark, frightful crisis with which we were confronted eighteen months ago broaden out into a somewhat clearer and more hopeful light.

Secret Sessions

[January 22, 1942

A Member of Parliament asked the Prime Minister whether a forthcoming debate on aerodrome defence would be in public or in secret, or part in public and part in secret. Replying to this question and to other questions which followed it, Mr. Churchill said: —

WE have only one desire, and that is to meet the convenience of the House. I think it will be necessary for the Secretary of State to make his statement in public, because there has been a lot of discussion about the matter in the country, and, after all, the House has certain duties to the country. Public opinion is affronted if discussion on an important topic is withheld. After the speech of the Secretary of State, representing the Government, it might be thought desirable that some speeches should be made by Members from the other side criticising it and so forth. I should have thought that after one or two of these speeches had been made it would be more convenient to go into Secret Session, in which case the operational side of this important matter could be more fully treated than in Public Session.

I think that after all the talk there has been we have a right to put our case, even the Government in time of war have some rights. We thought it would be very nice that those who wished to say things against the policy of the Government and to point out in public how many opportunities there were for improvement in our course of action should have their full run, and then, after that, if it were the wish of the House, we should go

15

into Secret Session, where something could be said which we should not like to say in the hearing of the enemy. I do not think we could have a better arrangement. I must say, about this Secret Session business, that it is often difficult to interpret the wishes of the House. When there is a suggestion to have a Session in secret there is a demand that it should be in public, and when there is a suggestion for a Public Session there is a demand that it should be secret. Now, when one suggests that it should be both public and secret, there is objection to that also.

The War Situation

TWO SPEECHES IN A HOUSE OF COMMONS DEBATE ON A
VOTE OF CONFIDENCE, WHICH WAS CARRIED BY
464 VOTES TO 1
JANUARY 27 AND 29, 1942

January 17. Mr. *Churchill and Lord Beaverbrook arrived back in England after a long flight from Bermuda, 3,287 miles in 18 hours.*

Germany announced the death of General von Reichenau, who had been in command of the Klin sector of the Moscow front.

Halfaya, last enemy stronghold in Cyrenaica, surrendered to Imperial troops.

January 18. U Saw, *Prime Minister of Burma, who had recently visited Britain, was arrested for complicity with the Japanese.*

January 20. *Russians announced their greatest victory of the war with the recapture of Mojaisk.*

January 22. *Japanese forces landed in New Guinea.*

General Rommel, German commander in Libya, made a surprise attack on British forces and reinforced by aircraft reoccupied Agedabia.

January 24. *United States naval units attacked 100-ship enemy convoy in Macassar Straits, sinking several ships and damaging others.*

General Rommel continued his offensive in Libya, wresting initiative from the British.

January 26. *American troops landed in Northern Ireland.*

January 27. Mr. *Churchill opened three-day war debate in the House of Commons.*

Admiralty announced the loss, on November 25, of the battleship Barham *in the Mediterranean.*

17

January 28.   *Announced that the Japanese had lost nine transports in the Macassar Straits.*

Lord Beaverbrook revealed that Britain's gun production had reached 30,000 a year and was still increasing.

January 29.   *House of Commons Vote of Confidence in the Government was carried by 464 to 1.*

[*January 27, 1942, at the opening of the debate*

F ROM time to time in the life of any Government there come occasions which must be clarified. No one who has read the newspapers of the last few weeks about our affairs at home and abroad can doubt that such an occasion is at hand.

Since my return to this country, I have come to the conclusion that I must ask to be sustained by a Vote of Confidence from the House of Commons. This is a thoroughly normal, constitutional, democratic procedure. A Debate on the war has been asked for. I have arranged it in the fullest and freest manner for three whole days. Any Member will be free to say anything he thinks fit about or against the Administration or against the composition or personalities of the Government, to his heart's content, subject only to the reservation which the House is always so careful to observe about military secrets. Could you have anything freer than that? Could you have any higher expression of democracy than that? Very few other countries have institutions strong enough to sustain such a thing while they are fighting for their lives.

I owe it to the House to explain to them what has led me to ask for their exceptional support at this time. It has been suggested that we should have a three days' Debate of this kind in which the Government would no doubt be lustily belaboured by some of those who have lighter burdens to carry, and that at the end we should separate without a Division. In this case sections of the Press which are hostile — and there are some whose hostility is pronounced — could declare that the Government's credit was broken, and it might even be hinted, after all that has passed and all the discussion there has been, that it had been privately intimated to me that I should be very reckless if I asked for a Vote of Confidence from Parliament.

And the matter does not stop there. It must be remembered that these reports can then be flashed all over the world, and that they are repeated in enemy broadcasts night after night in order to show that the Prime Minister has no right to speak for the nation and that the Government in Britain is about to collapse. Anyone who listens to the fulminations which come from across the water knows that that is no exaggeration. Of course, these statements from foreign sources would not be true, but neither would it be helpful to anyone that there should be any doubt about our position.

There is another aspect. We in this Island for a long time were alone, holding aloft the torch. We are no longer alone now. We are now at the centre and among those at the summit of 26 United Nations, comprising more than three-quarters of the population of the globe. Whoever speaks for Britain at this moment must be known to speak, not only in the name of the people — and that I feel pretty sure I may — but in the name of Parliament and, above all, of the House of Commons. It is a genuine public interest that requires that these facts should be made manifest afresh in a formal way.

We have had a great deal of bad news lately from the Far East, and I think it highly probable, for reasons which I shall presently explain, that we shall have a great deal more. Wrapped up in this bad news will be many tales of blunders and short-comings, both in foresight and action. No one will pretend for a moment that disasters like these occur without there having been faults and shortcomings. I see all this rolling towards us like the waves in a storm, and that is another reason why I require a formal, solemn Vote of Confidence from the House of Commons, which hitherto in this struggle has never flinched. The House would fail in its duty if it did not insist upon two things, first, freedom of debate, and, secondly, a clear, honest, blunt vote thereafter. Then we shall all know where we are, and all those with whom we have to deal, at home and abroad, friend or foe, will know where we are and where they are. It is because we are to have a free debate, in which perhaps 20 to 30 Members can take part, that I demand an expression of opinion from the 300 or 400 Members who will have to sit silent. It is because things have gone badly and worse is to come that I demand a Vote of Confidence. This will be placed on the Paper to-day, to be moved at a later stage. I do not see why this should hamper anyone. If a Member has helpful criticisms to make, or even severe corrections to administer, that may be perfectly consistent with thinking that in respect of the Administration, such as it is, he might go farther and fare worse. But if an hon. Gentleman dislikes the Government very much and feels it in the public interest that it should be broken up, he ought to have the manhood to testify his convictions in the Lobby. There is no need to be mealy-mouthed in debate. There is no objection to anything being said, plain, or even plainer, and the Government will do their utmost to conform to any standard which may be set in the course of the debate. But no one need be mealy-mouthed in debate, and no one should be chicken-hearted in voting. I have voted against Governments I have been elected to support, and, looking back, I have sometimes felt very glad that I did so. Everyone in these rough times must do what he thinks is his duty

The House of Commons, which is at present the most powerful representative Assembly in the world, must also — I am sure, will also — bear in mind the effect produced abroad by all its proceedings. We have also to remember how oddly foreigners view our country and its way of doing things. When Rudolf Hess flew over here some months ago he firmly believed that he had only to gain access to certain circles in this country for what he described as "the Churchill clique" to be thrown out of power and for a Government to be set up with which Hitler could negotiate a magnanimous peace. The only importance attaching to the opinions of Hess is the fact that he was fresh from the atmosphere of Hitler's intimate table. But, I can assure you that since I have been back in this country I have had anxious inquiries from a dozen countries, and reports of enemy propaganda in a score of countries, all turning upon the point whether His Majesty's present Government is to be dismissed from power or not. This may seem silly to us, but in those mouths abroad it is hurtful and mischievous to the common effort. I am not asking for any special, personal favours in these circumstances, but I am sure the House would wish to make its position clear; therefore I stand by the ancient, constitutional, Parliamentary doctrine of free debate and faithful voting.

Now I turn to the account of the war, which constitutes the claim I make for the support and confidence of the House. Three or four months ago we had to cope with the following situation. The German invaders were advancing, blasting their way through Russia. The Russians were resisting with the utmost heroism. But no one could tell what would happen, whether Leningrad, Moscow or Rostov would fall, or where the German winter line would be established. No one can tell now where it will be established, but now the boot is on the other leg. We all agree that we must aid the valiant Russian Armies to the utmost limit of our power. His Majesty's Government thought, and Parliament upon reflection agreed with them, that the best aid we could give to Russia was in supplies of many kinds of raw materials and of munitions, particularly tanks and aircraft. Our Forces at home and abroad had for long been waiting thirstily for these weapons. At last they were coming to hand in large numbers. At home we have always the danger of invasion to consider and to prepare against. I will speak about the situation in the Middle East presently. Nevertheless we sent Premier Stalin — for that I gather is how he wishes to be addressed; at least, that is the form in which he telegraphs to me — exactly what he asked for. The whole quantity was promised and sent. There has been, I am sorry to say, a small lag due to bad weather, but it will be made up by the early days of February. This was a decision of major strategy and policy, and anyone can see that it was right to put it first when they watch the wonderful achievements, unhoped for, undreamed of by us because we little knew the Russian strength, but all the more glorious as they are seen — the wonderful achievements of the Russian Armies. Our munitions were of course only a contribution to the Russian victory, but they were an encouragement in Russia's darkest hour. Moreover, if we had not shown a loyal effort to help our Ally, albeit at a heavy sacrifice to ourselves, I do not think our relations with Premier Stalin and his great country would be as good as they are now. There would have been a lack of comradeship, and the lack of comradeship might have spread reproaches on all sides. Far from regretting what we did for Russia, I only wish it had been in our power — but it was not — to have done more.

Three or four months ago, at a time when the German advance was rolling onwards, we were particularly concerned with the possibility of the Germans forcing the Don River, the capture of Rostov and the invasion of the Caucasus, and the reaching of the Baku oil wells before the winter by the Panzer spearheads of the German Army. Everyone who has been giving careful study and independent thought to this war knows how deep an anxiety that was in all our breasts three or four months ago. Such an advance would not only have given the Germans the oil which they are beginning seriously to need, but it would have involved the destruction of the Russian Fleet and the loss of the command of the Black Sea. It would have affected the safety of Turkey, and it would, in due course, have exposed to the gravest dangers Persia, Iraq, Syria and Palestine, and beyond those countries, all of which are now under our control, it would have threatened the Suez Canal, Egypt and the Nile Valley. At the same time as this menace defined itself with hideous and increasing reality as it seemed, General Rommel, with his army of ten German and Italian divisions entrenched in his fortified positions at and behind the Halfaya Pass, was preparing to make a decisive attack on Tobruk as a preliminary to a renewed advance upon Egypt from the West. The Nile Valley was therefore menaced simultaneously by a direct attack from the West and by a more remote but in some ways more deadly attack from the North. In such circumstances it is the classical rule of war, reinforced by endless examples — and some exceptions — that you prepare to fight a delaying action against one of the two attacks and concentrate, if possible, overwhelming strength against the other and nearer attack. We therefore approved General Auchinleck's plans for building up a delaying force in the vast region from Cyprus to the Caspian Sea, along what I may call the Levant-Caspian front, and preparing installations, airfields and communications upon which larger forces could be based, as time and transport allowed. On the other flank, the Western flank, we prepared to set upon Rommel and try to make a good job of him. For the sake of this battle in the Libyan Desert we concentrated everything we could lay our hands on, and we submitted to a very long delay, very painful to bear over here, so that all preparations could be perfected. We hoped to recapture Cyrenaica and the important airfields round Benghazi. But General Auchinleck's main objective was more simple. He set himself to destroy Rommel's army. Such was the mood in which we stood three or four months ago. Such was the broad strategical decision we took.

Now, when we see how events, which so often mock and falsify human effort and design, have shaped themselves, I am sure this was a right decision.

General Auchinleck had demanded five months' preparation for his campaign, but on 18th November he fell upon the enemy. For more than two months in the desert the most fierce, continuous battle has raged between scattered bands of men armed with the latest weapons, seeking each other dawn after dawn, fighting to the death throughout the day and then often long into the night. Here was a battle which turned out very differently from what was foreseen. All was dispersed and confused. Much depended on the individual soldier and the junior officer. Much, but not all; because this battle would have been lost on 24th November if General Auchinleck had not intervened himself, changed the command, and ordered the ruthless pressure of the attack to be maintained without regard to risks or consequences. But for this robust decision we should now be back on the old line from which we had started, or perhaps farther back. Tobruk would possibly have fallen, and Rommel might be marching towards the Nile. Since then the battle has declared itself. Cyrenaica has been regained. It has still to be held. We have not succeeded in destroying Rommel's army, but nearly two-thirds of it are wounded, prisoners or dead.

Perhaps I may give the figures to the House. In this strange, sombre battle of the desert, where our men have met the enemy for the first time — I do not say in every respect, because there are some things which are not all that we had hoped for, but upon the whole — have met him with equal weapons, we have lost in killed, wounded and captured about 18,000 officers and men, of whom the greater part are British. We have in our possession 36,500 prisoners, including many wounded, of whom

10,500 are Germans. We have killed and wounded at least 11,500 Germans and 13,000 Italians — in all a total, accounted for exactly, of 61,000 men. There is also a mass of enemy wounded, some of whom have been evacuated to the rear or to the Westward — I cannot tell how many. Of the forces of which General Rommel disposed on 18th November, little more than one-third now remains, while 852 German and Italian aircraft have been destroyed, and 336 German and Italian tanks. During this battle we have never had in action more than 45,000 men, against enemy forces — if they could be brought to bear — much more than double as strong. Therefore, it seems to me that this heroic, epic struggle in the desert, though there have been many local reverses and many ebbs and flows, has tested our manhood in a searching fashion, and has proved not only that our men can die for King and country — everyone knew that — but that they can kill.

I cannot tell what the position at the present moment is on the Western front in Cyrenaica. We have a very daring and skilful opponent against us and, may I say across the havoc of war, a great General. He has certainly received reinforcements. Another battle is even now in progress, and I make it a rule never to try and prophesy beforehand how battles will turn out. I always rejoice that I have made that rule. Naturally, one does not say that we have not a chance, because that is apt to be encouraging to the enemy and depressing to our own friends. In the general upshot, the fact remains that, whereas a year ago the Germans were telling all the neutrals that they would be in Suez by May, when some people talked of the possibility of a German descent upon Assiut, and many people were afraid that Tobruk would be stormed and others feared for the Nile Valley, Cairo, Alexandria and the Canal, we have conducted an effective offensive against the enemy and hurled him backward, inflicting upon him incomparably more — well, I should not say incomparably, because I have just given the comparison, but far heavier losses and damage — than we have suffered ourselves. Not only has he had three times our losses on the battlefield, approximately, but the blue waters of the Mediterranean have, thanks to the enterprise of the Royal Navy, our submarines and Air Force, drowned a large number of the reinforcements which

The War Situation, January 27, 1942

have been continually sent. This process has had further important successes during the last few days. Whether you call it a victory or not, it must be dubbed up to the present, although I will not make any promises, a highly profitable transaction, and certainly is an episode of war most glorious to the British, South African, New Zealand, Indian, Free French and Polish soldiers, sailors and airmen who have played their part in it. The prolonged, stubborn, steadfast and successful defence of Tobruk by Australian and British troops was an essential preliminary, over seven hard months, to any success which may have been achieved.

Let us see what has happened on the other flank, the Northern flank, of the Nile Valley. What has happened in Palestine, Syria, Iraq and Persia? There we must thank Russia. There the valour of the Russian Armies has warded off dangers which we saw and which we undoubtedly ran. The Caucasus and the precious oilfields of Baku, the great Anglo-Persian oilfields, are denied to the enemy. Winter has come. Evidently we have the time to strengthen still further our Forces and organisations in those regions. Therefore, I present to you, in laying the whole field open and bare and surveying it in all its parts, for all are related, a situation in the Nile Valley, both West and East, incomparably easier than anything we have ever seen, since we were deserted by the French Bordeaux-Vichy Government and were set upon by Italy. The House will not fail to discern the agate points upon which this vast improvement has turned. It is only by the smallest margin that we have succeeded so far in beating Rommel in Cyrenaica and destroying two-thirds of his forces. Every tank, every aircraft squadron was needed. It is only by the victories on the Russian flank on the Black Sea coast that we have been spared the overrunning of all those vast lands from the Levant to the Caspian, which in turn give access to India, Persia, the Persian Gulf, the Nile Valley and the Suez Canal.

I have told the House the story of these few months, and hon. Members will see from it how narrowly our resources have been strained and by what a small margin and by what strokes of fortune — for which we claim no credit — we have survived — so far. Where should we have been, I wonder, if we had yielded to the clamour which was so loud three or four months ago that we should invade France or the Low Countries? We can still see on the walls the inscription, "Second Front Now." Who did not feel the appeal of that? But imagine what our position would have been if we had yielded to this vehement temptation. Every ton of our shipping, every flotilla, every aeroplane, the whole strength of our Army would be committed, and would be fighting for life on the French shores or on the shores of the Low Countries. All these troubles of the Far East and the Middle East might have sunk to insignificance compared with the question of another and far worse Dunkirk.

Here, let me say, I should like to pay my tribute to one who has gone from us since I left this country, Mr. Lees-Smith, who, I remember, spoke with so much profound wisdom on this point at a moment when many opinions were in flux about it. His faithful, selfless and wise conduct of the important work which he discharged in this House was undoubtedly of great assistance to us all, not only to the Government but to us all, in the various stages of the war. His memory as a distinguished Parliamentarian will long find an honoured place in the recollection of those who had the fortune to be his colleagues.

Sometimes things can be done by saying "Yes," and sometimes things can be done by saying "No." Yet I suppose there are some of those who were vocal and voluble, and even clamant, for a second front to be opened in France, who are now going to come up bland and smiling and ask why it is that we have not ample forces in Malaya, Burma, Borneo and Celebes. There are times when so many things happen, and happen so quickly, and time seems to pass in such a way that you can neither say it is long or short, that it is easy to forget what you have said three months before. You may fail to connect it with what you are advocating at the particular moment. Throughout a long and variegated Parliamentary life this consideration has led me to try and keep a watchful eye on that danger myself. You never can tell. There are also people who talk and bear themselves as if they had prepared for this war with great armaments and long, careful preparation. But that is not true. In two and a half years of fighting we have only just managed to keep our heads above water. When I was called upon to be Prime Minister, now nearly two years ago, there were not many applicants for the job. Since then, perhaps, the market has improved. In spite of the shameful negligence, gross muddles, blatant incompetence, complacency, and lack of organising power which are daily attributed to us — and from which chidings we endeavour to profit — we are beginning to see our way through. It looks as if we were in for a very bad time, but provided we all stand together, and provided we throw in the last spasm of our strength, it also looks, more than it ever did before, as if we were going to win.

While facing Germany and Italy here and in the Nile Valley, we have never had any power to provide effectively for the defence of the Far East. My whole argument so far has led up to that point. It may be that this or that might have been done which was not done, but we have never been able to provide effectively for the defence of the Far East against an attack by Japan. It has been the policy of the Cabinet at almost all costs to avoid embroilment with Japan until we were sure that the United States would also be engaged. We even had to stoop, as the House will remember, when we were at our very weakest point, to close the Burma Road for some months. I remember that some of our present critics were very angry about it, but we had to do it. There never has been a moment, there never could have been a moment, when Great Britain or the British Empire, single-handed, could fight Germany and Italy, could wage the Battle of Britain, the Battle of the Atlantic and the Battle of the Middle East — and at the same time stand thoroughly prepared in Burma, the Malay Peninsula, and generally in the Far East against the impact of a vast military Empire like Japan, with more than 70 mobile divisions, the third navy in the world, a great air force, and the thrust of 80 or 90 millions of hardy, warlike Asiatics. If we had started to scatter our forces over these immense areas in the Far East, we should have been ruined. If we had moved large armies of troops urgently needed on the war fronts to regions which were not at war and might never be at war, we should have been altogether wrong. We should have cast away the chance, which has now become something more than a chance, of all of us emerging safely from the terrible plight in which we have been plunged.

We therefore have lain — I am putting it as bluntly as I can —

for nearly two years under the threat of an attack by Japan with which we had no means of coping. But as time has passed the mighty United States, under the leadership of President Roosevelt, from reasons of its own interest and safety but also out of chivalrous regard for the cause of freedom and democracy, has drawn ever nearer to the confines of the struggle. And now that the blow has fallen it does not fall on us alone. On the contrary, it falls upon united forces and united nations, which are unquestionably capable of enduring the struggle, of retrieving the losses, and of preventing another such stroke ever being delivered again.

There is an argument with which I will deal as I pass along to pursue my theme. It is said by some, "If only you had organized the munitions production of this country properly and had had a Minister of Production (and that is not a question which should be dogmatised upon either way) it would have made everything all right. There would have been enough for all needs. We should have had enough supplies for Russia, enough well-equipped squadrons and divisions to defend the British Islands, to sustain the Middle East, and to arm the Far East effectively." But that is really not true. As a matter of fact, our munitions output is gigantic, has for some time been very large indeed, and is bounding up in a most remarkable manner. In the last year, 1941, although we were at war in so many theatres and on so many fronts, we have produced more than double the munitions equipment of the United States, which was arming heavily, though of course a lap behind on the road. This condition will naturally be rapidly removed as the full power of American industry comes into full swing. But in the last six months, thanks to the energies of Lord Beaverbrook and the solid spadework done by his predecessors and the passage of time — Lord Beaverbrook particularly asks me to say — I should have said it anyway — that our munitions output has risen in the following respects: We are producing more than twice as many far more complicated guns every month as we did in the peak of the 1917–18 war period, and the curve is rising. The guns are infinitely more complicated. Tank production has doubled in the last six months. Small arms production is more than twice what it was six months ago. Filled rounds of ammunition have doubled in the last six months. I could go on with the catalogue, but these are not doublings from early very small totals, they are doublings from the totals we boasted about, as far as we dared, six months ago. There has been an immense leap forward. In aircraft production there is a steady increase not only in the numbers but also in the size and quality of the aircraft, though I must say there has not been all the increase which I had hoped for.

But all this has nothing to do with the preparations it was open to us to make in Malaya and Burma and generally in the Far East. The limiting factor has not been troops or even equipment. The limiting factor has been transport, even assuming we had wished to take this measure and had had this great surplus. From the time that this present Government was formed, from the moment it was formed I may say, every scrap of shipping we could draw away from our vital supply routes, every U-boat escort we could divert from the Battle of the Atlantic, has been busy to the utmost capacity to carry troops, tanks and munitions from this Island to the East. There has been a ceaseless flow, and as for aircraft they have not only been moved by sea but by every route, some very dangerous and costly routes, to the Eastern battlefields. The decision was taken, as I have explained, to make our contribution to Russia, to try to beat Rommel, and to form a stronger front from the Levant to the Caspian. It followed from that decision that it was in our power only to make a moderate and partial provision in the Far East against the hypothetical danger of a Japanese onslaught. Sixty thousand men, indeed, were concentrated at Singapore, but priority in modern aircraft, in tanks, and in anti-aircraft and anti-tank artillery, was accorded to the Nile Valley.

For this decision in its broad strategic aspects, and also for the diplomatic policy in regard to Russia, I take the fullest personal responsibility. If we have handled our resources wrongly, no one is so much to blame as me. If we have not got large modern air forces and tanks in Burma and Malaya to-night, no one is more accountable than I am. Why then should I be called upon to pick out scapegoats, to throw the blame on generals or airmen or sailors? Why then should I be called upon to drive away loyal and trusted colleagues and friends to appease the clamour of certain sections of the British and Australian Press, or in order to take the edge off our reverses in Malaya and the Far East, and the punishment which we have yet to take there? I should be ashamed to do such a thing at such a time, and if I were capable of doing it, believe me, I should be incapable of rendering this country or this House any further service.

I say that without in the slightest degree seeking to relieve myself from my duty and responsibility to endeavour to make continual improvements in Ministerial positions. It is the duty of every Prime Minister to the House, but we have to be quite sure that they are improvements in every case, and not only in every case but in the setting. I could not possibly descend to what the German radio repeatedly credits me with — an attempt to get out of difficulties in which I really bear the main load by offering up scapegoats to public displeasure. Many people, many very well-meaning people, begin their criticisms and articles by saying, "Of course, we are all in favour of the Prime Minister because he has the people behind him. But what about the muddles made by this or that Department; what about that general or this Minister?" But I am the man that Parliament and the nation have got to blame for the general way in which they are served, and I cannot serve them effectively unless, in spite of all that has gone wrong, and that is going to go wrong, I have their trust and faithful aid.

I must linger for a moment on our political affairs, because we are conducting the war on the basis of a full democracy and a free Press, and that is an attempt which has not been made before in such circumstances. A variety of attacks are made upon the composition of the Government. It is said that it is formed upon a party and political basis. But so is the House of Commons. It is silly to extol the Parliamentary system and then, in the next breath, to say, "Away with party and away with politics." From one quarter I am told that the leaders of the Labour party ought to be dismissed from the Cabinet. This would be a return to party Government pure and simple. From opposite quarters it is said that no one who approved of Munich should be allowed to hold office. To do that would be to cast a reflection upon the great majority of the nation at that time, and also to deny the strongest party in the House any proportionate share in the National Government, which again, in turn, might cause inconvenience. Even my right hon. Friend the leader of the Liberal party, the Secretary of State for Air [Sir Archibald Sinclair] whose help to-day I value so much and with whom, as a lifelong friend, it is a pleasure to work, even he has not escaped unscathed. If I were to show the slightest weakness in dealing with these opposite forms of criticism, not only should I deprive myself of loyal and experienced colleagues, but I should destroy the National Government and rupture the war-time unity of Parliament itself.

Other attacks are directed against individual Ministers. I have been urged to make an example of the Chancellor of the Duchy of Lancaster, who is now returning from his mission in the Far East. Thus, he would be made to bear the blame for our misfortunes. The position of the Chancellor of the Duchy of Lancaster at the head of the Council which he had been instructed to form at Singapore was rendered obsolete by the decision which I reached with the President of the United States to set up a Supreme Commander for the main fighting zone in the Far East. The whole conception of a Supreme Commander is that, under the direction of the Governments he serves, he is absolute master of all authorities in the region assigned to him. This would be destroyed if political functionaries representing the various nations — for it is not only this country which would be represented; others would have to be represented as well as ours — were clustered round him. The function of the Chancellor of the Duchy was therefore exhausted by the appointment of General Wavell to the Supreme Command. I may say that regret was expressed at his departure by the New Zealand and Australian Governments, and still more by the Council he formed at Singapore, which, in a localised and subordinate form, it has been found necessary to carry on. When I am invited, under threats of unpopularity to myself or the Government, to victimise the Chancellor of the Duchy, and throw him to the wolves, I say to those who make this amiable suggestion, I can only say to them, "I much regret that I am unable to gratify your wishes" — or words to that effect. [*Laughter*]

The outstanding question upon which the House should form ·its judgment for the purposes of the impending Division is whether His Majesty's Government were right in giving a marked priority in the distribution of the forces and equipment we could send overseas, to Russia, to Libya, and, to a lesser extent, to the Levant-Caspian danger front, and whether we were right in accepting, for the time being, a far lower standard of forces and equipment for the Far East than for these other theatres.

The first obvious fact is that the Far Eastern theatre was at peace and that the other theatres were in violent or imminent war. It would evidently have been a very improvident use of our limited resources — as I pointed out earlier — if we had kept large masses of troops and equipment spread about the immense areas of the Pacific or in India, Burma, and the Malay Peninsula, standing idle, month by month and perhaps year by year, without any war occurring. Thus we should have failed in our engagements to Russia, which has meanwhile struck such staggering blows at the German Army, and we should have lost the battle in Cyrenaica, which we have not yet won, and we might now be fighting defensively well inside the Egyptian frontier. There is the question on which the House should make up its mind. We had not the resources to meet all the perils and pressures that came upon us.

But this question, serious and large as it is by itself, cannot be wholly decided without some attempt to answer the further question — what was the likelihood of the Far Eastern theatre being thrown into war by a Japanese attack? I have explained how very delicately we walked, and how painful it was at times, how very careful I was every time that we should not be exposed single-handed to this onslaught which we were utterly incapable of meeting. But it seemed irrational to suppose that in the last six months — which is what I am principally dealing with — the Japanese, having thrown away their opportunity of attacking us in the autumn of 1940, when we were so much weaker, so much less well-armed, and all alone, should at this period have plunged into a desperate struggle against the combined Forces of the British Empire and the United States. Nevertheless, nations, like individuals, commit irrational acts, and there were forces at work in Japan, violent, murderous, fanatical and explosive forces, which no one could measure.

On the other hand, the probability, since the Atlantic Conference, at which I discussed these matters with Mr. Roosevelt, that the United States, even if not herself attacked, would come into a war in the Far East, and thus make final victory sure, seemed to allay some of these anxieties. That expectation has not been falsified by the event. It fortified our British decision to use our limited resources on the actual fighting fronts. As time went on, one had greater assurance that if Japan ran amok in the Pacific, we should not fight alone. It must also be remembered that over the whole of the Pacific scene brooded the great power of the United States Fleet, concentrated at Hawaii. It seemed very unlikely that Japan would attempt the distant invasion of the Malay Peninsula, the assault upon Singapore, and the attack upon the Dutch East Indies, while leaving behind them in their rear this great American Fleet. However, to strengthen the position as the situation seemed to intensify, we sent the *Prince of Wales* and the *Repulse* to form the spearpoint of the considerable battle forces which we felt ourselves at length able to form in the Indian Ocean. We reinforced Singapore to a considerable extent, and Hong Kong to the extent which we were advised would be sufficient to hold the island for a long time. Besides this in minor ways we took what precautions were open to us. On 7th December the Japanese, by a sudden attack, delivered while their envoys were still negotiating at Washington, crippled for the time being the American Pacific Fleet, and a few days later inflicted very heavy naval losses on us by sinking the *Prince of Wales* and the *Repulse*.

For the time being, therefore, naval superiority in the Pacific and in the Malaysian Archipelago has passed from the hands of the two leading naval Powers into the hands of Japan. How long it will remain in Japanese hands is a matter on which I do not intend to speculate. But at any rate it will be long enough for Japan to inflict very heavy and painful losses on all of the United Nations who have establishments and possessions in the Far East. The Japanese no doubt will try to peg out claims and lodgments over all this enormous area, and to organise, in the interval before they lose command of the seas, a local command of the air which will render their expulsion and destruction a matter of considerable time and exertion.

The End of the Beginning

Here I must point out a very simple strategic truth. If there are 1,000 islands and 100 valuable military key-points and you put 1,000 men on every one of them or whatever it may be, the Power that has the command of the sea and carries with it the local command of the air can go around to every one of these places in turn, destroy or capture their garrisons, ravage and pillage them, ensconce themselves wherever they think fit, and then pass on with their circus to the next place. It would be vain to suppose that such an attack could be met by local defence. You might disperse 1,000,000 men over these immense areas and yet only provide more prey to the dominant Power. On the other hand, these conditions will be reversed when the balance of sea power and air power changes, as it will surely change.

Such is the phase of the Pacific war into which we have now entered. I cannot tell how long it will last. All I can tell the House is that it will be attended by very heavy punishment which we shall have to endure, and that presently, if we persevere, as I said just now about the Russian front, the boot will be on the other leg. That is why we should not allow ourselves to get rattled because this or that place has been captured, because, once the ultimate power of the United Nations has been brought to bear, the opposite process will be brought into play, and will move forward remorselessly to the final conclusion, provided that we persevere, provided that we fight with the utmost vigour and tenacity, and provided, above all, that we remain united.

Here I should like to express, in the name of the House, my admiration of the splendid courage and quality with which the small American Army, under General MacArthur, has resisted brilliantly for so long, at desperate odds, the hordes of Japanese who have been hurled against it by superior air power and superior sea power. Amid our own troubles, we send out to General MacArthur and his soldiers, and also to the Filipinos, who are defending their native soil with vigour and courage, our salute across the wide spaces which we and the United States will presently rule again together. Nor must I fail to pay a tribute, in the name of the House, to the Dutch, who, in the air and with their submarines, their surface craft, and their solid

34

fighting troops, are playing one of the main parts in the struggle now going on in the Malaysian Archipelago.

We have to turn our eyes for a moment to the hard-fought battle which is raging upon the approaches to Singapore and in the Malay Peninsula. I am not going to make any forecast about that now, except that it will be fought to the last inch by the British, Australian and Indian troops, which are in the line together, and which have been very considerably reinforced. The hon. Member for the Eye Division of Suffolk (Mr. Granville) had a very sound military idea the other day, when he pointed out the importance of sending reinforcements of aircraft to assist our ground forces at Singapore and in Burma. I entirely agree with him. In fact, we anticipated his suggestion. Before I left for the United States, on 12th December, the moment, that is to say, when the situation in Singapore and Pearl Harbour had disclosed itself, it was possible to make a swift redistribution of our Forces. The moment was favourable. General Auchinleck was making headway in Cyrenaica; the Russian front not only stood unbroken but had begun the advance in a magnificent counter-attack, and we were able to order a large number of measures, which there is no need to elaborate, but which will be capable of being judged by their results as the next few weeks and the next few months unfold in the Far East.

When I reached the United States, accompanied by our principal officers and large technical staffs, further important steps were taken by the President, with my cordial assent, and with the best technical advice we could obtain, to move from many directions everything that ships could carry and all air power that could be flown transported and serviced to suitable points. The House would be very ill-advised to suppose that the seven weeks which have passed since 7th December have been weeks of apathy and indecision for the English-speaking world. Odd as it may seem, quite a lot has been going on. But we must not nourish or indulge light and extravagant hopes or suppose that the advantages which the enemy has gained can soon or easily be taken from him. However, to sum up the bad and the good together, in spite of the many tragedies past and future, and with all pity for those who have suffered and will suffer, I must profess my profound thankfulness for what has happened throughout the whole world in the last two months.

I now turn for a short space — I hope I am not unduly wearying the House, but I feel that the war has become so wide that there are many aspects that must be regarded — to the question of the organisation, the international, inter-Allied or inter-United Nations organisation, which must be developed to meet the fact that we are a vast confederacy. To hear some people talk, however, one would think that the way to win the war is to make sure that every Power contributing armed forces and every branch of these armed forces is represented on all the councils and organisations which have to be set up, and that everybody is fully consulted before anything is done. That is in fact the most sure way to lose a war. You have to be aware of the well-known danger of having "more harness than horse," to quote a homely expression. Action to be successful must rest in the fewest number of hands possible. Nevertheless, now that we are working in the closest partnership with the United States and have also to consider our alliances with Russia and with China, as well as the bonds which unite us with the rest of the 26 United Nations and with our Dominions, it is evident that our system must become far more complex than heretofore.

I had many discussions with the President upon the Anglo-American war direction, especially as it affects this war against Japan, to which Russia is not yet a party. The physical and geographical difficulties of finding a common working centre for the leaders of nations and the great staffs of nations which cover the whole globe are insuperable. Whatever plan is made will be open to criticism and many wild objections. There is no solution that can be found by which the war can be discussed from day to day fully by all the leading military and political authorities concerned. I have, however, arranged with President Roosevelt that there should be a body in Washington called the Combined Chiefs of the Staff Committee, consisting of the three United States Chiefs of the Staff, men of the highest distinction, and three high officers representing and acting under the general instructions of the British Chiefs of the Staff Committee in London. This body will advise the President, and in the event of divergence of view between the British and American Chiefs of the Staff or their representatives, the difference must be adjusted by personal agreement between him and me as representing our respective countries. We must also concert together the closest association with Premier Stalin and Generalissimo Chiang Kai-shek as well as with the rest of the Allied and Associated Powers. We shall, of course, also remain in the closest touch with one another on all important questions of policy.

In order to wage the war effectively against Japan, it was agreed that I should propose to those concerned the setting-up of a Pacific Council in London, on the Ministerial plane, comprising Great Britain, Australia, New Zealand and the Dutch Government. Assisted by the British Chiefs of the Staff and the great staff organisations beneath them, I was to try to form and focus a united view. This would enable the British Commonwealth to act as a whole and form plans — plans which are at present far advanced — for collaboration at the appropriate levels in the spheres of Defence, Foreign Affairs and Supply. Thus the united view of the British Commonwealth and the Dutch would be transmitted, at first, on the Chiefs of the Staff level, to the combined Chiefs of the Staff Committee sitting in Washington. In the event of differences between the members of the Pacific Council in London, dissentient opinions would also be transmitted. In the event of differences between the London and Washington bodies, it would be necessary for the President and me to reach an agreement. I must point out that it is necessary for everybody to reach an agreement, for nobody can compel anybody else.

The Dutch Government, which is seated in London, might be willing to agree to this arrangement, but the Australian Government desired and the New Zealand Government preferred that this Council of the Pacific should be in Washington, where it would work alongside the Combined Chiefs of the Staff Committee. I have therefore transmitted the views of these two Dominions to the President, but I have not yet received, nor do I expect for a few days to receive, his reply. I am not, therefore, in a position to-day to announce, as I had hoped, the definite and final arrangements for the Pacific Council.

I should like to say, however, that underlying these structural arrangements are some very practical and simple facts upon which there is full agreement. The Supreme Commander has assumed control of the fighting areas in the South-West Pacific called the "A. B. D. A." area — A. B. D. A. — called after the countries which are involved, not the countries which are in the area but the countries which are involved in the area, namely, America, Britain, Dutch and Australasia. We do not propose to burden the Supreme Commander with frequent instructions. He has his general orders, and he has addressed himself with extraordinary buoyancy to his most difficult task, and President Roosevelt and I, representing, for my part, the British Government, are determined that he shall have a chance and a free hand to carry it out. The action in the Straits of Macassar undertaken by forces assigned to this area has apparently had very considerable success, of the full extent of which I am not yet advised. The manner in which General Wavell took up his task, the speed with which he has flown from place to place, the telegrams which he has sent describing the methods by which he was grappling with the situation and the forming of the central organism which was needed to deal with it all this has made a most favourable impression upon the high officers, military and political, whom I met in the United States. This is all going on. Our duty, upon which we have been constantly engaged for some time, is to pass reinforcements of every kind, especially air, into the new war zone, from every quarter and by every means, with the utmost speed.

In order to extend the system of unified command which has been set up in the "A.B.D.A." area — that is to say, the South-West Pacific, where the actual fighting is going on — in order to extend that system to all areas in which the forces of more than one of the United Nations — for that is the term we have adopted — will be operating, the Eastward approaches to Australia and New Zealand, which have been styled the Anzac area, are under United States command, and the communications between the Anzac area and America are a United States responsibility, while the communications across the Indian Ocean and from India remain a British responsibility. All this is now working, while the larger constitutional, or semi-constitutional, discussions and structural arrangements are being elaborated by telegrams passing to and fro between so many Governments. All this is now working fully and actively from hour to hour, and it must not, therefore, be supposed that any necessary military action has been held up pending the larger structural arrangements which I have mentioned.

Now I come to the question of our own Empire or Commonwealth of Nations. The fact that Australia and New Zealand are in the immediate danger zone reinforces the demand that they should be represented in the War Cabinet of Great Britain and Northern Ireland. We have always been ready to form an Imperial War Cabinet containing the Prime Ministers of the four Dominions. Whenever any of them have come here they have taken their seats at our table as a matter of course. Unhappily, it has not been possible to get them all here together at once. General Smuts may not be able to come over from South Africa, and Mr. Mackenzie King could unfortunately stay only for a short time. But Mr. Fraser was with us, and it was a great pleasure to have him, and we had a three months' visit from Mr. Menzies, which was also a great success, and we were all very sorry when his most valuable knowledge of our affairs and the war position, and his exceptional abilities, were lost. For the last three months we have had Sir Earle Page representing the Commonwealth Government at Cabinets when war matters and Australian matters were under discussion and also, in similar circumstances, upon the Defence Committee. As a matter of fact this has always been interpreted in the most broad and elastic fashion. The Australian Government have now asked specifically "that an accredited representative of the Commonwealth Government should have the right to be heard in the War Cabinet in the formulation and the direction of policy." We have of course agreed to this. New Zealand feels bound to ask for similar representation, and the same facilities will of course be available to Canada and South Africa. The presence at the Cabinet table of Dominion representatives who have no power to take decisions and can only report to their Governments evidently raises some serious problems, but none, I trust, which cannot be got over with good will. It must not, however, be supposed that in any circumstances the presence of Dominion representatives for certain purposes could in any way affect the collective responsi-

The End of the Beginning

bility of His Majesty's Servants in Great Britain to Crown and Parliament.

I am sure we all sympathise with our kith and kin in Australia now that the shield of British and American sea power has, for the time being, been withdrawn from them so unexpectedly and so tragically, and now that hostile bombers may soon be within range of Australian shores. We shall not put any obstacle to the return of the splendid Australian troops who volunteered for Imperial service to defend their own homeland or whatever part of the Pacific theatre might be thought most expedient. We are taking many measures in conjunction with the United States to increase the security of Australia and New Zealand, and to send them reinforcements, arms and equipment by the shortest and best routes. I always hesitate to express opinions about the future, because things turn out so very oddly, but I will go so far as to say that it may be that the Japanese, whose game is what I may call "to make hell while the sun shines," are more likely to occupy themselves in securing their rich prizes in the Philippines, the Dutch East Indies and the Malayan Archipelago and in seizing island bases for defensive purposes for the attack which is obviously coming towards them at no great distance of time — a tremendous onslaught which will characterise the future in 1942 and 1943. (I do not think we can stretch our views beyond those dates, but, again, we must see how we go.) I think they are much more likely to be arranging themselves in those districts which they have taken or may probably take than to be planning a serious mass invasion of Australia. That would seem to be a very ambitious overseas operation for Japan to undertake in the precarious and limited interval before the British and American navies regain — as they must certainly regain, through the new building that is advancing, and for other reasons — the unquestionable command of the Pacific Ocean. However, everything in human power that we can do to help Australia, or persuade America to do, we will do; and meanwhile I trust that reproaches and recriminations of all kinds will be avoided, and that if any are made, we in Britain shall not take part in them.

Let me, in conclusion, return to the terrific changes which have occurred in our affairs during the last few months and particularly in the last few weeks. We have to consider the prospects of the war in 1942 and also in 1943, and, as I said just now, it is not useful to look farther ahead than that. The moment that the United States was set upon and attacked by Japan, Germany and Italy — that is to say, within a few days of December 7, 1941 — I was sure it was my duty to cross the Atlantic and establish the closest possible relationship with the President and Government of the United States, and also to develop the closest contacts, personal and professional, between the British Chiefs of Staff and their trans-Atlantic deputies, and with the American Chiefs of Staff who were there to meet them.

Having crossed the Atlantic, it was plainly my duty to visit the great Dominion of Canada. The House will have read with admiration and deep interest the speech made by the Prime Minister of Canada yesterday on Canada's great and growing contribution to the common cause in men, in money, and in materials. A notable part of that contribution is the financial offer which the Canadian Government have made to this country. The sum involved is one billion Canadian dollars, about £225,000,000. I know the House will wish me to convey to the Government of Canada our lively appreciation of their timely and most generous offer. It is unequalled in its scale in the whole history of the British Empire, and it is a convincing proof of the determination of Canada to make her maximum contribution towards the successful prosecution of the war.

During those three weeks which I spent in Mr. Roosevelt's home and family, I established with him relations not only of comradeship, but, I think I may say, of friendship. We can say anything to each other, however painful. When we parted he wrung my hand, saying, "We will fight this through to the bitter end, whatever the cost may be." Behind him rises the gigantic and hitherto unmobilised power of the people of the United States, carrying with them in their life and death struggle the entire, or almost the entire, Western hemisphere.

At Washington, we and our combined staffs surveyed the whole scene of the war, and we reached a number of important practical decisions. Some of them affect future operations and cannot, of course, be mentioned, but others have been made public by declaration or by events. The vanguard of an American Army has already arrived in the United Kingdom. Very considerable forces are following as opportunity may serve. These forces will take their station in the British Isles and face with us whatever is coming our way. They impart a freedom of movement to all forces in the British Isles greater than we could otherwise have possessed. Numerous United States fighter and bomber squadrons will also take part in the defence of Britain and in the ever-increasing bombing offensive against Germany. The United States Navy is linked in the most intimate union with the Admiralty, both in the Atlantic and the Pacific. We shall plan our naval moves together as if we were literally one people.

In the next place, we formed this league of 26 United Nations in which the principal partners at the present time are Great Britain and the British Empire, the United States, the Union of Socialist Soviet Republics of Russia, and the Republic of China, together with the stout-hearted Dutch, and the representatives of the rest of the 26 Powers. This Union is based on the principles of the Atlantic Charter. It aims at the destruction of Hitlerism in all its forms and manifestations in every corner of the globe. We will march forward together until every vestige of this villainy has been extirpated from the life of the world.

Thirdly, as I have explained at some length, we addressed ourselves to the war against Japan and to the measures to be taken to defend Australia, New Zealand, the Netherlands East Indies, Malaya, Burma, and India against Japanese attack or invasion.

Fourthly, we have established a vast common pool of weapons and munitions, of raw materials and of shipping, the outline of which has been set forth in a series of memoranda which I have initialled with the President. I had a talk with him last night on the telephone, as a result of which an announcement has been made in the early hours of this morning in the United States, and I have a White Paper for the House which will be available, I think, in a very short time. Many people have been staggered by the figures of prospective American output of war weapons which the President announced to Congress, and the Germans have affected to regard them with incredulity. I can only say that Lord Beaverbrook and I were made acquainted beforehand with all the bases upon which these colossal programmes were founded, and that I myself heard President Roosevelt confide their specific tasks to the chiefs of American industry, and heard these men accept their prodigious tasks and declare that they would and could fulfil them. Most important of all is the multiplication of our joint tonnage at sea. The American programmes were already vast. They have been increased in the proportion of 100 to nearly 160. If they are completed, as completed I believe they will be, we shall be able to move across the ocean spaces in 1943 armies two, three or even four times as large as the considerable forces we are able to handle at sea at the present time.

I expect — and I have made no secret of it — that we shall both of us receive severe ill-usage at the hands of the Japanese in 1942, but I believe we shall presently regain the naval command of the Pacific and begin to establish an effective superiority in the air, and then later on, with the great basic areas in Australasia, in India and in the Dutch East Indies, we shall be able to set about our task in good style in 1943. It is no doubt true that the defeat of Japan will not necessarily entail the defeat of Hitler, whereas the defeat of Hitler would enable the whole forces of the United Nations to be concentrated upon the defeat of Japan. But there is no question of regarding the war in the Pacific as a secondary operation. The only limitation applied to its vigorous prosecution will be the shipping available at any given time.

It is most important that we should not overlook the enormous contribution of China to this struggle for world freedom and democracy. If there is any lesson I have brought back from the United States that I could express in one word, it would be "China." That is in all their minds. When we feel the sharp military qualities of the Japanese soldiery in contact with our own troops, although of course very few have as yet been engaged, we must remember that China, ill-armed or half-armed, has, for four and a half years, single-handed, under its glorious leader Chiang Kai-shek, withstood the main fury of Japan. We shall pursue the struggle hand in hand with China, and do everything in our power to give them arms and supplies, which is all they need to vanquish the invaders of their native soil and play a magnificent part in the general forward movement of the United Nations.

Although I feel the broadening swell of victory and liberation bearing us and all the tortured peoples onwards safely to the final goal, I must confess to feeling the weight of the war upon me even more than in the tremendous summer days of 1940. There are so many fronts which are open, so many vulnerable points to defend, so many inevitable misfortunes, so many shrill voices raised to take advantage, now that we can breathe more freely, of all the turns and twists of war. Therefore, I feel entitled to come to the House of Commons, whose servant I am, and ask them not to press me to act against my conscience and better judgment and make scapegoats in order to improve my own position, not to press me to do the things which may be clamoured for at the moment but which will not help in our war effort, but, on the contrary, to give me their encouragement and to give me their aid. I have never ventured to predict the future. I stand by my original programme, blood, toil, tears and sweat, which is all I have ever offered, to which I added, five months later, "many shortcomings, mistakes and disappointments." But it is because I see the light gleaming behind the clouds and broadening on our path, that I make so bold now as to demand a declaration of confidence of the House of Commons as an additional weapon in the armoury of the United Nations.

[January 29, 1942, at close of debate

No one can say that this has not been a full and free Debate. No one can say that criticism has been hampered or stifled. No one can say that it has not been a necessary Debate. Many will think it has been a valuable Debate. But I think there will be very few who upon reflection will doubt that a Debate of this far-reaching character and memorable importance, in times of hard and anxious war, with the state of the world what it is, our relationships to other countries being what they are, and our own safety so deeply involved — very few people will doubt that it should not close without a solemn and formal expression of the opinion of the House in relation both to the Government and to the prosecution of the war.

In no country in the world at the present time could a Government conducting a war be exposed to such a stress. No dictator country fighting for its life would dare allow such a discussion. They do not even allow the free transmission of news to their peoples, or even the reception of foreign broadcasts, to which we are all now so hardily inured. Even in the great democracy of the United States the Executive does not stand in the same direct, immediate, day-to-day relation to the Legislative body as we do. The President, in many vital respects independent of the Legislature, Commander-in-Chief of all the Forces of the Republic, has a fixed term of office, during which his authority can scarcely be impugned. But here in this country the House of Commons is master all the time of the life of the Administration. Against its decisions there is only one appeal, the appeal to the nation, an appeal it is very difficult to make under the conditions of a war like this, with a register like this, with air raids and invasion always hanging over us.

Therefore, I say that the House of Commons has a great responsibility. It owes it to itself and it owes it to the people and the whole Empire, and to the world cause, either to produce an effective, alternative Administration by which the King's Government can be carried on, or to sustain that Government in the enormous tasks and trials which it has to endure. I feel myself very much in need of that help at the present time, and I am sure I shall be accorded it in a manner to give encouragement and comfort, as well as guidance and suggestion. I am sorry that I have not been able to be here throughout the whole Debate, but I have read every word of the Debate, except what has been spoken and has not yet been printed, and I can assure the House that I shall be ready to profit to the full from many constructive and helpful lines of thought which have been advanced, even when they come from the most hostile quarters. I shall not be like that saint to whom I have before referred in this House, but whose name I have unhappily forgotten, who refused to do right because the devil prompted him. Neither shall I be deterred from doing what I am convinced is right by the fact that I have thought differently about it in some distant, or even in some recent past.

When events are moving at hurricane speed and when scenes change with baffling frequency, it would be disastrous to lose that flexibility of mind in dealing with new situations on which I have often been complimented, which is the essential counterpart of a consistent and unswerving purpose. Let me take an instance. During my visit to America, events occurred which altered in a decisive way the question of creating a Minister of Production. President Roosevelt has appointed Mr. Donald Nelson to supervise the whole field of American production. All the resources of our two countries are now pooled, in shipping, in munitions, and in raw materials, and some similar office, I will not say with exactly the same scope, but of similar scope, must be created here, if harmonious working between Great Britain and the United States is to be maintained upon this very high level. I have been for some weeks carefully considering this, and the strong opinions which have been expressed in the House, even though I do not share their reasoning in all respects, have reinforced the conclusions with which I returned from the United States. I will not of course anticipate any advice that it may be my duty to tender to the Crown.

I was forced to inflict upon the House two days ago a very lengthy statement, which cost me a great deal of time and trouble, in the intervals of busy days and nights, to prepare. I do not desire to add to it to any important extent. It would not be possible for me to answer all the criticisms and inquiries which have been made during this Debate. I have several times pointed out to the House the disadvantage I lie under, compared with the leaders of other countries who are charged with general war direction, in having to make so many public statements, and the danger that in explaining fully our position to our friends we may also be stating it rather too fully to our enemies. Moreover, the Lord Privy Seal, in his excellent speech yesterday, has already replied to a number of the controversial issues which were raised. There are therefore only a few points with which I wish to deal to-day, but they are important points.

The first is the advantage, not only to Britain but to the Empire, of the arrival of powerful American Army and Air Forces in the United Kingdom. First of all, this meets the desire of the American people and of the leaders of the Republic that the large mass of trained and equipped troops which they have under arms in the United States shall come into contact with the enemy as close and as soon as possible. Secondly, the presence of these forces in these Islands imparts a greater freedom of movement overseas, to theatres where we are already engaged, of the mature and seasoned divisions of the British Home Army. It avoids the difficulty of reinforcing theatres where we are engaged with troops of another nation, and all the complications of armament and command which arise therefrom. Therefore we must consider this arrival of the American Army as giving us a latitude of manœuvre which we have not hitherto possessed. Thirdly, the presence in our Islands of a Force of heavy but unknown strength, and the establishment of a broader bridgehead between us and the New World, constituted an additional deterrent to invasion at a time when the successful invasion of these Islands is Hitler's last remaining hope of total victory. Fourthly — and here I address myself to what has been said about aiding and succouring Australia and New Zealand — the fact that well-equipped American divisions can be sent into these Islands so easily and rapidly will enable substantial supplies of weapons and munitions, now being made in the United States for our account, to be sent direct on the other side of the world to Australia and New Zealand, to meet the new dangers of home defence which are cast upon them by the Japanese war. Lastly, this whole business cannot do Mr. de Valera any harm, and it may even do him some good. It certainly offers a measure of protection to Southern Ireland, and to Ireland as a whole, which she could not otherwise enjoy. I feel sure that the House will find these reasons, or most of them, solid and satisfactory.

The course of this Debate has mainly turned upon the admitted inadequacy of our preparations to meet the full onslaught of the new and mighty military opponent who has launched against us his whole force, his whole energies and fury in Malaya and in the Far East. There is not very much I wish to add, and that only by way of illustration, to the connected argument which I deployed to the House on Tuesday. The speeches of the hon. Members for Kidderminster (Sir J. Wardlaw-Milne) and Seaham (Mr. Shinwell) dwelt from different angles upon this all-important issue. I do not, of course, pretend that there may not have been avoidable shortcomings or mistakes, or that some oversight may not have been shown in making use of our resources, limited though those resources were. While I take full responsibility for the broad strategic dispositions, that does not mean that scandals, or inefficiency or misbehaviour of functionaries at particular moments and particular places, occurring on the spot, will not be probed or will be covered by the general support I gave to our commanders in the field.

I am by no means claiming that faults have not been committed in the minor sphere, and faults for which the Government are blameworthy. But when all is said and done, the House must not be led into supposing that even if everything on the spot had gone perfectly — which is rare in war — they must not be led into supposing that this would have made any decisive difference to the heavy British and American forfeits which followed inexorably from the temporary loss of sea power in the Pacific, combined with the fact of our being so fully extended elsewhere. Even that is not exhaustive, because, before the defeat of Pearl Harbour — I am speaking of eight or nine months ago — our ability to defend the Malay Peninsula was seriously prejudiced by the incursion of the Japanese into French Indo-China and the steady building-up of very powerful forces and bases there. Even at the time when I went to meet the President In Newfoundland the invasion of Siam seemed imminent, and probably it was due to the measures which the President took as the result of our conversations that this attack was staved off for so long, and might well have been staved off indefinitely. In ordinary circumstances, if we had not been engaged to the last ounce in Europe and the Nile Valley, we should ourselves, of course, have confronted the Japanese aggression into Indo-China with the strongest possible resistance from the moment when they began to build up a large military and air power. We were not in a position to do this.

If we had gone to war with Japan to stop the Japanese coming across the long ocean stretches from their own country, and establishing themselves within close striking distance of the Malay Peninsula and Singapore, we should have had to fight alone, perhaps for a long time, the whole of the Japanese attacks upon our loosely-knit establishments and possessions in this vast Oriental region. As I said on Tuesday, we have never had the power, and we never could have had the power, to fight Germany, Italy and Japan single-handed at the same time. We therefore had to watch the march of events with an anxiety which increased with the growth of the Japanese concentrations, but at the same time was offset by the continuous approach of the United States ever nearer to the confines of the War. It must not be supposed that endless, repeated consultations and discussions were not held by the Staffs, by the Defence Committee, by Ministers, and that Staff conferences were not held at Singapore. Contact was maintained with Australia and New Zealand, and with the United States to a lesser degree.

All this went on; but, when all was said and done, there was the danger, and the means of meeting it had yet to be found. Ought we not in that interval to have considered the question which the House must ask itself — I want to answer the case quite fairly — whether, in view of that menace, apart from minor precautions, many of which were taken and some of which were not, we ought not to have reduced our aid in munitions to Russia? A part of what we sent to Russia would have made us, I will not say safe, because I do not think that that was possible, in view of what happened at sea, but far better prepared in Burma and Malaya than we were. Figures were mentioned by the hon. Member for Seaham yesterday. He will not expect me to confirm or deny those figures, but, taking them as a basis, half of that would have made us far better off, and would have dazzled the eyes of Sir Robert Brooke-Popham, who so repeatedly asked for more supplies of all those commodities of which we were most short. We did not make such a reduction in Russian supplies and I believe that the vast majority of opinion in all parts of the House, and in the country, endorses our decision now, even after the event. If they had to go back, they would take it again, even although they see now what serious consequences have arisen.

I entirely agree about the vital importance of the Burma Road and of fighting with every means in our power to keep a strong hand-grasp with the Chinese Armies and the closest contact with their splendid leader Chiang Kai-shek. Nothing has prevented the employment of Indian troops in that area, except the use of them in other theatres and the immense difficulties of transport in those regions. So much for the Russian policy, which, for good or for ill, has played a very great part in the thoughts and actions of the people of this country in this struggle, and I believe has played a very important part — not by any means a decisive part, but a very important part — in the crushing defeats which have been inflicted on the German army and the possible demoralisation of the wicked régime which uses that army.

But, apart from Russia, what about the campaign in Libya? What were the reasons which made that a necessary operation? First, we had to remove, and probably we have removed, the menace to the Nile Valley from the West for a considerable time, thus liberating important forces and still more important transport to meet what seemed to be an impending attack through the Caucasus from the North. Secondly, this was the only place where we could open a second front against the enemy. Everyone will remember, conveniently short as memories may be, the natural and passionate impatience which our prolonged inactivity aroused in all our hearts while Russia seemed to be being battered to pieces by the fearful machinery of the German army. There is no doubt whatever that, although our offensive in Libya was on a small scale compared with the mighty struggle on the Russian front, it nevertheless drew important German air forces from that front. They were moved at a most critical moment in that battle and transferred to the Mediterranean theatre. Thirdly, this second front in the Western Desert afforded us the opportunity of fighting a campaign against Germany and Italy on terms most costly to them. If there be any place where we can fight them with marked advantage, it is in the Western Desert and Libya, because not only, as I explained, have we managed to destroy two-thirds of their African army and a great amount of its equipment and air power, but also to take a formidable toll of all their reinforcements of men and materials, and above all of their limited shipping across the Mediterranean by which they were forced to maintain themselves. The longer they go on fighting in this theatre the longer that process will go on, and there is no part of the world where you have a chance of getting better results for the blood and valour of your soldiers.

For these reasons, I am sure that it was a sound decision, and one with which all our professional advisers agreed, to take the offensive in the Western Desert and to do our utmost to make it a success. We have been over this ground in Cyrenaica already. The first time we took a quarter of a million Italian prisoners without serious loss to ourselves. The second time we have accounted for 60,000 men, including many Germans, for the loss of only one-third to ourselves. Even if we have to do part of it a third time, as seems possible, in view of the tactical successes of the enemy attacks upon our armoured brigade last week, there seems no reason why the campaign should not retain its profitable character in the war in North East Africa and become a festering sore, a dangerous drain, upon the German and Italian resources.

This is the question: Should we have been right to sacrifice all this, to stand idly on the defensive in the Western Desert and send all our available Forces to garrison Malaya and guard against a war against Japan which nevertheless might not have taken place, and which, I believe, did take place only through the civil Government being overwhelmed by a military *coup d'état?* That is a matter of opinion, and it is quite easy for those who clamoured eagerly for opening an offensive in Libya to dilate upon our want of foresight and preparedness in the Far East. That is a matter on which anyone can form an opinion, and those are lucky who do not have to form one before the course of events is known.

I come now to this battle which is raging in Johore. I cannot tell how it will go or how the attack upon the Island of Singapore will go, but a steady stream of reinforcements, both air and troops, has flowed into the island for several weeks past. The forces which have been sent were, of course, set in motion within a few days, and some within a few hours, of the Japanese declaration of war. To sum up, I submit to the House that the main strategic and political decision to aid Russia, to deliver an offensive in Libya and to accept a consequential state of weakness in the then peaceful theatre of the Far East, was sound, and will be found to have played a useful part in the general course of the War, and that this is in no wise invalidated by the unexpected naval misfortunes and the heavy forfeits which we have paid, and shall have to pay, in the Far East. For this Vote of Confidence, on that I rest.

The End of the Beginning

There is, however, one episode of a tactical rather than a strategic character about which many questions have been asked, both here and in another place, and to which it is not easy to refer. I mean, of course, the dispatch from this country of the *Prince of Wales* during November last and, secondly, the operation which led to the sinking of the *Prince of Wales* and of the *Repulse,* which had started earlier. This sinking took place on 9th December. It was the policy of the War Cabinet and the Defence Committee, initiated by the Naval Staff, to build up in the Indian Ocean, and base mainly on Singapore, a battle squadron to act, it was hoped, in co-operation with the United States fleet in general protective work in Far Eastern waters. I am not at liberty to state how these plans stand at the present time, but the House may be assured that nothing has been left undone, which was in our power, to repair the heavy losses which have been sustained. My right hon. Friend the Member for East Edinburgh (Mr. Pethick-Lawrence) has asked very properly why the *Prince of Wales* and *Repulse* were sent to Eastern waters if they could not be properly protected by aircraft. The answer to this question is that the decision to send those ships in advance to the Far East was taken in the hope, primarily, of deterring the Japanese from going to war at all, or, failing that, of deterring her from sending convoys into the Gulf of Siam, having regard to the then position of the strong American fleet at Hawaii.

After long and careful consideration it was decided, in view of the importance of having in Far Eastern waters at least one ship which could catch or kill any individual vessel of the enemy — the Americans then not having a new battleship available — to send the *Prince of Wales.* Moreover, she was the only ship available at the moment which could reach the spot in time for any deterrent effect to be produced. The intention was that these two fast ships, whose arrival at Cape Town was deliberately not concealed, should not only act as a deterrent upon Japan coming into the war but a deterrent upon the activities of individual heavy ships of the enemy, our ships being able to choose their moment to fight. The suggestion of the hon. and gallant Member for Epsom (Sir A. Southby) that the Naval Staff desired to send an aircraft-carrier and were overruled by me is as mischievous as it is untrue. It was always the intention that any fast ships proceeding to the Far East should be accompanied by an aircraft-carrier. Unfortunately, at the time, with the exception of an aircraft-carrier in home waters, not a single ship of this type was available. Through a succession of accidents, some of very slight consequence, all of them, except the one with the Home Fleet, were under repair. Accordingly, the *Prince of Wales* and the *Repulse* arrived at Singapore, and it was hoped they would shortly leave again for secret bases and the broad waters, which would enable them to put a continuous restraining preoccupation on all the movements of the enemy. That is the first phase of the story.

I now come to the further question of why, the presence of the two ships having failed to achieve the deterrent object, Pearl Harbour having occurred, and the Japanese having begun war, they were sent North from Singapore to oppose the Japanese landings from the Gulf of Siam on the Kra Peninsula. Admiral Tom Phillips, as Vice-Chief of the Naval Staff, was fully acquainted with the whole policy I have described, and had sailed in the *Prince of Wales* to carry it out. On 8th December he decided, after conferring with his captain and staff officers, that in the circumstances, and in view of the movement of Japanese transports with a weak fighting escort towards the Kra Peninsula, drastic and urgent naval action was required. This action, if successful, would have presented the Army with a good prospect of defeating the landings and possibly of paralysing the invasion of Malaya at its birth. The stakes on both sides were very high. The prize was great if gained; if lost, our danger most grievous. Admiral Phillips was fully aware of the risk, and he took steps for air reconnaissance to see whether there was an enemy aircraft-carrier about, and for fighter protection up to the limit of the short-range fighters available. Only after he left harbour was he informed that fighter protection could not be provided in the area in which he intended to operate, but in view of the low visibility he decided to stand on. Later, in accordance with his predetermined plans, he turned back, because the weather began to clear, and he knew he had been sighted. However, later still, during his retirement, a further landing more to the South of the peninsula was reported, presenting an even more serious threat to Malaya, and he decided to investigate this. It was on returning from this investigation, which proved to be negative, that his force was attacked, not, as has been supposed, by torpedo or bomber aircraft flown off a carrier, but by very long-range shore-based heavy two-engined torpedo bombers from the main Japanese aerodromes 400 miles away.

In the opinion of the Board of Admiralty, which it is my duty to pronounce, the risks which Admiral Phillips took were fair and reasonable, in the light of the knowledge which he had of the enemy, when compared with the very urgent and vital issues at stake on which the whole safety of Malaya might have depended. I have given an account of this episode. No doubt the Admiralty will have its own inquiry for the purpose of informing itself and of studying the lessons, but I could not bring myself, on the first day that this matter was mentioned, when the information I had was most scanty, to pronounce condemnation on the audacious, daring action of Admiral Tom Phillips in going forward, although he knew of the risks he ran, when the prize might have been 20,000 of the enemy drowned in the sea, and a relief from the whole catalogue of misfortunes which have since come upon us, and have still to come.

I have finished, and it only remains for us to act. I have tried to lay the whole position before the House as far as public interest will allow, and very fully have we gone into matters. On behalf of His Majesty's Government, I make no complaint of the Debate, I offer no apologies, I offer no excuses, I make no promises. In no way have I mitigated the sense of danger and impending misfortunes of a minor character and of a severe character which still hang over us, but at the same time I avow my confidence, never stronger than at this moment, that we shall bring this conflict to an end in a manner agreeable to the interests of our country, and in a manner agreeable to the future welfare of the world. I have finished. Let every man act now in accordance with what he thinks is his duty in harmony with his heart and conscience.

NOTE

The Vote of Confidence was carried by 464 to 1.

The Defence of Rangoon

A MESSAGE SENT TO SIR REGINALD DORMAN-SMITH
THE GOVERNOR OF BURMA
FEBRUARY 2, 1942

January 30. *Hitler made a speech preparing the German people for hard times, but promising a Spring offensive.*
Rommel's forces recaptured Benghazi.
January 31. *British troops withdrew from Malaya mainland to Singapore and siege of Island began.*

[*February 2, 1942*

AGAINST the sombre background of difficulty and danger in the Far East have stood out in cheering relief the brilliant exploits of the American Volunteer Group and the Royal Air Force in the defence of Rangoon — the vital gateway on which not only Burma itself but no less our brave Chinese allies rely for the reinforcements which we mean to send them in steadily increasing measure. The victories they have won in the air over the paddy fields of Burma may well prove to have been comparable in character, if not in scale, with those won over the orchards and hop fields of Kent in the Battle of Britain.

To these brave men, who have achieved in the air protection of this great port, the thanks of all the United Nations are due, but no less thanks are due also to those who, under cover of this protection, are daily working in the face of danger under your inspiring and cheerful leadership to keep the port fully at work. To all — to the dock labourers, the Port Commission, the civil defence workers, the shipping firms, the railway staffs, and not least the lowly municipal workers whose perseverance in their tasks alone preserves a bombarded city from disease — to all, Burmans, Indians, Chinese and Europeans, private citizens and officials alike, I gladly and gratefully pay tribute.

Imperial War Cabinet

[February 5, 1942

*In reply to a Member of Parliament who asked when the new
Imperial War Cabinet or Directorate would begin to function
and whether it had been decided who would be its members, the
Prime Minister said: —*

THE proposals for associating Dominion representatives with
the War Cabinet do not involve any change in the United Kingdom membership of the War Cabinet. The proposal of the
Australian Government was that they should have a representative at the War Cabinet who should have the right to be heard
in the formulation and direction of policy. I replied that we
were in agreement with this proposal, and for a good many
months past Sir Earle Page has been exercising these rights. We
have informed the Governments of Canada, New Zealand and
the Union of South Africa that the same facilities are available
for them if they wish to take advantage of them. We have as yet
had no formal reply from New Zealand. I understand that
Canada and South Africa are satisfied with the existing arrangements for consultation — indeed they expressed themselves
strongly on this point — and do not at present wish to attach
special representatives to the War Cabinet here.

So far as I gather the request of the Australian Government
makes no change in what has actually been going on here since
Sir Earle Page arrived, and been going on with very satisfactory
results.

Service Pay and Allowances and the Minister of War Production

STATEMENTS TO THE HOUSE OF COMMONS
FEBRUARY 10, 1942

February 4.	*Lord Beaverbrook appointed to newly-created post of Minister of War Production and Sir Andrew Duncan became Minister of Supply.*
February 5.	*Japan claimed that the big offensive against Singapore had begun.*
February 7.	*Naval base at Singapore partly evacuated and docks flooded.*
	Announced that Dr. Todt, builder of Germany's roads and fortifications, had been killed in an air crash.
February 9.	*Japanese landed in force north-west of Singapore.*
	Former French liner, Normandie, *caught fire and capsized at New York while being converted for war.*
February 10.	*General Chiang Kai-shek arrived in India for conference on war strategy.*

[February 10, 1942

I HAVE two statements to make to the House, one on Service Pay and Allowances, and the other on the new office of Minister of Production.

I take, first, the question of Service Pay and Allowances. As was promised before Christmas, His Majesty's Government have given careful consideration to the remuneration of the Armed Forces and have examined the various suggestions which at that time were put forward in debate in the House. We regard the improved War Service Grants Scheme, which was introduced as

57

recently as last October, as an effective and flexible instrument for ensuring that the families of fighting men shall be guarded against hardship. We have, nevertheless, decided as a result of our review to make certain improvements relating both to current conditions and to post-war needs. Details of the improvements are contained in a White Paper which will be available to-day, and which I ask hon. Members to study.

There are three proposals designed to meet the wish expressed in the House for immediate improvement in the position of those with family responsibilities. In the first place, the Government have accepted the suggestion for a reduction, at the expense of the Exchequer, of 3s. 6d. in the compulsory allotments from their own pay made by men claiming family or dependent's allowances, thus increasing the total family resources by 3s. 6d. per week. The cost to the public of this improvement will be £17,500,000 a year. The second improvement is an increase in all children's allowances of 1s. per week per child, and the third a similar increase in the allowances paid to certain classes of dependent. The annual cost to the public of these improvements in allowances will be £5,000,000 more.

We have sought also for the best way of meeting the criticism — about which I must say that I personally always felt much concerned and very much disturbed — that Service men are at a disadvantage, by comparison with civilians, in regard to the provision which they are able to make for the financial needs which they will have to face after the war. To my mind, it would be a very anomalous and invidious situation if those who had worn uniform had no nest-egg and everybody else had one as a result of savings from higher pay or through the Income Tax credits. We have decided to institute a system of post-war credits under which a sum of 6d. per day, or approximately £9 a year, will be set aside for all other ranks and ratings; the sixpences will be accumulated on behalf of the men, and will form a nest-egg available for use after the war and after discharge from the Forces. It is the intention of the Government that the introduction of this credit shall not prejudice the question, when the time comes to consider it, of granting a war gratuity to the Forces on appropriate lines. The cost to the public of this bonus will be £32,500,000 a year.

We have thus sought to combine immediate improvement in those cases where family responsibilities constitute a claim for the most sympathetic treatment possible, with a general provision for the difficult days which may face many of us when the war is over. The total cost, both current and deferred, of these improvements is £55,000,000 a year, and this figure will rise as the Forces expand further to over £60,000,000 a year. These are large figures, but I have no doubt that the burden which they represent will be patiently and cheerfully borne.

[MINISTER OF PRODUCTION]

Now I come to the question of the Office of the Minister of Production, which has occupied a good deal of my thoughts following the recent Debate. I ask no pardon for going a little into the past, because I am anxious to place my action in the recollection of the House. During the latter part of the last war I was at the head of the Ministry of Munitions, which comprised, not only what is now called the Ministry of Supply, but also the Ministry of Aircraft Production, which latter was in many ways an enclave of its own. The burden did not appear too great, and the work went forward without more than the usual volume of complaints and criticisms. The Ministry of Munitions did not cover the Admiralty, nor various outlying branches of production, including merchant shipbuilding, which was then under the Ministry of Shipping.

Having seen this system in action at close quarters, I was, naturally, inclined to recommend it to Parliament before the war, and when I became Prime Minister I looked for an opportunity of restoring it. In October, 1940, the air bombardment being at its height, there was advantage in placing at the head of Home Security a Minister who had special knowledge of London, which up till then had sustained the brunt and continued to do so for some time afterwards. Accordingly, my right hon. friend the Member for South Hackney (Mr. Morrison), who was then Minister of Supply, became Home Secretary. This enabled me to offer Lord Beaverbrook, who was then Minister of Aircraft Production, the double office of Minister of Aircraft Production and Minister of Supply, which, of course, comprised four-fifths of the entire field of war production. Unfortunately,

The End of the Beginning

Lord Beaverbrook's health at that time was seriously affected, and he did not feel able, in spite of my insistence, to undertake any additional burdens. I therefore made the arrangements, which I explained to Parliament in January, 1941, by which the three Supply Departments of Ministry of Supply, Ministry of Aircraft Production, and the Controller's Department of the Admiralty remained separate and independent, but were grouped together for common purposes by the Production Executive, over which my right hon. Friend the Minister of Labour [Mr. Ernest Bevin] presided. This was the first time that the Admiralty had come so fully into the common system, and it is a tribute to the manner in which my right hon. Friend the Minister of Labour has discharged his difficult duties, that they are now ready and willing to take a further step towards unification.

I do not feel that this system has worked badly, and I do not accept the many complaints that have been made against it. The entry of the United States into the war, the far-reaching measures of the pooling of Anglo-American resources, and the appointment of Mr. Donald Nelson over the whole sphere of American war production, created an entirely new situation Lord Beaverbrook had established very close and intimate connections with the chiefs of American production. He enjoys the confidence and the good will of the President. In shaping the new organisation, it was natural that he should be the British representative in the various pooling arrangements which were made, and which I laid before Parliament in a White Paper a fortnight ago. It followed from this, again quite naturally, that he should be put into a position, broadly speaking, similar to that occupied by Mr. Donald Nelson, and that someone should be able to speak to the United States representing British war production as a whole. I found myself, therefore, drawn to the conclusion before I left America that there should be a Minister of Production and that Lord Beaverbrook should be that Minister. I was very much fortified on the general question by the undoubted wish of the House and of the Press that such an officer and such an office should be created, and I have accordingly taken all necessary steps to bring the policy into effect.

It should be pointed out on the one hand that we are not now creating a Ministry of Munitions of nominally one Department under one executive head over a large portion of war supplies. On the contrary, the Departments retain their separate identities under their respective chiefs. A War Cabinet Minister, Lord Beaverbrook, will exercise general supervision and guidance over them and will concert and co-ordinate their actions. Moreover, the Controller's Department of the Admiralty will come within the scope of the new Office, except in so far as warship design and the fixing of naval programmes are concerned. In addition, certain productive or distributive functions exercised by the Board of Trade and by the Ministry of Works and Buildings are also brought within the scope of the Minister of Production. A White Paper will be available in the Vote Office later to-day which will set forth the scope and powers of the new Office in more precise detail. I should like to point out, however, that this Paper is not to be read as if it were a Parliamentary Statute on which courts of law would pronounce after elaborate argument, but as a practical division of functions, and a guide under which men of good will, having common objects in view, will work together in the public interest and for the maximum prosecution of the war effort. I will content myself by reading the four opening paragraphs of this White Paper, leaving the more technical and departmental aspects to the study of the House at their leisure:

"1. The Minister of Production is the War Cabinet Minister charged with prime responsibility for all the business of war production in accordance with the policy of the Minister of Defence and the War Cabinet. He will carry out all the duties hitherto exercised by the Production Executive excepting only those relating to man-power and labour.

"2. These duties include the allocation of available resources of productive capacity and raw materials (including arrangements for their import) , the settlement of priorities of production where necessary, and the supervision and guidance of the various Departments and Branches of Departments concerned.

"3. Notwithstanding anything in this paper, the responsibilities to Parliament of the Ministers in charge of Departments concerned with production for the administration of their Departments remain unaltered, and any Ministerial Head of a Department has the right to appeal either to the Minister of

Defence or to the War Cabinet in respect of the proper discharge of such responsibilities.

"4. The Minister of Production will also be the Minister responsible for handling, on behalf of the War Cabinet, discussions on the Combined Bodies set up here and in the United States to deal with Munitions Assignments and Raw Materials as between the Allies."

I commend this scheme to the House. It is certainly capable of modification in practice, but I hope it will be given a fair trial by all concerned.

Mr. Hore-Belisha then asked: Why are questions of man-power and labour excluded from this proposal? If the Production Executive is to lapse, surely the co-ordination over the whole field of supply will be less complete than it was before, in the absence of this essential factor?

Mr. Churchill continued: —

Of course, that is all provided for in the White Paper. I was only dealing with the general lay-out in these remarks. The right hon. Gentleman will see in paragraphs 8, 9 and 10 that it states:

"8. The Minister of Labour and National Service is the War Cabinet Minister who will in future, under the general authority of the War Cabinet, discharge the functions hitherto performed by the Production Executive in regard to man-power and labour. These functions include the allocation of man-power resources to the Armed Forces and Civil Defence, to war production, and to civil industry, as well as general labour questions in the field of production.

"9. As part of his function of dealing with demands for and allocating man-power, the Minister of Labour and National Service has the duty of bringing to notice any direction in which he thinks that greater economy in the use of man-power could be effected, and for this purpose his officers will have such facilities as they require for obtaining information about the utilisation of labour.

"10. All labour questions between the Production Departments and the Ministry of Labour will be settled between the

Minister of Labour and the Minister of Production, or such officers as they may appoint. The three Supply Departments will retain their existing separate labour organisations."

The Minister of Production and the Minister of Labour will work in the closest co-operation. The Minister of Labour will carry out the policy of the War Cabinet. He finds and supplies the labour, and he follows it up and sees that it is not used uneconomically. That is exactly what he does at the present time. He does that in the same way as the Chancellor of the Exchequer, under the direction of the Cabinet, supplies money, follows it up, and sees that it is not used uneconomically. The position is not exactly the same, but I think one may compare the two.

It is stated in paragraph 16 of the White Paper: "The Minister of Supply will answer for the Minister of Production in the House of Commons over the whole range of his responsibilities." With regard to the difficulties that hon. Members may experience in deciding whether a question should be put to the Minister of Supply in his capacity of Minister of Supply or as responsible for answering for the Minister of Production, that no doubt raises some nice questions, but if those were the only difficulties that we had to encounter I should feel very much relieved.

I suggest that the White Paper should be read and studied, and that then, if there is a desire for a Debate, it should be conveyed to the Government through the usual channels, with which I have no doubt my hon. Friend can get himself into touch. And if and when a Debate has been decided upon, then we can see whether one or two or three days shall be devoted to it.

" *Through the Storm* "

AN ADDRESS BROADCAST
FEBRUARY 15, 1942

February 12. German *warships,* Scharnhorst, Gneisenau *and* Prinz Eugen, *dashed through the Channel from Brest to Germany. British lost 42 planes and Germans 18 in sea and air battle in vain British attempt to sink the ships.*

February 13. *Detailed report of American fleet's raid on Japanese islands revealed that the enemy had lost 16 ships, including an aircraft carrier.*

February 15. *With food, water and ammunition exhausted, Singapore surrendered, the Japanese claiming 60,000 prisoners.*

[*February 15, 1942*

NEARLY six months have passed since at the end of August I made a broadcast directly to my fellow-countrymen; it is therefore worth while looking back over this half-year of struggle for life, for that is what it has been, and what it is, to see what has happened to our fortunes and to our prospects.

At that time in August I had the pleasure of meeting the President of the United States and drawing up with him the declaration of British and American policy which has become known to the world as the Atlantic Charter. We also settled a number of other things about the war, some of which have had an important influence upon its course. In those days we met on the terms of a hard-pressed combatant seeking assistance from a great friend who was, however, only a benevolent neutral.

In those days the Germans seemed to be tearing the Russian armies to pieces and striding on with growing momentum to Leningrad, to Moscow, to Rostov, and even farther into the heart of Russia. It was thought a very daring assertion when the President declared that the Russian armies would hold out till the winter. You may say that the military men of all countries — friend, foe, and neutral alike — were very doubtful whether this would come true. As for us, our British resources were stretched to the utmost. We had already been for more than a whole year absolutely alone in the struggle with Hitler and Mussolini. We had to be ready to meet a German invasion of our own Island; we had to defend Egypt, the Nile Valley and the Suez Canal. Above all we had to bring in across the Atlantic in the teeth of the German and Italian U-boats and aircraft the food, raw materials and finished munitions without which we could not live, without which we could not wage war. We have to do all this still.

It seemed our duty in those August days to do everything in our power to help the Russian people to meet the prodigious onslaught which had been launched against them. It is little enough we have done for Russia, considering all she has done to beat Hitler and for the common cause. In these circumstances, we British had no means whatever of providing effectively against a new war with Japan. Such was the outlook when I talked with President Roosevelt in the middle of August on board the good ship *Prince of Wales,* now, alas, sunk beneath the waves. It is true that our position in August, 1941, seemed vastly better than it had been a year earlier in 1940, when France had just been beaten into the awful prostration in which she now lies, when we were almost entirely unarmed in our own Island, and when it looked as if Egypt and all the Middle East would be conquered by the Italians who still held Abyssinia and had newly driven us out of British Somaliland. Compared with those days of 1940, when all the world except ourselves thought we were down and out for ever, the situation the President and I surveyed in August, 1941, was an enormous improvement. Still, when you looked at it bluntly and squarely — with the United States neutral and fiercely divided, with the Russian armies falling back with grievous losses, with the German military power triumphant and unscathed, with the Japanese menace assuming an uglier shape each day — it certainly seemed a very bleak and anxious scene.

The End of the Beginning

How do matters stand now? Taking it all in all, are our chances of survival better or are they worse than in August, 1941? How is it with the British Empire or Commonwealth of Nations? Are we up or down? What has happened to the principles of freedom and decent civilisation for which we are fighting? Are they making headway, or are they in greater peril? Let us take the rough with the smooth, let us put the good and bad side by side, and let us try to see exactly where we are. The first and greatest of events is that the United States is now unitedly and whole-heartedly in the war with us. The other day I crossed the Atlantic again to see President Roosevelt. This time we met not only as friends, but as comrades standing side by side and shoulder to shoulder in a battle for dear life and dearer honour in the common cause and against a common foe. When I survey and compute the power of the United States and its vast resources and feel that they are now in it with us, with the British Commonwealth of Nations all together, however long it lasts, till death or victory, I cannot believe there is any other fact in the whole world which can compare with that. That is what I have dreamed of, aimed at and worked for, and now it has come to pass.

But there is another fact, in some ways more immediately effective. The Russian armies have not been defeated, they have not been torn to pieces. The Russian people have not been conquered or destroyed. Leningrad and Moscow have not been taken. The Russian armies are in the field. They are not holding the line of the Urals or the line of the Volga. They are advancing victoriously, driving the foul invader from that native soil they have guarded so bravely and love so well. More than that: for the first time they have broken the Hitler legend. Instead of the easy victories and abundant booty which he and his hordes had gathered in the West, he has found in Russia so far only disaster, failure, the shame of unspeakable crimes, the slaughter or loss of vast numbers of German soldiers, and the icy wind that blows across the Russian snow.

Here, then, are two tremendous fundamental facts which will in the end dominate the world situation and make victory possible in a form never possible before. But there is another heavy and terrible side to the account, and this must be set in the

66

balance against these inestimable gains. Japan has plunged into the war, and is ravaging the beautiful, fertile, prosperous, and densely populated lands of the Far East. It would never have been in the power of Great Britain while fighting Germany and Italy — the nations long hardened and prepared for war — while fighting in the North Sea, in the Mediterranean and in the Atlantic — it would never have been in our power to defend the Pacific and the Far East single-handed against the onslaught of Japan. We have only just been able to keep our heads above water at home; only by a narrow margin have we brought in the food and the supplies; only by so little have we held our own in the Nile Valley and the Middle East. The Mediterranean is closed, and all our transports have to go round the Cape of Good Hope, each ship making only three voyages in the year. Not a ship, not an aeroplane, not a tank, not an anti-tank gun or an anti-aircraft gun has stood idle. Everything we have has been deployed either against the enemy or awaiting his attack. We are struggling hard in the Libyan Desert, where perhaps another serious battle will soon be fought. We have to provide for the safety and order of liberated Abyssinia, of conquered Eritrea, of Palestine, of liberated Syria, and redeemed Iraq, and of our new ally, Persia. A ceaseless stream of ships, men, and materials has flowed from this country for a year and a half, in order to build up and sustain our armies in the Middle East, which guard those vast regions on either side of the Nile Valley. We had to do our best to give substantial aid to Russia. We gave it her in her darkest hour, and we must not fail in our undertaking now. How then in this posture, gripped and held and battered as we were, could we have provided for the safety of the Far East against such an avalanche of fire and steel as has been hurled upon us by Japan? Always, my friends, this thought overhung our minds.

There was, however, one hope and one hope only — namely that if Japan entered the war with her allies, Germany and Italy, the United States would come in on our side, thus far more than repairing the balance. For this reason, I have been most careful, all these many months, not to give any provocation to Japan, and to put up with Japanese encroachments, dangerous though they were, so that if possible, whatever happened, we should not find ourselves forced to face this new enemy alone. I could not be sure that we should succeed in this policy, but it has come to pass. Japan has struck her felon blow, and a new, far greater champion has drawn the sword of implacable vengeance against her and on our side.

I shall frankly state to you that I did not believe it was in the interests of Japan to burst into war both upon the British Empire and the United States. I thought it would be a very irrational act. Indeed, when you remember that they did not attack us after Dunkirk when we were so much weaker, when our hopes of United States help were of the most slender character, and when we were all alone, I could hardly believe that they would commit what seemed to be a mad act. To-night the Japanese are triumphant. They shout their exultation round the world. We suffer. We are taken aback. We are hard pressed. But I am sure even in this dark hour that "criminal madness" will be the verdict which history will pronounce upon the authors of Japanese aggression, after the events of 1942 and 1943 have been inscribed upon its sombre pages.

The immediate deterrent which the United States exercised upon Japan — apart of course from the measureless resources of the American Union — was the dominant American battle fleet in the Pacific, which, with the naval forces we could spare, confronted Japanese aggression with the shield of superior sea-power. But, my friends, by an act of sudden violent surprise, long-calculated, balanced and prepared, and delivered under the crafty cloak of negotiation, the shield of sea-power which protected the fair lands and islands of the Pacific Ocean was for the time being, and only for the time being, dashed to the ground. Into the gap thus opened rushed the invading armies of Japan. We were exposed to the assault of a warrior race of nearly eighty millions, with a large outfit of modern weapons, whose war lords had been planning and scheming for this day, and looking forward to it perhaps for twenty years — while all the time our good people on both sides of the Atlantic were prating about perpetual peace, and cutting down each other's navies in order to set a good example. The overthrow, for a while, of British and United States sea-power in the Pacific was like the breaking of some mighty dam; the long-gathered pent-up waters rushed down the peaceful valley, carrying ruin and devastation forward on their foam, and spreading their inundations far and wide.

No one must underrate any more the gravity and efficiency of the Japanese war machine. Whether in the air or upon the sea, or man to man on land, they have already proved themselves to be formidable, deadly, and, I am sorry to say, barbarous antagonists. This proves a hundred times over that there never was the slightest chance, even though we had been much better prepared in many ways than we were, of our standing up to them alone while we had Nazi Germany at our throat and Fascist Italy at our belly. It proves something else. And this should be a comfort and a reassurance. We can now measure the wonderful strength of the Chinese people who under Generalissimo Chiang Kai-shek have single-handed fought this hideous Japanese aggressor for four and a half years and left him baffled and dismayed. This they have done, although they were a people whose whole philosophy for many ages was opposed to war and warlike arts, and who in their agony were caught ill-armed, ill-supplied with munitions, and hopelessly outmatched in the air. We must not underrate the power and malice of our latest foe, but neither must we undervalue the gigantic, overwhelming forces which now stand in the line with us in this world-struggle for freedom, and which, once they have developed their full natural inherent power, whatever has happened in the meanwhile, will be found fully capable of squaring all accounts and setting all things right for a good long time to come.

You know I have never prophesied to you or promised smooth and easy things, and now all I have to offer is hard adverse war for many months ahead. I must warn you, as I warned the House of Commons before they gave me their generous vote of confidence a fortnight ago, that many misfortunes, severe torturing losses, remorseless and gnawing anxieties lie before us. To our British folk these may seem even harder to bear when they are at a great distance than when the savage Hun was shattering our cities and we all felt in the midst of the battle ourselves. But the same qualities which brought us through the awful jeopardy of the summer of 1940 and its long autumn and winter bombardment from the air, will bring us through this other new ordeal, though it may be more costly and will certainly be longer. One fault, one crime, and one crime only, can rob the United Nations and the British people, upon whose constancy this grand alliance came into being, of the victory upon which their lives and honour depend. A weakening in our purpose and therefore in our unity — that is the mortal crime. Whoever is guilty of that crime, or of bringing it about in others, of him let it be said that it were better for him that a millstone were hanged about his neck and he were cast into the sea.

Last autumn, when Russia was in her most dire peril, when vast numbers of her soldiers had been killed or taken prisoner, when one-third of her whole munitions capacity lay, as it still lies, in Nazi German hands, when Kiev fell, and the foreign Ambassadors were ordered out of Moscow, the Russian people did not fall to bickering among themselves. They just stood together and worked and fought all the harder. They did not lose trust in their leaders; they did not try to break up their Government. Hitler had hoped to find quislings and fifth columnists in the wide regions he overran, and among the unhappy masses who fell into his power. He looked for them. He searched for them. But he found none.

The system upon which the Soviet Government is founded is very different from ours or from that of the United States. However that may be, the fact remains that Russia received blows which her friends feared and her foes believed were mortal, and through preserving national unity and persevering undaunted, Russia has had the marvellous come-back for which we thank God now. In the English-speaking world we rejoice in free institutions. We have free parliaments and a free press. This is the way of life we have been used to. This is the way of life we are fighting to defend. But it is the duty of all who take part in those free institutions to make sure, as the House of Commons and the House of Lords have done, and will I doubt not do, that the National Executive Government in time of war have a solid foundation on which to stand and on which to act; that the misfortunes and mistakes of war are not exploited against them; that while they are kept up to the mark by helpful and judicious criticism or advice, they are not deprived of the persisting power to run through a period of bad times and many cruel vexations and come out on the other side and get to the top of the hill.

To-night I speak to you at home; I speak to you in Australia and New Zealand, for whose safety we will strain every nerve; to our loyal friends in India and Burma; to our gallant Allies, the Dutch and Chinese; and to our kith and kin in the United States. I speak to you all under the shadow of a heavy and far-reaching military defeat. It is a British and Imperial defeat. Singapore has fallen. All the Malay Peninsula has been overrun. Other dangers gather about us out there, and none of the dangers which we have hitherto successfully withstood at home and in the East are in any way diminished. This, therefore, is one of those moments when the British race and nation can show their quality and their genius. This is one of those moments when it can draw from the heart of misfortune the vital impulses of victory. Here is the moment to display that calm and poise combined with grim determination which not so long ago brought us out of the very jaws of death. Here is another occasion to show — as so often in our long story — that we can meet reverses with dignity and with renewed accessions of strength. We must remember that we are no longer alone. We are in the midst of a great company. Three-quarters of the human race are now moving with us. The whole future of mankind may depend upon our action and upon our conduct. So far we have not failed. We shall not fail now. Let us move forward steadfastly together into the storm and through the storm.

The War Situation

February 17. As the war neared Australia, Mr. Curtin (Prime Minister) ordered total mobilisation of all resources.

[*February 17, 1942*

I SHALL deal first with the naval episode which has attracted attention in the last few days. In March last the two German cruisers *Scharnhorst* and *Gneisenau* took refuge in Brest harbour, where they were joined in May by the *Prinz Eugen* after the destruction of the *Bismarck*. The position of these three ships became a serious preoccupation for the Admiralty. They lay on the flank of our main convoy route to the East, and they could make a sortie at any time on to the Atlantic trade routes or into the Mediterranean. Accordingly, the Admiralty have pressed for their continued attack from the air in the hopes of disabling them and preventing their being repaired. This process continued for more than ten months, during which time the ships were undoubtedly hit several times and repair work was made very difficult. No less than 4,000 tons of bombs were dropped, and 3,299 bomber sorties were made upon them, with a loss of 247 Air Force personnel and 43 aircraft. As we were never in a position to know when some or all of these ships might put to sea, the situation entailed almost continuous naval precautions in the hope of being ready at all times to meet the various threats which these ships constituted. A further serious feature was the very grave subtraction from the bombing effort against Germany.

The bombing of these ships was, however, so severe that the Germans evidently came to the decision that they could not maintain them any longer at Brest and that they must return to Germany. We do not know whether this was for the purpose of effecting final repairs or to enable them to work up to full efficiency in the sheltered waters of the Baltic. However this may be, the Germans resolved to try to bring the ships back to Germany. This was a very hazardous operation. It could be done either by sailing round the British Isles and returning via Norway, or by a dash up the Channel. The Germans rejected the plan of returning Northabout, and preferred to run the admittedly serious risks of the Channel passage. In the Atlantic Ocean they would have run a great risk of being picked up by our extensive air reconnaissances from the shore and from aircraft-carriers, or of being slowed down by torpedo attacks and brought to action against overwhelming forces, as was the *Bismarck*. The Channel route, on the other hand, was a run of under 24 hours, part of which could be made in darkness, possibly by surprise, and they had the opportunity of choosing the weather which would be most favorable. The whole way through the Channel and along the Dutch coast they had the advantage of a powerful air umbrella. The dangers of running past the Dover batteries, under suitable weather conditions, were not great. Our slow convoys repeatedly traverse the Straits of Dover, and are repeatedly bombarded by the German guns on the French shore, but this has not stopped our convoy traffic. One great danger was mines, but this they might hope to avoid by energetic sweeping. There remained, therefore, the action of surface ships and aircraft. Air reconnaissance would show the Germans that neither heavy ships nor even cruisers were in these narrow waters, and, therefore, attacks by flotillas of destroyers and of small torpedo boats were all that need be expected, apart from the air.

Some people seem to think that heavy forces should have been stationed so as to be able to intercept them in the Channel or the North Sea. Had we done so, our ships would have been open to the same scale of air attack as were the German ships at Brest. Further, any such disposition would have dangerously weakened the preventive measures which we have to take to safeguard our convoys and guard the Northern passage, and to deal with other German heavy ships, *Tirpitz*, the *Lützow* and the *Scheer*. The Admiralty did not consider that the attempt to run through the Channel would be an impossible operation under the conditions which prevailed, and this was certainly a much less formidable matter than that the ships should break out on to the trade routes or into the Mediterranean. No one can doubt the vigor and courage with which the enemy squadron was attacked as soon as its movement was perceived, and, of course, everyone is very sorry that these ships were not sunk. The only questions which are open are, first: Why was their movement not detected shortly after daylight? and secondly, Was the contact and liaison between the Coastal Command and the Admiralty, and also between the other R.A.F. Commands and the Admiralty, as close as it should have been? At the suggestion of the Admiralty and of the Air Ministry, I have directed that an inquiry shall be held into these points. The inquiry will be secret. I doubt very much whether, when completed, its results will be suitable for publication. I am not prepared to give any information about the inquiry, or any undertaking that its results will be made public.

Although it may somewhat surprise the House and the public, I should like to state that, in the opinion of the Admiralty, with which I most cordially concur, this abandonment by the Germans of their position at Brest has been decidedly beneficial to our war situation. The threat to our convoy routes has been removed, and the enemy has been driven to leave his advantageous position. The diversion of our air bombing effort, which, though necessary, was so wasteful, is over. A heavier scale of attack on Germany is now possible, in which all the near misses will hit German and not French dwellings. Both the *Scharnhorst* and the *Gneisenau* have received damage in their passage which will keep them out of action for some time to come, after which they will have to be worked up in gunnery and other practices. Before they can again play any part in the war, the Royal Navy will be reinforced by various important units of the highest quality, and the same strengthening process is going forward in the Navy of the United States. Whatever smart of disappointment or annoyance may remain in our breasts that the final forfeit was not exacted, there is no doubt that the naval position in the Atlantic, so far from being worsened, is definitely eased.

The War Situation, February 17, 1942

I have also been asked whether the Government have a statement to make about the fall of Singapore. This extremely grave event was not unexpected, and its possibility was comprised within the scope of the argument I submitted to the House on the occasion of the Vote of Confidence three weeks ago. The House has, of course, many opportunities of discussing this and other aspects of the war situation. I am sure it would be a great mistake to try to discuss it to-day in the short time available. I have no information to give to the House other than that conveyed in the public press, nor would it be prudent to speculate in detail upon the various evil consequences which will follow from the fall of Singapore. Moreover, it would ill become the dignity of the Government and the House, and would render poor service to the Alliance of which we are a part, if we were drawn into agitated or excited recriminations at a time when all our minds are oppressed with a sense of tragedy and with the sorrow of so lamentable a misfortune. Perhaps, at a later date, when we are more fully informed and when a carefully considered statement can be made, the House may seek for a further Debate upon the situation in the Far East and the prospect of its being retrieved by the combined action of the Allied Powers concerned. I could certainly not take part in any such discussion now.

However, as some hon. Members may be otherwise inclined, and as I did not wish to prevent them from expressing their opinions, I decided to move the Adjournment, as I have done. The Government will, of course, listen to the Debate, if it takes place, but I hope I may be permitted to remind the House of the extremely serious situation in which we stand, of the use that is made in hostile and even in Allied countries of any loose or intemperate language into which anyone may be drawn, and of the importance of the House of Commons maintaining its reputation for firmness and courage in the face of adversity.

After questions and speeches by other Members of Parliament, Mr. Churchill made the following addition to his statement: —

I indicated how grave the position was in the Far East, and how terrible are the forfeits that have been and will be exacted from us. I certainly feel that the House should have a Debate;

there is not the slightest reason to object to a Debate; on the contrary, I will give every facility for a Debate and for a Division. The House is absolutely master. If its confidence is not extended to the Government, if it does not believe that the war is being well managed, if it thinks it can make arrangements which would lead to the war being better managed, it is the duty and the right of the House to express its opinion, as it can do in a proper and a constitutional manner. Therefore, as I say, I certainly consider that a matter of this kind should be the subject of a Debate, but at the present time I have absolutely no news which has not been published in the Press — no news of any importance or interest. I do not quite know when the news will be received, but still I think that during the course of the next series of Sitting Days there should be a Debate on the subject, and I hope it will be a long Debate. I do not know whether it can all take place in public. I am absolutely certain that I could say things to this House which would arouse hon. Members to the seriousness of the situation and to the way in which the dangers may be aggravated by action we may take or fail to take, but I do not think I could say them in public at all. Let us say then that there will be a Debate. I was only deprecating that it should be held now as it seems in a mood of panic. I think that a very excited Debate taking place here to-day, while our minds are oppressed by what has happened, may easily have the effect of causing a bad and very unfavourable reaction all over the world. That is what I said. I stick to it. I think it would have been a bad thing to have a Debate to-day. I certainly do not think I could undertake to prepare a full statement on this matter by the third Sitting Day.

I must ask the House to realise the enormous burdens falling on me, not by my work as Minister of Defence, but by repeated and constant attendance on this House, which I never expected I should have to face, but which I will face. But I think I should be more prepared to make a statement next week. I hope that some information will come in which will enable me to make it. I beg that the Debate shall be absolutely frank, measured only by regard to the public interest. I beg that it shall be searching; I beg, I implore hon. Gentlemen — their manhood and honour require it — that they shall give effect to their opinions. There is one point. I have been asked about the Inquiry. What I propose is that Mr. Justice Bucknill should preside, and that Air Chief Marshal Sir Edgar Ludlow-Hewitt and Vice-Admiral Sir Hugh Binney should represent the two Services concerned. I hope that the Inquiry will be quickly conducted. Of course, if anyone is found to have been guilty of a dereliction of duty, obviously disciplinary action will follow. Certainly, in that case, I am sure it will be possible to make some statement to the House; but I do not want this Inquiry, which deals with our secret matters of defence around these Islands upon which our lives and safety depend, to be subject to a fought-out discussion and wrangling and intricate debate in the same way as has been done in time of peace, when a submarine like the *Thetis* was lost. I think it would be a great pity to do that. I hope the House will realise that there is a very great desire to do as well as possible among all those who are serving them, whether in the House or in the Forces.

I think that a Debate held to-day in excitement, and pierced with charges and counter-charges interchanged across the House at this moment of great anxiety and distress, would undoubtedly be contributing to what I might have called the "rattling" process which is going on in some parts of the Press, not only in the Press in this country, but freely telegraphed both to Australia and the United States, which tends to give a feeling of insecurity, which I am quite sure the House would agree is detrimental.

Heart of Austria

A SPEECH OUTSIDE NO. 10, DOWNING STREET, WHEN SIR GEORGE FRANCKENSTEIN, FORMERLY AUSTRIAN MINISTER IN LONDON, PRESENTED ON BEHALF OF AUSTRIANS IN BRITAIN A TRAILER CANTEEN TO THE WOMEN'S VOLUNTARY SERVICE FEBRUARY 18, 1942

[February 18, 1942

IT is not without deep emotion that I attend this simple ceremony. Here we see the heart of Austria, although trampled down under the Nazi and Prussian yoke. We can never forget here in this island that Austria was the first victim of Nazi aggression. We know that happy life which might have been led by scores of millions in central Europe. We remember the charm, beauty, and historic splendour of Vienna, the grace of life, the dignity of the individual; all the links of past generations which are associated in our minds with Austria and with Vienna.

Sir George Franckenstein, you are here as a link with us between the dark past, the haggard present, and what I still believe will be the glorious future. We shall struggle on and fight on. The people of Britain will never desert the cause of the freeing of Austria from the Prussian yoke. We shall go forward. Many long miles have to be marched and many leagues at sea to be covered by ships; many millions of miles of aeroplane flights be accomplished; great heart effort will be needed from large masses of human beings — but we have three-quarters of the human race upon our side. Only our own follies can deprive us of victory; and in the victory of the Allies, Free Austria shall find her honoured place.

Red Army's Anniversary

[*February 23, 1942*

THE twenty-fourth anniversary of the foundation of the Red Army is being celebrated to-day after eight months of a campaign which has reflected the greatest glory on its officers and men, and has enshrined its deeds in history for all time. On this proud occasion I convey to you, the Chairman of the Defence Committee of the U.S.S.R., and to all members of the Soviet forces, an expression of the admiration and gratitude with which the people of the British Empire have watched their exploits, and of our confidence in the victorious end of the struggle which we are waging together against the common foe.

Changes in the Government

February 19. War Cabinet reduced from nine to seven. Sir Stafford Cripps became Lord Privy Seal and Leader of the House of Commons, and Mr. Oliver Lyttelton Minister of State in charge of war production in place of Lord Beaverbrook, detailed for America on special duties. Mr. Attlee became Deputy Prime Minister and Dominions Secretary. Mr. Arthur Greenwood left the Government.

February 20. Battle for Java started with the Japanese invasion of the Island of Bali. Japanese also landed in Timor, directly threatening Port Darwin (Australia).

February 22. More Government changes. Sir James Grigg replaced Capt. David Margesson as Secretary of State for War, Col. J. J. Llewellyn replaced Lt.-Col. Moore-Brabazon as Minister of Aircraft Production, Lord Cranborne became Colonial Secretary, and Mr. Hugh Dalton President of the Board of Trade.

February 23. Stalin issued an inspiring message on the 24th anniversary of the Red Army, promising the freeing of all Russian territory.

President Roosevelt, in a national broadcast, stated that the United States would soon take up the offensive "in distant lands and waters."

February 24. Big Russian victory in the Staraya Russa area of the North.

Rangoon, preparing for attack, evacuated all civilians.

Mr. Churchill opened a debate on the War.

SINCE we last met here there has been a major reconstruction of the War Cabinet and among Ministers of Cabinet rank. There will be further changes, not only consequential changes, among the Under-Secretaries, but these I have not yet had time to consider in all their bearings. After nearly two years of strain and struggle, it was right and necessary that a Government called into being in the crash of the Battle of France should undergo both change and reinvigoration. I regret very much the loss of loyal and trusted colleagues, with whom I have come through so many hard times and who readily placed their resignations in my hand, in order to facilitate a reconstruction of the Government. They had, of course, no greater share of responsibility than the rest of the Administration for the disasters which have fallen upon us in the Far East. Nevertheless, I am sure that we have achieved a more tensely-braced and compact Administration to meet the new dangers and difficulties which are coming upon us, and I believe that that is the general opinion of the House and of the country.

Attention is naturally concentrated upon the War Cabinet, and no doubt comparisons will be made with the War Cabinet of the last war. I have on previous occasions given the reasons why I do not believe that a war cabinet entirely composed of Ministers without Departments is practicable or convenient. In other ways, however, the resemblance is fairly close. During most of the period from December, 1916, to November, 1918, the Lloyd George War Cabinet consisted of six or seven Ministers, of whom one only had departmental duties, namely, Mr. Bonar Law, Chancellor of the Exchequer, Leader of the House, and Leader of the Conservative Party. In addition, Mr. Balfour, the Foreign Secretary, although not in name a member of the War Cabinet, was so to all practical purposes, and was in fact a far more powerful politician than any of its members except the Prime Minister and the Chancellor of the Exchequer. The new War Cabinet consists of seven members, of whom three have no Department. One is Prime Minister, one is Deputy Prime Minister with the Dominions Office, and one is Foreign

Secretary. In the seventh case, the Minister of Labour and National Service replaces the Chancellor of the Exchequer of the former model. I think this is right. In the last 25 years Labour has made immense advances in the State, and it is desirable, both on personal and on public grounds, that this office, which serves all Departments, should be included.

There may prove to be other points of resemblance. It is now the fashion to speak of the Lloyd George War Cabinet as if it gave universal satisfaction and conducted the war with unerring judgment and unbroken success. On the contrary, complaints were loud and clamant. Immense disasters, such as the slaughter of Passchendaele, the disaster at Caporetto in 1917, the destruction of the Fifth Army after March 21st, 1918 — all these and others befell that rightly famous Administration. It made numerous serious mistakes. No one was more surprised than its members when the end of the War came suddenly in 1918, and there have even been criticisms about the character of the Peace which was signed and celebrated in 1919. Therefore we, in this difficult period, have other calls upon us besides that of living up slavishly to the standards and methods of the past, instructive and on the whole encouraging as they unquestionably are.

Let me explain how the duties are divided. The members of the War Cabinet are collectively and individually responsible for the whole policy of the country, and they are the men who are alone held accountable for the conduct of the war. However, they have also particular spheres of superintendence. The Leader of the Labour Party, as head of the second largest party in the National Government, acts as Deputy Prime Minister in all things, and in addition will discharge the duties of the Dominions Secretary, thus meeting, without an addition to our numbers, the request pressed upon us from so many quarters that our relations with the Dominions, apart from those between His Majesty's various Prime Ministers, on which the Dominions are most insistent, shall be in the hands of a member of the War Cabinet.

The Lord President of the Council presides over what is, in certain aspects, almost a parallel Cabinet concerned with home affairs. Of this body a number of Ministers of Cabinet rank are

Changes in the Government, February 24, 1942

regular members, and others are invited as may be convenient. An immense mass of business is discharged at their frequent meetings, and it is only in the case of a serious difference or in very large questions that the War Cabinet as such is concerned. The Minister of State, who will soon be returning from Cairo, has, as his sphere of superintendence, the whole process of production in all its aspects. The White Paper which had been issued upon this subject is superseded and withdrawn, and I am not sure that the new arrangements will require to be defined so formally in a paper constitution. In these circumstances the Supplementary Estimate which was presented on 17th February for the purpose of asking this House to give financial effect to the arrangements set out in the White Paper of 10th February is no longer appropriate, and accordingly it is proposed, with the permission of the House, not to proceed with that Estimate. While the new revised arrangements now contemplated are taking shape, we shall arrange and see what are the best plans, financial and otherwise, appropriate to the altered circumstances. The special spheres of the remaining members of the War Cabinet are defined by the offices they hold.

My right hon. Friend the former Minister without Portfolio (Mr. Arthur Greenwood), who has played a fine part in all affairs connected with this war, was busy with further plans for post-war reconstruction. The reduction in the size of the War Cabinet, which was held to be desirable in many quarters, has led to the elimination of this office. I must ask the House for a certain amount of time, though there will be no delay, before I am able to submit a scheme for this essential task of preparation for reconstruction. Even though we must now prepare ourselves for an evident prolongation of the war through the intervention of Japan, the whole of this preparatory work, of this preliminary work, for the post-war period must go forward, because no one can be sure that, as in the last war, victory may not come unexpectedly upon us. The seven members of the War Cabinet can sit together either as the War Cabinet of the United Kingdom of Great Britain and Northern Ireland, responsible to the Crown and to Parliament, or they can sit in a larger gathering with representatives from the Dominions and India. Both series of meetings will continue regularly, as before.

The End of the Beginning

The Pacific War Council has also come into being, on which the representatives of the Dominions specially concerned, namely, Australia and New Zealand, and of India and the Netherlands, sit under my chairmanship or under that of my Deputy, the Dominions Secretary. I am very glad to say that Generalissimo Chiang Kai-shek has just accepted an invitation which I tendered him that a representative of China should join this Council. I recently explained to the House the relation of this body to the Chiefs of Staff Committee in London, and the relation of both of these bodies to the Combined Chiefs of Staff Committee in Washington. I can only say that all this inevitably complicated machinery, where many are concerned and oceans divide, is working swiftly and smoothly. The results, as I will presently explain, depend upon factors far more potent and massive than any machinery, however well devised, which we can immediately bring into being.

I will now, with the permission of the House, speak a little about my own part in it. At the time when I was called upon by the King to form the present Government we were in the throes of the German invasion of France and the Low Countries. I did not expect to be called upon to act as Leader of the House of Commons. I therefore sought His Majesty's permission to create and assume the style or title of Minister of Defence, because obviously the position of Prime Minister in war is inseparable from the general supervision of its conduct and the final responsibility for its result. I intended at that time that Mr. Neville Chamberlain should become Leader of the House and take the whole of the House of Commons work off my hands. This proposal was not found to be acceptable. I had myself to take the Leadership of the House as well as my other duties. I must admit that this Parliamentary task has weighed upon me heavily. During the period for which I have been responsible I find to my horror that I have made more than 25 lengthy speeches to Parliament in Public or in Secret Session, to say nothing of answering a great number of questions and dealing with many current emergencies. I have greatly valued the honour of leading the House, which my father led before me, and in which my public life has been spent for so long; and I have always taken the greatest trouble to give it the best possible service, and even in very rough periods I have taken most particular care of its rights and interests.

Although I feel a great sense of relief in laying down this burden, I cannot say that I do so without sorrow. I am sure, however, it is in the public interest, and I am also sure that my right hon. and learned friend the Member for East Bristol (Sir S. Cripps), the new Lord Privy Seal, will prove to the House that he is a respecter of its authority and a leader capable of dealing with all the incidents, episodes and emergencies of House of Commons and Parliamentary life. I shall, of course, as Prime Minister, remain always at the service of the House should the occasion require it, and I shall hope, from time to time, though I trust not too often, to seek their permission to give them a general appreciation of the progress of the War.

Let me now speak of the office, or title, which I hold as Minister of Defence. About this there seem to be many misunderstandings. Perhaps the House will bear with me while I explain the method by which the War has been and will be conducted. I may say, first of all, that there is nothing which I do or have done as Minister of Defence which I could not do as Prime Minister. As Prime Minister, I am able to deal easily and smoothly with the three Service Departments, without prejudice to the constitutional responsibilities of the Secretaries of State for War and Air and the First Lord of the Admiralty. I have not, therefore, found the need of defining formally or precisely the relationship between the office of Minister of Defence when held by a Prime Minister and the three Service Departments. I have not found it necessary to define this relationship as would be necessary in the case of any Minister of Defence who was not also Prime Minister. There is, of course, no Ministry of Defence, and the three Service Departments remain autonomous. For the purpose of maintaining general supervision over the conduct of the War, which I do under the authority of the War Cabinet and the Defence Committee, I have at my disposal a small staff, headed by Major-General Ismay, which works under the long-established procedure and machinery of the pre-war Committee of Imperial Defence, and forms a part of the War Cabinet secretariat.

While, as I have said, I take constitutional responsibility for everything that is done or not done, and am quite ready to take the blame when things go wrong — as they very often do, and as they are very likely to do in future in many ways — I do not, of course, conduct this war from day to day myself; it is conducted from day to day, and in its future outlook, by the Chiefs of Staff Committee, namely, the First Sea Lord, the Chief of the Imperial General Staff, and the Chief of the Air Staff. These officers sit together every day, and often twice a day. They give executive directions and orders to the Commanders-in-Chief in the various theatres. They advise me, they advise the Defence Committee and the War Cabinet, on large questions of war strategy and war policy. I am represented on the Chiefs of Staff Committee by Major-General Ismay, who is responsible for keeping the War Cabinet and myself informed on all matters requiring higher decision. On account of the immense scope and complexity of the task, when fighting is going on literally all over the world, and when strategy and supply are so closely intermingled, the Chiefs of Staff Committee are assisted by a Vice-Chiefs of Staff Committee, which relieves them of a great mass of important questions of a secondary order. At the disposal of the Chiefs of Staff Committee and of the Vice-Chiefs Committee are the Joint Planning Staffs and Joint Intelligence Staffs of the three Services, consisting of specially-selected officers. In addition, there are the three General Staffs of the Army, Navy and Air Force, between whom constant collaboration proceeds at all levels where combined operations are involved. I think it necessary to put this matter in some detail before the House, because, although it sounds complicated, it is necessary to understand it.

Each of the three Chiefs of Staff has, it must be remembered, the professional executive control of the Service he represents. When, therefore, they meet together, they are not talking in a vacuum, or in theory. They meet together in a position to take immediate and responsible action, in which each can carry out his share, either singly or in combination. I do not think there has ever been a system in which the professional heads of the Fighting Services have had a freer hand or a greater or more direct influence, or have received more constant and harmonious support from the Prime Minister and the Cabinet under which they serve. It is my practice to leave the Chiefs of Staff alone to do their own work, subject to my general supervision, suggestion and guidance. For instance, in 1941, out of 462 meetings of the Chiefs of Staff Committee, most of them lasting over two hours, I presided at only 44 myself. In addition, however, there are, of course, the meetings of the Defence Committee, at which the Service Ministers are present, as well as other Ministerial members, and there are the Cabinet meetings at which the Chiefs of Staff are present when military matters are discussed. In my absence from this country, or should I be at any time incapacitated, my Deputy has acted and will act for me. Such is the machinery which, as Prime Minister and Minister of Defence, I have partly elaborated and partly brought into existence. I am satisfied that it is the best that can be devised to meet the extraordinary difficulties and dangers through which we are passing. There is absolutely no question of making any change in it of a serious or fundamental character as long as I retain the confidence of the House and of the country. However tempting it might be to some when much trouble lies ahead to step aside adroitly and put someone else up to take the blows, the heavy and repeated blows, which are coming, I do not intend to adopt that cowardly course, but, on the contrary, to stand to my post and persevere in accordance with my duty as I see it.

I now turn to the general situation of the War. It had always been my hope that the United States would enter the war against Germany without Japan being immediately involved on the other side. The greatest forbearance was shown by both the English-speaking countries in the face of constant Japanese encroachments. These efforts proved vain; and, at a moment fixed by the war leaders in Japan, the sudden violent attacks were made upon Hawaii, the Philippines, the Dutch East Indies, and Malaya. Thereupon, an entirely new situation supervened. The conversion of the giant power of the United States to war purposes is only in its early stage, and the disaster at Pearl Harbour and our own naval losses have given Japan for the time being — but only for the time being — the command of, or, at least, the superiority in, the Far Eastern seas.

Great Britain and the British Empire were engaged almost to

their full strength, in their powers and in their equipment, with Germany in the Atlantic, with Germany as a potential invader, and with Germany and Italy in the Libyan Desert, which protects Egypt and the Suez Canal. The shipping to nourish the large Armies we had in the Middle East has to go round the Cape, and, as I said the other day, can make only three voyages in the year. Our shipping losses since the War began have been very heavy. In the last few months there has been a most serious increase in shipping losses, and our anti-U-boat flotillas and naval light forces of all kinds have been and are strained to the utmost limit, by the need of bringing in the food by which we live and the materials for the munitions with which we fight and the convoys which carry our troops so continually and in such great numbers to the various seats of war.

In addition to these actual burdens and perils, there remains the front, from the Levant to the Caspian, covering the approaches to India from the West, as well as the most important oilfields of Baku and Persia. A few months ago it seemed that this theatre would become dominant in our thoughts. At the same time, a heavy invasion enterprise was mounted by the enemy against Egypt. The extraordinary successes of the valiant Russian Armies, whose prowess we all honoured yesterday, has given us a breathing-space in both directions. As lately as October and November we were not only fully extended but, indeed, over-stretched, and I cannot imagine what our position would have been if we had yielded to the pressure which at one time was so vehement to open a new front in France or in the Low Countries.

Upon this situation, which I have so very briefly outlined to the House, there suddenly came the impact of Japan, a new combatant, long scheming and preparing, with a warlike population of 80,000,000, several millions of trained soldiers, and a vast amount of modern material. This mighty impact fell upon our wide, prosperous, but lightly-defended possessions and establishments throughout the Far East, all of which had, rightly, been kept at the very lowest level on account of the imperative requirements of the European and African theatres. I saw that some gentlemen who escaped from Penang announced to the world with much indignation that there was not a single anti-aircraft gun in the place. Where should we have been, I should like to know, if we had spread our limited anti-aircraft guns throughout the immense, innumerable regions and vulnerable points of the Far East, instead of using them to preserve the vital life of our ports and factories here, and of our fortresses which were under continuous attack, and all our operations with the field Armies in the Middle East?

The House and the nation must face the blunt and brutal fact that if, having entered a war, yourself ill-prepared, you are struggling for life with two well-armed countries, one of them possessing the most powerful military machine in the world, and, then, at the moment when you are in full grapple, a third major antagonist with far larger military forces than you possess suddenly springs upon your comparatively undefended back, obviously your task is heavy and your immediate experiences will be disagreeable. From the moment that Japan attacked, we set in motion to the Far East naval forces, aircraft, troops and equipment on a scale limited only by the available shipping. All these forces and supplies were diverted from or came from theatres which already needed them, and both our margin of safety and the advance of our operations have been notably, though not, I trust, decisively, affected.

Before I left for the United States early in December most of the principal orders had been given, and in fact we managed to reinforce Singapore by over 40,000 men, together with large quantities of anti-aircraft and anti-tank artillery, all of which were withdrawn, as I have said, from other points where they were sorely needed or even actively engaged. This was especially true in regard to modern aircraft. Unfortunately, before enough of these latter could arrive in the Malay Peninsula, although there was no delay in giving orders and many daring expedients were adopted by the commanders, before they arrived in the Malay Peninsula, the airfields in Singapore Island were already under the fire of the Japanese artillery from Johore, from which we had been driven out. We were not therefore able to repeat the air fighting from an island base which has been so remarkable a feature of the prolonged defence of Malta, now under increasingly severe attack. Nevertheless, the speedy reinforcement of Singapore by no less than nine convoys would be judged a splendid achievement if the resultant defence had been crowned with success.

I have no news whatever from Singapore to give to the House, I have no information with which I can supplement such accounts — very scanty — as have appeared in the newspapers. I am therefore unable to make any statement about it, and for that reason, as I have no material for going into details, I do not propose to ask the House to go into Secret Session, and this Debate will be conducted throughout in public. I will, however, say this: Singapore was, of course, a naval base rather than a fortress. It depended upon the command of the sea, which again depends upon the command of the air. Its permanent fortifications and batteries were constructed from a naval point of view. The various defence lines which had been constructed in Johore were not successfully held. The field works constructed upon the island itself to defend the fortress were not upon a sufficiently large scale. I shall certainly not attempt at this stage to pass any judgment upon our troops or their commanders, 73,000 of whom are stated by the enemy to be prisoners of war. Certainly larger numbers than that were in the fortress at the time of the attack. I shall not attempt, I say, to pass judgment. I think it would be a very unseasonable moment and a very ungracious task. We have more urgent work to do. We have to face the situation resulting from this great loss of the base, and the troops, and the equipment of a whole Army. We have to face the situation resulting from that, and from the great new Japanese war which has burst upon us.

There is little more that I can usefully say at this juncture upon the progress of the general war. Certainly it would be very foolish to try and prophesy its immediate future. It is estimated that there are 26 Japanese divisions in the A.B.D.A. area, as it has been called, and we must remember that these divisions can be moved and supplied with far less tonnage, at far less expense, than is the case where European or United States troops are concerned. We have not so many. In the A.B.D.A. area I have mentioned the enemy have for the time being a waning command of the sea. They have the command of the air, which makes it costly and difficult for our air reinforcements to establish themselves and secure dominance. They are in many cases destroyed upon the ground before they can effectively come into action. We must, therefore, expect many hard and adverse experiences, which will be all the more difficult to bear because they are unaccompanied by the sense of imminent national, domestic danger — that feeling of being in the business ourselves — which brought out all the best qualities of our people a year and a half ago.

If I were to dilate upon our hopes, these might soon be falsified, and I might be mocked by those who proved themselves wise by our failures. If, on the other hand, I painted the picture in its darkest hues, very great despondency might be spread among our ardent and growing Forces, and the enemy might be encouraged. I therefore say no more at this moment. Moreover, although it does not necessarily rest with me to do more than offer an opinion, I would deprecate a long series of speeches in the House censuring or explaining in detail the many tragedies which are occurring in the Far East, and I am not sure that we can afford to indulge ourselves too freely, having regard to the perils that beset us and to the ears that listen. On the other hand, if we look forward across the considerable period of immediate punishment through which we must make our way in consequence of the sudden onslaught of Japan — if we look forward through that and across that to the broad and major aspects of the War — we can see very clearly that our position has been enormously improved, not only in the last two years but in the last few months. This improvement is due, of course, to the wonderful strength and power of Russia, and to the accession of the United States, with its measureless resources, to the common cause. Our position is in fact improved beyond any measure which the most sanguine would have dared to predict.

Beyond this phase of tribulation, which may be shorter or longer in accordance with our exertions and behaviour, there arises the prospect of ultimate victory for Britain, for the United States, for Russia and China, and indeed, for all the United Nations — victory complete over the foes that have fallen upon them. The ordeal through which we have to pass will be tormenting and protracted, but if everyone bends to the task with unrelenting effort and unconquerable resolve, if we do not weary by the way or fall out among ourselves or fail our Allies, we have a right to look forward across a good many months of sorrow and suffering to a sober and reasonable prospect of complete and final victory.

I will venture to end by repeating to the House the very words I used myself when I resigned from Mr. Asquith's Government on 15th November, 1915. I apologise for quoting myself, but I have found comfort in reading them because of the occasion, because of what happened then, and because of our own position now. I said:

"There is no reason to be discouraged about the progress of the war. We are passing through a bad time now, and it will probably be worse before it is better, but that it will be better, if we only endure and persevere, I have no doubt whatever. The old wars were decided by their episodes rather than by their tendencies. In this war the tendencies are far more important than the episodes. Without winning any sensational victories we may win this war. We may win it even during the continuance of extremely disappointing and vexatious events. It is not necessary for us, in order to win the war, to push the German lines back over all the territory they have absorbed, or to pierce them. While the German lines extend far beyond their frontiers, while their flag flies over conquered capitals and subjugated provinces, while all the appearances of military success attend their arms, Germany may be defeated more fatally in the second or third year of the war than if the Allied army had entered Berlin in the first."

Actually, as we now know, Germany was not defeated until the fifth year of the last war, and we are already far advanced into the third year of this present struggle; but, excepting in this respect, provided that you add Japan to Germany in each case, I find comfort in this passage which comes back to me like an echo from the past, and I commend it respectfully to the consideration of the House.

Speed Up the Ships

A MESSAGE TO A CONFERENCE OF EMPLOYERS
AND WORKERS IN THE TRANSPORT INDUSTRY
FEBRUARY 27, 1942

[February 27, 1942

I AM glad to have an opportunity at this crucial moment of sending a message to the representatives of the Port Transport Industry attending the Conference, and through them to all the employers and workers in our ports. There is no need for me to emphasize that shipping is the vital factor in our defence and in our war; you all know it, and know too that the developments of the past few months have imposed still greater demands upon our shipping resources.

The supplies which we have promised to Russia must be sent, and sent on time; the needs of the Allied forces in the Middle and Far East must be met; the munitions, the food, and the materials essential to our life and effort here at home must continue to be brought in. And all this at a time when our Merchant Navy has to face new dangers from a fresh enemy striking at our communications in distant oceans.

We are building ships as fast as we can. The United States is building many more. But we must do now without delay everything which is in our power to increase our resources and expand our shipping space. That is the supreme contribution which the ports can make, by turning our ships around even more quickly, and by ensuring that not a moment is lost in loading or discharging cargoes.

Every day that is saved in the ports represents a solid addition to our Merchant Fleet. Our men fighting oversea and our people working at home rely on you in the ports to give this help, just as they rely on the Navy and the merchant seamen to bring their supplies to them. I know you will not fail them. Nothing must stand that may hamper or delay the working of the ports. Any customs or rules that can safely be dispensed with must be suspended. Any prejudices that may still exist among employers or men must be put on one side.

There can be only one aim — namely, to get the ships out to sea again quicker than ever before. You are meeting now to contrive ways and means of getting this done, and I am sure that with energetic leadership from employers and supervisors and whole-hearted comradeship from the men, you will win.

Sir Stafford Cripps's Mission to India

A STATEMENT TO THE HOUSE OF COMMONS
MARCH 11, 1942

February 28. *British paratroops landed at Havre (France), destroyed important radio-location post and brought back prisoners.*

Japanese troops landed at three points in Java.

March 2. *General Wavell handed over command of operations in the Netherlands East Indies to the Dutch and resumed command in India and Burma.*

March 3. *R.A.F. bombed Renault factories in Paris, which were turning out armaments for Germany. Vichy stated 600 were killed.*

March 4. *More American troops, the largest contingent so far, arrived in Northern Ireland.*

Sir Archibald Sinclair, introducing the Air Estimates in the House of Commons, promised an early resumption of the bombing offensive on Germany.

March 5. *National Service extended to men up to 45 and girls of 18–19. Officially stated that 150,000 women a month were being placed in war jobs.*

Japanese advanced across the center of Java, cutting off Sourabaya.

March 6. *New Defence Regulations made civilians liable for any work necessary to resist invaders.*

Batavia captured by Japanese troops.

March 7. *Fall of Bandoeng, Dutch military headquarters in Java, gave Japanese complete possession of the island after little more than a week's fighting.*

95

The End of the Beginning

March 8.   *Japanese made their first landing on the main-*
             land of New Guinea.
             R.A.F. developed Western air offensive with
             daylight raid on a big factory near Paris and
             a heavy night attack on Krupps works near
             Essen.
March 9.   *Rangoon evacuated and "scorched" in face*
             of Japanese advance in Burma. General Alex-
             ander took over Burma command from Gen-
             eral Hutton.
March 10.   *Mr. Anthony Eden, Foreign Secretary,*
             shocked the world with a report to the House
             of Commons of the atrocities committed by
             Japanese on prisoners and civilians at Hong
             Kong.
March 11.   *Mr. Churchill announced that a plan to settle*
             the India problem had been prepared by the
             Government and that Sir Stafford Cripps had
             agreed to take it personally to India for deci-
             sion.

[*March 11, 1942*

THE crisis in the affairs of India arising out of the Japanese
advance has made us wish to rally all the forces of Indian life
to guard their land from the menace of the invader. In August,
1940, a full statement was made about the aims and policy we
are pursuing in India. This amounted, in short, to a promise
that, as soon as possible after the war, India should attain Dominion status, in full freedom and equality with this country
and the other Dominions, under a Constitution to be framed by
Indians, by agreement among themselves, and acceptable to the
main elements in Indian national life. This was, of course, subject to the fulfilment of our obligations for the protection of
minorities, including the depressed classes, and of our treaty
obligations to the Indian States, and to the settlement of certain
lesser matters arising out of our long association with the fortunes of the Indian sub-continent.

96

However, in order to clothe these general declarations with precision and to convince all classes, races and creeds in India of our sincere resolve, the War Cabinet have agreed unitedly upon conclusions for present and future action which, if accepted by India as a whole, would avoid the alternative dangers either that the resistance of a powerful minority might impose an indefinite veto upon the wishes of the majority, or that a majority decision might be taken which would be resisted to a point destructive of internal harmony and fatal to the setting-up of a new Constitution. We had thought of setting forth immediately the terms of this attempt, by a constructive British contribution, to aid India in the realisation of full self government; we are, however, apprehensive that to make a public announcement at such a moment as this might do more harm than good. We must first assure ourselves that our scheme would win a reasonable and practical measure of acceptance, and thus promote the concentration of all Indian thought and energies upon the defence of the native soil. We should ill serve the common cause if we made a declaration which would be rejected by essential elements in the Indian world, and which provoked fierce constitutional and communal disputes at a moment when the enemy is at the gates of India.

Accordingly, we propose to send a member of the War Cabinet to India, to satisfy himself upon the spot, by personal consultation, that the conclusions upon which we are agreed, and which we believe represent a just and final solution, will achieve their purpose. My right hon. and learned Friend the Lord Privy Seal and Leader of the House (Sir Stafford Cripps) has volunteered to undertake this task. He carries with him the full confidence of His Majesty's Government, and he will strive in their name to procure the necessary measure of assent, not only from the Hindu majority, but also from those great minorities, amongst which the Moslems are the most numerous and on many grounds pre-eminent.

The Lord Privy Seal will, at the same time, consult with the Viceroy and the Commander-in-Chief upon the military situation, bearing always in mind the paramount responsibility of His Majesty's Government by every means in their power to shield the peoples of India from the perils which now beset them.

The End of the Beginning

We must remember that India has a great part to play in the world's struggle for freedom, and that her helping hand must be extended in loyal comradeship to the valiant Chinese people, who have fought alone so long. We must remember also that India is one of the bases from which the strongest counterblows must be struck at the advance of tyranny and aggression.

My right hon. Friend will set out as soon as convenient and suitable arrangements can be made. I am sure he will command in his task the heartfelt good wishes of all parts of the House and that, meanwhile, no word will be spoken or debates be held, here or in India, which would add to the burden he has assumed in his mission, or lessen the prospects of a good result. During my right hon. and learned Friend's absence from this House, his duties as Leader will be discharged by my right hon. Friend the Foreign Secretary.

Duties of the Minister of Production

[March 12, 1942

MY right hon. and gallant Friend the present Minister of State (Capt. Oliver Lyttelton) will be appointed Minister of Production. The Minister of Production is the Minister charged with chief responsibility — I may here interpolate the fact that, in the White Paper, publication of which was withdrawn, the expression "prime responsibility" is used. "Prime" in the dictionary is capable of meaning either "chief" or "primary." It is in the sense of "chief" rather than "primary" that the word is used. The word "primary" might conflict with the departmental responsibility of the Prime Minister. He is charged, as I say, with chief responsibility on behalf of the War Cabinet, for the business of war production as a whole, subject, of course, to the policy of the Minister of Defence and of the War Cabinet itself. Subject to the position of the Admiralty, which I will mention later, he will have full effective powers to concert and supervise the activities of the Production Departments, including the adjustment of existing programmes and the initiation of future policy.

No new Ministry, incorporating the existing Supply Departments, will be set up. Subject to the performance by the Minister of Production of the duties assigned to him, the Ministers in charge of the Supply Departments will continue to be responsible to the War Cabinet and to Parliament for the administration of their Departments. That is the general position: but the House will no doubt expect some closer definition of the Minister's responsibilities in regard to specific matters.

He will be responsible for the duties hitherto discharged by the Production Executive, including the settlement of production priorities, the regional boards, and the allocation of industrial capacity, except shipyard capacity (which will be allocated as heretofore by the Admiralty). He will direct the work of the

British representatives on the combined bodies set up here and in the United States, to provide for the most effective utilisation of the joint resources of the United Nations in munitions and raw materials. He will organise, in co-operation with the Dominions and other Empire Governments, the general planning of the production of raw materials, machine tools and finished munitions in the Empire.

As regards raw materials and machine tools required for war production in this country, he will be responsible for planning the development of home resources, for arranging the import programmes, and for settling the allocation and release of stocks. He will determine the scope and extent of the building programmes.

In all matters connected with the allocation, distribution and efficient use of labour within the field of war production, the Minister of Production and the Minister of Labour and National Service will work together; the latter being generally responsible for the supply of labour, and the former for determining the relative importance of the various demands for labour for war production.

As regards the Admiralty, the position is that the Board will continue to control the design, construction and armament of all naval vessels, and the naval programmes, subject only to the approval of the Minister of Defence and the War Cabinet. The Board of Admiralty will also remain responsible for the construction and defensive equipment of merchant vessels, and for their repair in this country, but will be advised by the Minister of War Transport about such matters as the types of merchant vessels to be constructed. In all other respects the functions of the Minister of Production will extend to the field of production for which the Admiralty is primarily responsible.

It is not intended to issue a White Paper on this occasion. I had hoped that the Leader of the House would be able to arrange for a Debate on the scope of the duties of the Minister of Production next week. I am sorry to say that the illness of my right hon. and gallant Friend the Minister of State may impose some little delay, as he wishes himself to make a statement upon the view he takes of his duties, and also to reply to any suggestions and questions that may occur to the House.

The Minister of State in the Middle East

March *13.* Mr. Curtin, Prime Minister of Australia, in a broadcast, expressed his hope of closer co-operation with the United States in the Pacific.

March *14.* Officially announced that *12* Allied warships, including H.M.S. Exeter, and at least *9* Japanese warships were sunk in a great battle off Java.

March *15.* Hitler, in a Berlin speech, blamed the winter for the failure of the German campaign in Russia.

March *17.* General MacArthur, leader of the heroic American resistance in the Philippines, arrived in Australia to take over supreme command of the military forces at the request of the Commonwealth Government.

March *18.* Lord Halifax, Ambassador to Washington, disclosed that British tank output had doubled since August.

March *19.* Mr. Casey, Australian Minister in Washington, appointed Minister of State to represent the British War Cabinet in the Middle East.

March *21.* Malta, subjected to the heaviest air raids of the year, destroyed *17* aircraft.

March *22.* Sir Stafford Cripps arrived in India with the Government plan to solve the Indian problem.

[*March 19, 1942*

HIS Majesty has been pleased to approve the appointment of the Right Honourable Richard Gardiner Casey, D.S.O., M.C., to be Minister of State. Mr. Casey will be a member of the War Cabinet of the United Kingdom, and will represent the War

Cabinet in the Middle East, where he will concert, on their behalf, the measures necessary for the prosecution of the War in that area, other than the conduct of operations. Mr. Casey will be described as Minister of State in the Middle East. Mr. Casey is at present Australian Minister in Washington, and I wish, on behalf of His Majesty's Government, to express our thanks to the Commonwealth Government for their consent to release Mr. Casey at this juncture from his important duties in the United States.

Defence of a Convoy

MESSAGE SENT TO THE COMMANDER-IN-CHIEF, MEDITERRA-
NEAN FLEET, FOLLOWING THE SUCCESSFUL DEFENCE OF A
CONVOY FROM ALEXANDRIA TO MALTA
MARCH 24, 1942

[March 24, 1942

I SHALL be glad if you will convey to Admiral Vian and all who sailed with him the admiration which I feel at this resolute and brilliant action by which the Malta convoy was saved. That one of the most powerful modern battleships afloat, attended by two heavy and four light cruisers and a flotilla, should have been routed and put to flight with severe torpedo and gunfire injury in broad daylight by a force of five British light cruisers and destroyers constitutes a naval episode of the highest distinction, and entitles all ranks and ratings concerned, and above all their Commander, to the compliments of the British nation.

The Outlook for 1942

A SPEECH TO THE CENTRAL COUNCIL
OF THE CONSERVATIVE PARTY, AT
CAXTON HALL, LONDON
MARCH 26, 1942

March 25.	*Japanese troops occupied the strategically important Andaman Islands in the Bay of Bengal.*
March 26.	*Mr. Churchill told the Conservative Party that the Battle of the Atlantic had worsened for the time being, but that we could not lose the war except through our own fault.*

[*March 26, 1942*

A YEAR, almost to a day, has passed since I addressed you here. We had then made our great recovery after the collapse of France. Our Air Force had won the Battle of Britain. We had endured, and were still enduring, the full fury of the German air raids. The position in Egypt was secure, and we were cheered by the long series of victories by which General Wavell destroyed the Italian armies in North Africa. But perhaps you will remember that I went out of my way to warn you that we could not expect to have successes unchequered by reverses.

Since then we have had an almost unbroken series of military misfortunes. We were driven out of Cyrenaica, and have now only partly re-established ourselves there. We were driven out of Greece and Crete. We have been attacked by a new and most formidable antagonist in the Far East. Hong Kong has fallen; the Malay Peninsula and the possessions of the brave Dutch in the East Indies have been overrun. Singapore has been the scene of the greatest disaster to British arms which our history records. The Allied squadrons in the Netherlands East Indies have been virtually destroyed in the action off Java. Burma is invaded;

The Outlook for 1942, March 26, 1942

Rangoon has fallen; very hard fighting is proceeding in Upper Burma. Australia is threatened; India is threatened. The Battle of the Atlantic, upon which all the time our power to live and carry on the war effort depends, after turning markedly in our favour for five or six months, has now for the time being — but only for the time being — worsened again.

Can you wonder that such a melancholy tale, which I do not fear to tell or to face, should have caused widespread distress and anxiety throughout our country and Empire? Yet it is in such moments that fortitude and courage are the only means of safety. I cannot offer this morning any guarantee that we are at the end of our misfortunes. We were engaged in a deadly grapple with two heavily-armed opponents, both of whom had been preparing for years, and bending their whole national life to the fulfilment of a gospel of war. Beginning as we did, ill-prepared, we had gathered and engaged and employed all our resources to make head against these two Powers, Germany and Italy, when suddenly a third great Power, armed to the teeth, with a population of 80,000,000, with three or four millions of trained soldiers formed into an army of at least two millions, with a powerful, efficient navy and air force and a heavy outfit of munitions — I say outfit and not output — fell upon our eastern possessions, which our bitter needs in the West had forced us to leave so insufficiently guarded. In such a situation it would be foolish for us not to be prepared for further heavy blows, and I am not here to speak smooth words or make cheering promises. But this I will venture to say, that just as last year I warned you that you could not expect to have successes unchequered by reverses, so now in 1942 we need not expect to have reverses unrelieved by successes.

There is another side to the picture, there is another column in the account which has to be added up. When we look back over the sombre year that has passed, and forward to the many trials that lie before us, no one can doubt for a moment the improvement in our war position. A year ago we were alone: now three of the greatest nations in the world are sworn to us in close alliance, and are fighting at our side in all their growing power. Whereas a year ago all we could do was to fight stubbornly and doggedly on, as we had done when we were alone in former

The End of the Beginning

wars — and not without ultimate success — we have now at our side mighty allies. Whereas when we met here last year it was impossible to state any definite method by which we could come out victorious, except our confidence that that would be the end, it now seems very likely that we and our allies of the United Nations cannot lose this war, and with it all that makes life worth living, except through our own fault or their own fault, through failure to use our combined strength, overwhelming strength when fully mobilised and organised, and to use the multiplying opportunities which, as the months pass by, will present themselves to us. We must therefore examine searchingly and repeatedly our own conduct and the character and quality of our war effort in every form and direction. We must make sure our fellow-countrymen and our allies have the best service from us that we can give.

We are certainly aided by a great volume of criticism and advice from which it will always be our endeavour to profit in the highest degree. Naturally when one is burdened by the very hard labour of the task and its cares, sorrows, and responsibilities, there may sometimes steal across the mind a feeling of impatience at the airy and jaunty detachment of some of those critics who feel so confident of their knowledge and feel so sure of their ability to put things right. If I should be forced — as I hope I shall not be — to yield to such a temptation, I hope you will remember how difficult it is to combine the attitude of proper meekness and humility towards assailants at home with those combative and pugnacious qualities, with the spirit of offensive and counter-attack, which we feel were never more needful than now against the common enemy.

We have succeeded in preserving our traditional free institutions, free speech, full and active Parliamentary government, a free Press. We have done that under conditions which at times were more strained and convulsive than have ever beset a civilised State. But there is one limit which I must ask shall be respected. I cannot allow, while I bear the responsibility, a propaganda to disturb the Army, which is now so strong and solid; or to weaken the confidence of the country and the armed forces in the quality and character of our devoted corps of officers, guard or line, staff or regimental, to whom we must all look, not only as the leaders of audacious enterprises abroad but as our indispensable weapon against invasion here at home.

I am perpetually asked to devote more time and attention to the rebuilding of the post-war world, and measures, some of them elaborate and all of them carefully thought out, have been taken to prepare by study and planning for that most important and longed-for period. But as you will, I am sure, agree, we must be, above all things, careful that nothing diverts or distracts our thoughts or our fullest energies from the task of national self-preservation and of inter-allied duty which will require the total concentration for an indefinite period of all that we can give.

I will not therefore enter on these subjects to-day, except to say that a few weeks ago one of our leading intellectuals, a great thinker — and as the father of our new President once said, one of the great difficulties about great thinkers is that they so often think wrong — asked in public whether I was working for the new England or the old. It is an easy question to answer, for you as well as for myself: we are working for both. The new England, or the new Britain, for we have our Welsh and Scottish friends represented [a voice: "And Northern Ireland"] — and Northern Ireland which we never forget — the new Britain and the old Britain have always dwelt side by side in our land, and it is by the union and inter-play of the new impulses and the great traditions both working together that we have managed to solve peacefully, yet finally, problems which have ruined for ever the unity of many a famous State.

It is by this dual process that we have contrived to build up over generations that basis of life with its rights and tolerances, its individual freedom, its collective associations, and, above all, its infinite power of self-improvement and national progress, that decent way of life which the broad masses of our people share and for which they now show themselves prepared to fight, and if need be to die.

This is a very hard war. Its numerous and fearful problems reach down to the very foundations of human society. Its scope is world wide, and it involves all nations and every man, woman, and child in them. Strategy and economics are interwoven. Sea, land, and air are but a single service. The latest refinements of science are linked with the cruelties of the Stone Age. The work-

The End of the Beginning

shop and the fighting line are one. All may fall, all will stand together. We must aid each other, we must stand by each other. We must confront our perils and trials with that national unity which cannot be broken, and a national force which is inexhaustible. We must confront them with resilience and ingenuity which are fearless, and above all with that inflexible will-power to endure and yet to dare for which our island race has long been renowned. Thus, and thus alone, can we be worthy champions of that grand alliance of nearly thirty States and nations which without our resistance would never have come into being, but which now has only to march on together until tyranny is trampled down.

In all this the Conservative Party has a vital part to play. Now is the time for all its characteristic qualities to come increasingly into action. Now is the time for it to impart to our affairs and our national life those elements of stability and firmness, that power to plough through the evil days till the whole result is gained. Now is the time, and without this aid it might be that all the strength of embattled democracy would be cast away. The time has not come to form judgments about the past: all our thoughts, all our will-power must be concentrated on what lies around us and before us. Yet, as your leader, I shall hope that when the whole story has been told it will be said of the Conservative Party in Parliament and throughout the land: They strove for peace — too long, but when war came they proved themselves the main part of the rock on which the salvation of Britain was founded and the freedom of mankind regained.

Free Denmark

A SPEECH AT NO. 10, DOWNING STREET, WHEN RECEIVING A
CHEQUE FOR £38,300 PRESENTED BY THE FREE DANES TO
PROVIDE GREAT BRITAIN WITH FIGHTER AEROPLANES
APRIL 9, 1942

March 28. *Combined British force made "Zeebrugge" raid on St. Nazaire, German naval base in France. Old destroyer filled with explosives rammed the dock gate and blew up.*

March 29. *Britain's proposals for India — being discussed by Sir Stafford Cripps with the Indian leaders — were published. They provided for Dominion status after the War, when an elected body would frame a new constitution.*

April 1. *First meeting of the Pacific War Council held in the White House at Washington.*

April 2. *Situation deteriorated in Burma, where the Japanese were actively assisted by Burmese rebels.*

In India, General Wavell was called into Sir Stafford Cripps's discussions to consider Nationalist demand for Indian control of defence.

April 4. *General Wavell discussed defence plans with Indian leaders.*

April 5. *Japanese lost 27, out of 75, planes in surprise attempt to bomb Colombo (Ceylon).*

April 8. *Mr. Harry Hopkins, President Roosevelt's personal representative, and General Marshall, Chief of Staff, U.S. Army, arrived in London.*

April 9. *Admiralty announced that Japanese aircraft had sunk 10,000-ton cruisers* Dorsetshire *and* Cornwall *in the Indian Ocean.*

United States forces withdrew from Bataan Peninsula (Philippines) to fortress island of Corregidor.

I AM very glad you devoted your munificent contribution to the Air Force, because that is the part of our armed attack which is most constantly in contact with the enemy. We have, as it seems, a very long road to trek. The arrival of a new enemy fresh, and very powerful, has prolonged the journey which Europe must travel, but has also brought us new friends far more powerful, once they have been given the time to realise their strength.

Therefore, I feel I may say with very good confidence that the day of the liberation of Europe can be looked and hoped for by all whose nations are in bondage at the present time. We shall never give in. We shall never weary. It is not seen how we can easily be destroyed. When we look at the times through which we have passed, we can see how much more we are now in power to continue our unrelenting struggle against the vile, dark, criminal forces which have laid their foul grip on Western Europe and on Christian civilisation.

We shall never pause in our struggle, nor will our great American and Russian allies, and I have very little doubt that the day will come — perhaps sooner than it would be prudent or sensible to hope — when Denmark will be free from the grip in which she has been held, and when she will resume her independent, honoured, and ancient place among the free peoples and States of Europe.

We here in England who hope to take part in the work of liberation and are resolved to do so, shall always be particularly grateful for the assistance we have received from the Danes and the moral support we have from the Danish nation, because of our connexion with the beautiful Queen Alexandra, who was for so many years the object of admiration, the cynosure of the British nation.

We never have forgotten those days, nor have we forgotten the longer days in the past when our armies served together. We shall do our utmost to repay your country with good results. Good weather is needed to turn this splendid cheque for £38,000 into the first heavy thunder drops of the storm which has to beat upon this odious tyranny.

A Message to Sir Stafford Cripps in India

APRIL 11, 1942

April 10. *Sinking of British aircraft-carrier* Hermes *by Japanese planes off Ceylon officially announced.*

April 11. *Sir Stafford Cripps announced that Britain's offer to India had been withdrawn after Indian parties had failed to reach agreement.*

[*April 11, 1942*

YOU have done everything in human power, and your tenacity, perseverance, and resourcefulness have proved how great was the British desire to reach a settlement. Even though your hopes have not been fulfilled, you have rendered a very important service to the common cause, and the foundations have been laid for the future progress of the peoples of India.

The War Situation

A STATEMENT TO THE HOUSE OF COMMONS
APRIL 13, 1942

[*April 13, 1942*

IT was thought convenient that I should deal with several points that were raised in the course of Questions in a brief statement at the end of them. With regard to the conversations in India and the mission of the Lord Privy Seal (Sir Stafford Cripps), it would be better to await the return of the Lord Privy Seal, who may be in a position to make a personal report to the House upon the very important mission with which he was charged. I will consider whether a White Paper can be laid, although a great deal has been made public already by both parties to the negotiations.

I have a Question which was asked by the hon. Member for South Croydon (Sir H. Williams) about the loss of the two 10,000-ton 8-inch gun cruisers *Dorsetshire* and *Cornwall* in the Indian Ocean. On 4th April superior Japanese naval forces which had entered the Indian Ocean were observed steering towards Ceylon. These forces comprised at least three battleships, including one of the modernised 16-inch Nagato type, and five aircraft-carriers, together with a number of heavy and light cruisers and destroyer flotillas. Severe air attacks were delivered on the harbours of Colombo and Trincomalee. As has been announced, the attacking aircraft suffered heavy losses at both places from the British fighter protection and anti-aircraft batteries. We also suffered to a lesser extent, but seriously, in our aircraft, and damage was done to shore establishments and to the few ships which remained in harbour. Besides these losses, the two 8-inch gun cruisers *Dorsetshire* and *Cornwall* and the aircraft-carrier *Hermes,* which had left harbour before the attack, were sunk at sea by enemy aircraft. The naval operations were under the command of Admiral Sir James Somerville, an officer who for the last two years has been commanding in the Western Mediterranean and has almost unrivalled experience of the conditions of modern naval war. Without giving the enemy useful information, I cannot make any statement about the strength of the forces at Admiral Somerville's disposal or of the reasons which led him to make the dispositions of his fleet, for which he was responsible. Nothing in these dispositions or in the consequences which followed from them have in any way weakened the confidence of the Admiralty in his judgment. I may, perhaps, add that it is quite impossible to afford continuous air protection by shore-based or carrier-borne aircraft to all His Majesty's ships at sea. Many scores are at sea every day without such protection, and unless these risks are taken, there is no means of carrying on the immense business of convoy and sea war which falls upon the Royal Navy.

I have had a Question also by the hon. Member for South Croydon and the hon. Member for Central Southwark (Mr. Martin) about the course of events in Malaya and Singapore. Major-General Gordon-Bennett's report has now been received. It is not suitable for publication. His Majesty's Government are, however, collecting information wherever it can be obtained. Thus, Sir Archibald Wavell has been instructed to appoint an officer to collect such information as is of value from persons who have escaped from Singapore to India, and to send it to this country. Moreover, Sir Archibald Wavell, as supreme commander of the United Nations Forces in the A.B.D.A. area during the major part of the operations in Malaya, will, no doubt, furnish a report or dispatch on what took place; but I cannot expect him to divert his attention from the immediate conduct of the war on the Eastern frontier of India at the present time. All the available information is being and will be examined in order to make sure that none of the lessons to be learned from the fighting in Malaya are neglected. I cannot, however, hold out any expectation that any report or White Book about the fighting in Malaya will be published within any foreseeable period. Still less would it be appropriate to attempt to pronounce judgment while many of those who took part in these events are prisoners of war and are not able to give their accounts of what happened. I may add, however, that I will seek an opportunity during the next fortnight or so to make a statement to the House on the present course of the war. This will have to be in Secret Session.

I have one announcement to make which may be of interest to the House, and I mention it, first of all, to the House as I am present here to-day. On 19th October, 1941, my hon. and gallant Friend the Member for North Portsmouth (Sir R. Keyes) was succeeded in charge of combined operations by Captain Lord Louis Mountbatten, G.C.V.O., D.S.O., R.N., with the title of Adviser on Combined Operations (A.C.O.), and the rank of Commodore, First Class. On 18th March, 1942, Captain Lord Louis Mountbatten was appointed Chief of Combined Operations (C.C.O.), which office carries with it the acting rank of Vice-Admiral and the honorary ranks of Lieutenant-General and Air Marshal. The Chief of Combined Operations attends the meetings of the Chiefs of Staff Committee, and is a full member whenever major issues are in question and also when his own combined operations, or any matters in which he is concerned, are under discussion.

In reply to further questions Mr. Churchill made these additional statements: —

Sir Stafford Cripps's Mission to India

I take this opportunity, which I am sure the House will approve, of saying how much we have admired the tenacity and ingenuity and patience with which he conducted these negotiations, and although I have no doubt he feels stricken a most cruel blow by the fact that success was not achieved, that does not in any way lessen the fact that we highly approve of his mission and his conduct of these difficult negotiations.

The Air Raid on Colombo

While the attack on Colombo was being delivered by the Japanese, our torpedo aircraft sallied out to attack the carriers from which the Japanese attack had been delivered, but owing to thunderstorms and low cloud in that vicinity, they did not make contacts on that day. The weather in the other parts of the Indian Ocean was not subject to those conditions of cloud and thunderstorms in which the Japanese carriers had shrouded themselves. Very valiant attacks were made by the torpedo aircraft that we possessed, and also by the fighter bomber aircraft which were on the spot in such numbers as were available. As has already been published, one of the Japanese carriers is said to have had near misses, but whether any damage was done I have no knowledge. I know this, however, that practically all the aircraft taking part in the attack were either shot down or seriously injured or rendered unserviceable. That was the result.

British Prisoners at Singapore

I cannot take any responsibility for various statements that are made by Major-General Gordon-Bennett. I have, I think, mentioned some figures in the past, and I am pretty confident that the closest examination of the figures will show that what the Government have said is correct.

Defence of Malaya

In the period before Japan declared war there were a number of reports of great length and in great detail from the officers in that theatre. There were also at least three or four conferences, some secret, to which the Dutch and other Powers were invited. There is an immense mass of technical material upon the subject, but all of it bears very intimately upon our war arrangements, and I cannot think that any advantage — in fact there would be great disadvantage — would attach to its publication. It would certainly show, speaking very generally, that an immense amount of study and discussion preceded these lamentable events, but study and discussion are not in themselves sufficient to prepare against attack by a superior force of the enemy, and the difficulty under which we have suffered has been to search for the necessary forces to make head against the new attack to which we have been subjected.

Use of Naval Strength

When you have the Pacific Ocean and the Indian Ocean, and the Japanese occupy an intermediate situation between the two, it is possible for them to use a large force on one side and a lighter force on the other, or vice versa. Consequently, the positions of our ships have to be related as far as possible to the information which we possess as to where the enemy's main strength lies. Certainly it would be impossible to carry on the immense business of convoy without His Majesty's ships — not capital ships in this case — being from time to time in situations where they have not got that support against air attack which everyone sees is eminently desirable.

Native Population of Malaya

All my information is to the effect that the people of Malaya were thoroughly friendly.

A Great Daylight Raid

A MESSAGE TO AIR MARSHAL HARRIS, CHIEF OF THE BOMBER
COMMAND, AFTER THE GREAT DAYLIGHT ATTACK BY THE
R.A.F. ON AUGSBURG
APRIL 20, 1942

[April 20, 1942

WE must plainly regard the attack of the Lancasters on the U-boat engine factory at Augsburg as an outstanding achievement of the Royal Air Force. Undeterred by heavy losses at the outset, the bombers pierced in broad daylight into the heart of Germany and struck a vital point with deadly precision. Pray convey the thanks of His Majesty's Government to the officers and men who accomplished this memorable feat of arms, in which no life was lost in vain.

Anzac Day, 1942

A MESSAGE TO MR. CURTIN, THE PRIME MINISTER
OF AUSTRALIA
APRIL 25, 1942

[April 25, 1942

GREETINGS to you on Anzac Day. We shall never forget the great comradeship of Gallipoli, with its imperishable memories.

Poland's Fight

A MESSAGE TO GENERAL SIKORSKI, THE POLISH PRIME MINISTER AND COMMANDER-IN-CHIEF, ON THE 151ST ANNIVERSARY OF THE POLISH CONSTITUTION MAY 4, 1942

[May 4, 1942

I DESIRE on behalf of His Majesty's Government and the British People to send you their best wishes for the restoration and the future greatness of Poland.

Poland has suffered much in the cause of Freedom, but her sons and daughters abroad and in Poland are continuing the struggle and contributing a valuable part to the Allied war effort. Their sacrifices and their contribution will not be forgotten at the time which I hope is not far distant when you lead the Polish armies back to a restored and independent Poland.

" *Evatt Is With Us* "

A MESSAGE TO MR. CURTIN, THE AUSTRALIAN PRIME MIN-
ISTER, ON THE OCCASION OF THE VISIT TO LONDON OF
DR. H. V. EVATT, THE AUSTRALIAN MINISTER FOR
EXTERNAL AFFAIRS
MAY 6, 1942

[*May 6, 1942*

EVATT is with us now. In the sure and certain hope that our hard striving will be crowned by victory, we send you our heartfelt good wishes.

The Landing on Madagascar

A STATEMENT TO THE HOUSE OF COMMONS
MAY 7, 1942

April 14. Sir Kingsley Wood introduced new budget aiming at £150,000,000 more from taxation. Changes included: Tax allowance on a wife's earnings raised, purchase tax on luxury goods doubled, increased taxation on tobacco, wines, spirits, beer and entertainment.
Vichy France announced new submission to Germany, with return of Laval as Chief of Government.

April 15. United States bombers made a 2,000-mile raid on Japanese bases in the Philippines, damaging ships, docks and aerodromes.

April 16. The King awarded the George Cross to Malta in recognition of the island's heroic defence.

April 17. R.A.F. made a daring daylight raid on Augsburg in Southern Germany.

April 18. United States planes bombed Tokio, Yokohama, Nagoya and Kobe.

April 20. Laval, in a broadcast speech, bitterly attacked Britain and pledged closer co-operation with Germany. Germans executed thirty French hostages as a reprisal for the blowing-up of a troop train.

April 21. Sir Stafford Cripps arrived back in London from his mission to India.

April 22. British commando troops raided the French coast near Boulogne.

April 26. Hitler assumed arbitrary legal powers as Supreme Law Lord to tighten up German home front.

April 30. Japanese captured Lashio, the western terminus of the Burma road to China.

The End of the Beginning

May 1.   *Hitler and Mussolini conferred at Salzburg on political and military problems.*

May 2.   *Japanese captured Mandalay, British troops retreating westward to avoid being cut off from India.*

May 5.   *British forces landed in the Vichy-controlled island of Madagascar and advanced against the naval base of Diego Suarez.*

Japanese troops, pushing north from Lashio, entered China.

The last United States stronghold in the Philippines, the island fortress of Corregidor, surrendered to the Japanese.

May 7.   *Mr. Churchill announced that French naval and military commanders in Madagascar had surrendered.*

Great naval battle in the Coral Sea between United States and Japanese fleets in which, it was subsequently revealed, fifteen Japanese ships, including a new aircraft-carrier, were lost and twenty-two others damaged, while the Americans lost the aircraft-carrier Lexington.

[*May 7, 1942*

I THOUGHT the House might wish to know at once the latest news from Madagascar. In order to prevent bloodshed as far as possible, very strong forces of all arms were employed, and preparations were made extending over the last three months. The landings were, as has already been made public, successfully accomplished, and by Tuesday evening our troops were in contact with the French forces in and before Diego Suarez, before the promontory of Antsirane and the promontory of Oronjia. The first assault on Antsirane at dawn yesterday was repulsed with losses which may have exceeded 1,000 men, but Major-General Sturges, of the Royal Marines, who commanded the troops on the island, attacked again during last night and captured the promontory. The French naval and military commanders surrendered, and the town of Diego Suarez was also occupied.

Early this morning a further attack was made on the Oronjia batteries, which command the entrance to the harbour. These have now surrendered, and a protocol is now being drawn up between the commanders of either side. The mine-sweepers of the powerful covering fleet under Admiral Syfret which had been assembled have already begun their work, and it is expected that the Fleet will enter the harbour of Diego Suarez at about 3.30 this afternoon.

These operations, which were not without risks of various kinds, have been carried out with great dash and vigour. The French also fought with much gallantry and discipline. We grieve that bloodshed has occurred between the troops of our two countries, whose people at heart are united against the common foe. We trust that the French nation in time will come to regard this episode as a recognisable step in the liberation of their country, including Alsace-Lorraine, from the German yoke.

Prime Minister for Two Years

A WORLD BROADCAST
MAY 10, 1942

I HAVE now served for two years exactly to a day as the King's First Minister. Therefore I thought it would be a good thing if I had a talk to you on the broadcast, to look back a little on what we have come through, to consider how we stand now, and to peer cautiously, but at the same time resolutely, into the future.

The tremendous period through which we have passed has certainly been full of anxieties and exertions; it has been marked by many misfortunes and disappointments. This time two years ago the Germans were beating down Holland and Belgium by unprovoked brutal, merciless invasion, and very soon there came upon us the total defeat of France and the fatal surrender at Bordeaux. Mussolini, the Italian miscalculator, thought he saw his chance of a cheap and easy triumph, and rich plunder for no fighting. He struck at the back of a dying France, and at what he believed was a doomed Britain. We were left alone — our quarter of a million Dunkirk troops saved, only disarmed; ourselves, as yet unarmed — to face the might of victorious Germany, to face also the carefully saved-up strength of an Italy which then still ranked as a first-class Power.

Here at home in this island, invasion was near; the Mediterranean was closed to us; the long route round the Cape, where General Smuts stands on guard, alone was open; our small, ill-equipped forces in Egypt and the Sudan seemed to await destruction. All the world, even our best friends, thought that our end had come. Accordingly, we prepared ourselves to conquer or to perish. We were united in that solemn, majestic hour; we were all equally resolved at least to go down fighting. We cast calculation to the winds; no wavering voice was heard; we hurled defiance at our foes; we faced our duty, and, by the mercy of God, we were preserved.

It fell to me in those days to express the sentiments and resolves of the British nation in that supreme crisis of its life. That was to me an honour far beyond any dreams or ambitions I had ever nursed, and it is one that cannot be taken away. For a whole year after the fall of France we stood alone, keeping the flag of freedom flying, and the hopes of the world alive. We conquered the Italian Empire, we destroyed or captured almost all Mussolini's African army; we liberated Abyssinia; we have so far successfully protected Palestine, Syria, Persia and Iraq from German designs. We have suffered grievous reverses in going to the aid of the heroic Greeks; we bore unflinching many a heavy blow abroad, and still more in our cities here at home; and all this time, cheered and helped by President Roosevelt and the United States, we stood alone, neither faltering nor flagging.

Where are we now? Can anyone doubt that if we are worthy of it, as we shall be, we have in our hands our own future? As in the last war, so in this, we are moving through many reverses and defeats to complete and final victory. We have only to endure and to persevere, to conquer. Now we are no longer unarmed; we are well armed. Now we are not alone; we have mighty allies, bound irrevocably by solemn faith and common interests to stand with us in the ranks of the United Nations. There can only be one end. When it will come, or how it will come, I cannot tell. But, when we survey the overwhelming resources which are at our disposal, once they are fully marshalled and developed — as they can be, as they will be — we may stride forward into the unknown with growing confidence.

During the time that we were all alone, we were steadily growing stronger. He would have been a bold man, however, who in those days would have put down in black and white exactly how we were going to win. But, as has happened before in our island history, by remaining steadfast and unyielding — stubborn, if you will — against a Continental tyrant, we reached the moment when that tyrant made a fatal blunder. Dictators, as well as democracies and parliamentary governments, make mistakes sometimes. Indeed, when the whole story is told, I believe it will be found that the Dictators, for all their preparations and pro-

The End of the Beginning

longed scheming, have made greater mistakes than the Democracies they have assailed. Even Hitler makes mistakes sometimes. In June last, without the slightest provocation, and in breach of a pact of non-aggression, he invaded the lands of the Russian people. At that time he had the strongest army in the world, trained in war, flushed with incredible unbroken success, and equipped with limitless munitions and the most modern weapons. He had also secured for himself the advantages of surprise and treachery. Thus he drove the youth and manhood of the German nation forward into Russia.

The Russians, under their warrior chief, Stalin, sustained losses which no other country or government has ever borne in so short a time and lived. But they, like us, were resolved never to give in. They poured out their own blood upon their native soil. They kept their faces to the foe. From the very first day to the end of the year, and on till to-night, they fought with unflinching valour. And, from the very first day when they were attacked, when no one could tell how things would go, we made a brotherhood with them, and a solemn compact to destroy Nazidom and all its works. Then Hitler made his second grand blunder. He forgot about the winter. There is a winter, you know, in Russia. For a good many months the temperature is apt to fall very low. There is snow, there is frost, and all that. Hitler forgot about this Russian winter. He must have been very loosely educated. We all heard about it at school; but he forgot it. I have never made such a bad mistake as that. So winter came, and fell upon his ill-clad armies, and with the winter came the valiant Russian counter-attacks. No one can say with certainty how many millions of Germans have already perished in Russia and its snows. Certainly more have perished than were killed in the whole four and a quarter years of the last war. That is probably an understatement. So besotted is this man in his lust for blood and conquest, so blasting is the power he wields over the lives of Germans, that he even blurted out the other day that his armies would be better clothed and his locomotives better prepared for their second winter in Russia than they were for their first.

There was an admission about the length of the war that struck a chill into German hearts as cold as the icy winds of Russia.

What will be the sufferings of the German manhood in this new bloodbath? What is there in front of Hitler now? Certain it is that the Russian armies are stronger than they were last year, that they have learnt by hard experience to fight the Germans in the field, that they are well-equipped, and that their constancy and courage are unquenched. That is what is in front of Hitler. What is he leaving behind him? He leaves behind him a Europe starving and in chains; a Europe in which his execution squads are busy in a dozen countries every day; a Europe which has learned to hate the Nazi name as no name has ever been hated in the recorded history of mankind; a Europe burning for revolt whenever the opportunity comes.

But this is not all he has left behind. We are on his tracks, and so is the great Republic of the United States. Already the Royal Air Force has set about it; the British, and presently the American, bombing offensive against Germany will be one of the principal features in this year's world war. Now is the time to use our increasingly superior air strength, to strike hard and continually at the home front in Germany, from which so much evil has leaked out upon the world, and which is the foundation of the whole enormous German invasion of Russia. Now, while the German armies will be bleeding and burning up their strength against the two-thousand-mile Russian line, and when the news of casualties by hundreds of thousands is streaming back to the German Reich, now is the time to bring home to the German people the wickedness of their rulers, by destroying under their very eyes the factories and seaports on which their war effort depends.

German propaganda has been constantly appealing of late to British public opinion to put a stop to these severe forms of warfare, which, according to the German view, should be the strict monopoly of the *Herrenvolk*. Herr Hitler himself has not taken at all kindly to this treatment, and he has been good enough to mingle terrible threats with his whinings. He warns us, solemnly, that if we go on smashing up the German cities, his war factories and his bases, he will retaliate against our cathedrals and historic monuments — if they are not too far inland. We have heard his threats before. Eighteen months ago, in September, 1940, when he thought he had an overwhelming Air Force at his command, he declared that he would rub out — that was the actual expression, rub out — our towns and cities. And he certainly had a good try. Now the boot is on the other leg. Herr Hitler has even called in question the humanity of these grim developments of war. What a pity this conversion did not take place in his heart before he bombed Warsaw, or massacred twenty thousand Dutch folk in defenceless Rotterdam, or wreaked his cruel vengeance upon the open city of Belgrade! In those days, he used to boast that for every ton of bombs we dropped on Germany, he would drop ten times, or even a hundred times, as many on Britain. Those were his words, and that was his belief. Indeed, for a time we had to suffer very severely from his vastly superior strength and utter ruthlessness.

But now it is the other way round. We are in a position to carry into Germany many times the tonnage of high explosives which he can send here, and this proportion will increase all the summer, all the autumn, all the winter, all the spring, all the summer, and so on, till the end! The accuracy of our bombing has nearly doubled, and, with continued practice, I expect it will improve still more. Moreover, at the same time, our methods of dealing with his raiders over here have more than repaid the immense care and science bestowed upon them, and the very large scale upon which they are applied. During the month of April we have destroyed one-tenth of all the raiding aircraft which have assailed our island; whereas, acting on a scale several times as big, the losses which we have suffered have been proportionately far smaller. We have waited long for this turning of the tables, and have taken whatever came to us meanwhile.

You will remember how the German propaganda films, seeking to terrorise neutral countries and glorying in devastating violence, were wont to show rows of great German bombers being loaded up with bombs, then flying in the air in battle array, then casting down showers of bombs upon the defenceless towns and villages below, choking them in smoke and flame. All this was represented from the beginning of the war to neutral countries as the German way of making war. All this was intended to make the world believe that resistance to the German will was impossible, and that subjugation and slavery were the safest and easiest road. Those days are gone. Though the mills of God grind slowly, yet they grind exceeding small. And for my part, I hail it as an example of sublime and poetic justice that those who have loosed these horrors upon mankind will now in their homes and persons feel the shattering strokes of just retribution.

We have a long list of German cities in which all the vital industries of the German war machine are established. All these it will be our stern duty to deal with, as we have already dealt with Lübeck, with Rostock, and half-a-dozen important places. The civil population of Germany have, however, an easy way to escape from these severities. All they have to do is to leave the cities where munitions work is being carried on — abandon their work, and go out into the fields, and watch their home fires burning from a distance. In this way they may find time for meditation and repentance; there they may remember the millions of Russian women and children they have driven out to perish in the snows, and the mass executions of peasantry and prisoners-of-war which in varying scales they are inflicting upon so many of the ancient and famous peoples of Europe. There they may remember that it is the villainous Hitlerite régime which is responsible for dragging Germany through misery and slaughter to ultimate ruin, and learn that the tyrant's overthrow is the first step to world liberation.

We now wait in what is a stormy lull, but still a lull, before the hurricane bursts again in full fury on the Russian front. We cannot tell when it will begin; we have not so far seen any evidences of those great concentrations of German masses which usually precede their large-scale offensives. They may have been successfully concealed, or may not yet have been launched eastward. But it is now the tenth of May, and the days are passing. We send our salutations to the Russian armies, and we hope that the thousands of tanks and aeroplanes which have been carried to their aid from Britain and America will be a useful contribution to their own magnificently developed and reorganised munitions resources.

There is, however, one serious matter which I must mention to you. The Soviet Government have expressed to us the view that the Germans in the desperation of their assault may make use of poison gas against the armies and people of Russia. We are ourselves firmly resolved not to use this odious weapon unless it is used first by the Germans. Knowing our Hun, however, we have not neglected to make preparations on a formidable scale. I wish now to make it plain that we shall treat the unprovoked use of poison gas against our Russian ally exactly as if it were used against ourselves, and if we are satisfied that this new outrage has been committed by Hitler, we shall use our great and growing air superiority in the West to carry gas warfare on the largest possible scale far and wide against military objectives in Germany. It is thus for Hitler to choose whether he wishes to add this additional horror to aerial warfare. We have for some time past been bringing our defensive and precautionary arrangements up to date, and I now give public warning, so that there may be no carelessness or neglect. Of one thing I am sure: that the British people, who have entered into the full comradeship of war with our Russian ally, will not shrink from any sacrifice or trial which that comradeship may require.

Meanwhile, our deliveries of tanks, aircraft and munitions to Russia from Britain and from the United States continue upon the full scale. We have the duty of escorting the northern convoys to their destination. Our sailors and merchant seamen face the fearful storms of the Arctic Circle, the lurking U-boats and shore-based aircraft, as well as attacks by German destroyers and surface craft, with their customary steadfastness and faithful courage. So far, though not without some loss both to the supply ships and their escorts, every convoy has successfully fought its way through, and we intend to persevere and fight it out on this northern route to the utmost of our strength.

Is there anything else we can do to take the weight off Russia? We are urged from many quarters to invade the continent of Europe and so form a second front. Naturally, I shall not disclose what our intentions are, but there is one thing I will say: I welcome the militant, aggressive spirit of the British nation so strongly shared across the Atlantic Ocean. Is it not far better that in the thirty-second month of this hard war we should find this general desire to come to the closest grips with the enemy, than that there should be any signs of war-weariness? Is it not far better that demonstrations of thousands of people should gather in Trafalgar Square demanding the most vehement and audacious attacks, than that there should be the weepings and wailings and peace agitations which in other lands and other wars have often hampered the action and vigour of governments? It is encouraging and inspiring to feel the strong heartbeats of a free nation, surging forward, stern and undaunted, in a righteous cause. We must not fail them, either in daring or in wisdom.

This week, two islands have been in our minds — one is very large, the other very small — Madagascar and Malta. We have found it necessary to take precautions to prevent Madagascar falling into enemy hands, by some dishonourable and feeble drifting or connivance by Vichy, like that which injured us so much in Indo-China. It is three months since the decision was taken, and more than two months since the expedition left these shores. Its first task was to secure the splendid harbour of Diego Suarez, in the northern part of Madagascar, which, if it had fallen into Japanese hands, might have paralysed all our communications with India and the Middle East. While the troops were on the sea, I must tell you I felt a shiver every time I saw the word "Madagascar" in the newspapers. All those articles with diagrams and measured maps, showing how very important it was for us to take Madagascar and forestall the Japanese, and be there "first for once," as they said, filled me with apprehension. There was no question of leakage, or breach of confidence. As they say, great minds think alike. But shrewd surmise may be as dangerous as leakage. And it was with considerable relief that I learned the difficulties of our soldiers and their losses had been exaggerated, and that the operation had been swiftly and effectually carried out.

We hold this island in trust; we hold it in trust for that gallant France which we have known and marched with, and whose restoration to her place among the great Powers of the world is indispensable to the future of Europe. Madagascar rests under the safeguard of the United Nations. Vichy, in the grip of the Germans, has been made to bluster and protest. The France that rose at St. Nazaire, and will one day rise in indescribable fury against the Nazis, understands what we have done and gives us its trust.

The smaller island is Malta, a tiny rock of history and romance. To-day we welcome back to our shores General Dobbie, for nearly two years the heroic defender of Malta. The burden which he has borne so honourably and for so long entitles him to release and repose. In Lord Gort we have a new impulse. His work at Gibraltar has been of the highest order. It was not his fault that our armies did not have their chance in France. He is a grand fighter. For the moment the terrific air attack on Malta has slackened. It looks as if a lot of enemy aircraft had moved eastward. I wonder why? If so, another intense air battle for Malta, upon which the enemy have concentrated such an immense preponderance of strength, and for which they have sacrificed so many of those aircraft which they now have to count more carefully every day — another intense air battle will have been definitely won. But other perils remain, and I know of no man in the British Empire to whom I would sooner entrust the combating and beating-down of those perils than Lord Gort.

If we look back to-day over the course of the war as it has so far unfolded, we can see that it seems to divide itself into four very clearly defined chapters. The first ended with the over-running by the Nazis of Western Europe and with the fall of France. The second chapter, Britain alone, ended with Hitler's attack upon Russia. I will call the third chapter which then began, "the Russian glory." May it long continue! The fourth chapter opened at Pearl Harbour, when the military party in Japan treacherously attacked the United States and Great Britain in the Far East. That is where we are now.

The aggression of Italy in 1940 had carried the war from Europe to Africa. The aggression of Japan has involved all Asia, including unconquerable China, and in one way or another has drawn in, or will draw in, the whole of the American Continent. Thus the struggle has become world-wide, and the fate of all states and nations and their future is at stake. This latest chapter — universal war — confronts us with many difficulties and immense complications. But is there any thoughtful sensible person who cannot see how vastly and decisively the awful balances have turned to the advantage of the cause of freedom? It is true that the Japanese, taking advantage of our preoccupations elsewhere, and of the fact that the United States had striven for so long to keep the peace, have seized more easily and more quickly than they expected their lands of booty and desire in the East Indian Archipelago. Henceforward they will find resistance stiffening on all their widely-spread fronts. They can ill afford losses such as those they have sustained in the naval action of the Coral Sea; so far we have no detailed accounts, but it is obvious, if only from the lies the Japanese have felt compelled to tell about the sinking of a battleship of the *Warspite* class, that a most vigorous and successful battle has been fought by the United States and Australian naval forces.

The Japanese war-lords cannot be indifferent to the losses of aircraft inflicted upon them at so many points, and particularly off the northern coasts of Australia, and in their repulse at Colombo and Trincomalee. At the start the pent-up, saved-up resources of Japan were bound to prevail in the Far Eastern theatre; but the strength of the United States, expressed in units of modern war power, actual and potential, is alone many times greater than the power of Japan. And we also shall make our contribution to the final defeat and punishment of this ambitious and greedy nation. Time will, however, be needed before the true strengths on either side of the Eastern war become manifest. I am not prone to make predictions, but I have no doubt to-night that the British and American sea power will grip and hold the Japanese, and that overwhelming air power, covering vigorous military operations, will lay them low. This would come to pass, of course, very much sooner, should anything happen to Hitler in Europe.

Therefore to-night I give you a message of good cheer. You deserve it, and the facts endorse it. But be it good cheer or be it bad cheer will make no difference to us; we shall drive on to the end, and do our duty, win or die. God helping us, we can do no other.

The Home Guard

[*May 12, 1942*

WHEN France fell out of the war two years ago and we were left alone, we were in imminent danger of invasion, and at that time we were not only destitute of an Army but we were an unarmed people. But at the same time that we reorganised our Army the Home Guard sprang into existence, and now we have the best part of 1,750,000 men trained to the use of arms, conscious of their military character and accustomed readily and rapidly to come together at any point, fixing their minds upon the possibilities of contact with the enemy, which are never to be excluded. This body, engaged in work of national importance during all the hours of the day, and often of the night, is nevertheless an invaluable addition to our armed forces and an essential part of the effective defence of the Island.

More especially is this true in view of the fact that airborne invasion becomes more and more a possibility and a feature of modern war. If in 1940 the enemy had descended suddenly in large numbers from the sky in different parts of the country, he would have found only little clusters of men, mostly armed with shotguns, gathered round our searchlight positions. But now, whenever he comes — if ever he comes — he will find, wherever he should place his foot, that he will immediately be attacked by resolute, determined men who have a perfectly clear intention and resolve — namely, to put him to death or compel his immediate surrender.

Therefore, to invade this island by air, apart from the difficulties of facing the Royal Air Force by daylight, is to descend into a hornet's nest. And I venture to think that there is no part of that nest where the stings are more ready and their effective power to injure more remarkable than here in the ancient Palace of Westminster, where, rifle in one hand and sometimes speech-notes in the other, we conduct the essential work of the Mother of Parliaments, and make clear that neither bombardment nor invasion will prevent our institutions functioning steadily, unbrokenly, throughout the storms of war.

" We See the Ridge Ahead "

A SPEECH FROM THE STEPS OF LEEDS TOWN HALL DURING
A TOUR OF THE CITY WITH DR. H. V. EVATT, THE AUSTRALIAN
MINISTER FOR EXTERNAL AFFAIRS
MAY 16, 1942

May 11.   *Germany made the first move in her spring offensive against Russia by launching a fierce attack against the Kerch peninsula.*

May 12.   *Russians attacked in the Kharkov sector to offset strategically German progress at Kerch.*

[*May 16, 1942*

IN the height of the second great war, it is a great pleasure to come to Leeds and bring to the citizens a word of thanks and encouragement in all the work they are doing to promote the common cause of many nations and in many lands. That cause appeals to the hearts of all those in the human race who are not already gripped by tyranny or who have not already been seduced to its insidious voice. That cause is shared by all the millions of our cousins across the Atlantic who are preparing night and day to have their will and rights respected. It appeals to the patient millions of China, who have suffered long from cruel aggression and still fight with faithful stubbornness. It appeals to the noble manhood of Russia, now at full grips with the murderous enemy, striking blow for blow and repaying better ones for blows struck at them. It appeals to all the people of Britain, without discrimination of class or party. It appeals to all the peoples of the British Empire throughout the world, and I have here at my side Dr. Evatt from Australia.

I voice on behalf of this vast gathering of men and women of Leeds our warmest message of good will and comradeship to

136

our kith and kin in Australia, who, like ourselves, lie under the menace of imminent enemy attack, and who, like ourselves, are going to strike a heavy and successful blow on all who spring upon us.

You have had your test in battle, but lately the enemy has not been so ready to come to this island: first, because a large portion of his air force is engaged against our Russian allies, and secondly because he knows that our arrangements for meeting him, thanks to the assistance of hundreds and thousands of active, willing minds and hands, are improving in power and efficiency every day. I have seen some of your factories this morning, though not as many as I should have liked to have seen, and I know well the great contribution which Leeds is making to the whole forward and upward thrust of the War.

We have reached a period in the War when it would be premature to say that we have topped the ridge, but now we see the ridge ahead. We see that perseverance, unflinching, dogged, inexhaustible, tireless, valiant, will surely carry us and our Allies, the great nations of the world, and the unfortunate nations who have been subjugated and enslaved, on to one of the most deep-founded movements of humanity which have ever taken place in our history. We see that they will come to the top of the ridge, and then they will have a chance not only of beating down and subduing those evil forces which have withstood us so long, which have twice let ruin and havoc loose on the world, but they will have that further and grander prospect that beyond the smoke of battle and the confusion of the fight we shall have the chance to settle our countries and the whole world together, moving forward together on the high road. That is the prospect that lies before us if we do not fail. And we shall not fail.

Here in the 33rd month of the War none of us is weary of the struggle. None of us is calling for any favours from the enemy. If he plays rough we can play rough too. Whatever we have got to take we will take, and we will give it back in even greater measure. When we began this war we were a peaceful and unarmed people. We had striven hard for peace. We had even gone into folly over our desire for peace, and the enemy started all primed-up and ready to strike. But now, as the months go by and the great machine keeps turning and the labour becomes

The End of the Beginning

skilled and habituated to its task, we are going to be the ones who have the modern scientific tackle. It is not now going to be a fight of brave men against men armed. It is going to be a fight on our side of people who have not only the resolve and the cause, but who also have the weapons.

We shall go forward together. The road upwards is stony. There are upon our journey dark and dangerous valleys through which we have to make and fight our way. But it is sure and certain that if we persevere — and we shall persevere — we shall come through these dark and dangerous valleys into a sunlight broader and more genial and more lasting than mankind has ever known.

Airgraphs from South Africa

THE PRIME MINISTER'S REPLY TO GENERAL SMUTS'S
AIRGRAPH LETTER ON THE OPENING OF THE
AIRGRAPH SERVICE FROM SOUTH AFRICA
TO GREAT BRITAIN
MAY 24, 1942

[*May 24, 1942*

P RAY accept, my dear friend, my best wishes for your birthday and my hope that you may long continue on the road we have travelled together. I was very much pleased to receive your letter inaugurating the airgraph service. I feel that this service, which shortens by so much the distance between our two countries, will be a great help and comfort to all who are striving for our common cause. With all good wishes.

One Thousand Bombers Raid Cologne

A MESSAGE TO THE AIR OFFICER COMMANDING-IN-CHIEF,
BOMBER COMMAND, FOLLOWING THE FIRST
1,000-BOMBER RAID ON GERMANY
MAY 31, 1942

May 18.   *Largest American Army contingent to date landed in Northern Ireland.*

May 22.   *United States Maritime Day celebrated by launching of 27 ships. President Roosevelt gave a warning that "it will be a long war."*

May 23.   *Hitler and Goering held an emergency council of war in Berlin with the chiefs of the German General Staff.*

Kerch Peninsula evacuated by Soviet troops.

May 27.   *Rommel's Army, heavily reinforced, began an offensive in Libya.*

Tojo, Japanese Premier, in a speech to the Diet, gave a "warning" to Australia, and said Japan was determined to destroy the influence of Britain and America.

Heydrich, German Gestapo chief in occupied countries, was seriously wounded when a bomb was thrown at his car in Prague.

May 28.   *General Wavell announced that more than four-fifths of the British and Indian forces engaged in Burma had reached India.*

May 29.   *1,000th day of the War.*

May 30.   *R.A.F. attacked Cologne with more than 1,000 bombers in the biggest air raid in history.*

I CONGRATULATE you and the whole of the Bomber Command upon the remarkable feat of organisation which enabled you to dispatch over 1,000 bombers to the Cologne area in a single night, and without confusion to concentrate their action over the target into so short a time as one hour and a half. This proof of the growing power of the British bomber force is also the herald of what Germany will receive, city by city, from now on.

Thanks to Labour

A LETTER TO MR. W. H. GREEN, M.P., CHAIRMAN OF THE LABOUR PARTY CONFERENCE, WHO AT THE CLOSE OF THE CONFERENCE HAD ASSURED THE PRIME MINISTER OF THE CONTINUED LOYALTY AND SUPPORT OF THE LABOUR MOVEMENT IN THE PROSECUTION OF THE WAR
MAY 31, 1942

10, Downing Street, S.W.1., *May 31, 1942*

DEAR Mr. Green, — The very kind expressions which you used about me at the Labour Conference, assuring me of the continuing loyalty of the Labour Party to the National Government which we formed together when our life and freedom hung by a thread two years ago, not only cheer my heart but — what is more important — help me in my work.

Every proof of national unity and strong combined action by our experienced democracy encourages the whole grand Alliance of the United Nations, and strikes its chill of doom and retribution into the guilty ranks of the Nazis.

I can assure you that inside the Cabinet and Government an absolutely healthy team spirit prevails, and that the supreme aim of winning the war and saving the world dominates all personal or party interests. Democracy based upon universal suffrage and free Parliamentary institutions expresses itself most effectively through party organisations. In time of peace these may correct and balance each other and promote a healthy and lively public opinion. In a war like this they must all march together, for only in this way will the shortest and surest road be found out of our many troubles and dangers.

For all your aid in this high duty I thank you and your friends and comrades.

Yours very faithfully,
WINSTON S. CHURCHILL.

The Battle in Libya

A STATEMENT TO THE HOUSE OF COMMONS
JUNE 2, 1942

June 1. R.A.F. made a 1,000-bomber raid on Essen and the Ruhr.

General Cruwell, one of Rommel's chief assistants, was captured during fierce fighting in Libya.

Three Japanese submarines were destroyed in an unsuccessful attack on Sydney Harbour.

[June 2, 1942

I THOUGHT the House would wish to have some news of the important and very severe battle which has now been proceeding for a week in the Libyan desert. Accordingly, I asked General Auchinleck for a statement. I do not think I can do better than read it out in his actual words:

"On the evening of 26th May, General Rommel launched the German Afrika Korps to the attack. He was at pains to explain, in an order of the day issued to all Italian and German troops in his pay, that in the course of great operations they were to carry through a decisive attack against our forces in Libya, and that for this purpose he had made ready and equipped a force superior in numbers, with perfected armament and a powerful air force to give it support. In conclusion, he hailed His Majesty the King of Italy and Emperor of Ethiopia, the Duce of the Roman Empire, and the Fuehrer of Great Germany. We had foreseen this attack, and were ready for it.

"From captured documents it is clear that Rommel's object was to defeat our armoured forces and capture Tobruk. The main ingredients of his plan were, first, to capture our defended locality at Bir Hacheim held by our gallant Allies the Free French; secondly, to pass round by the South of Bir Hacheim the German Afrika Korps, comprising the 15th and 21st German Armoured Divisions, to be followed closely by the German 90th (Light) Division, and the 20th Italian Mobile Corps, comprising the 132nd Ariete Armoured Division and the 101st Trieste Motorised Division; thirdly, to attack in strength our positions running South from the coast at Gazala to the Capuzzo Road. These were held by the South African and 50th British Divisions, the latter including battalions of the East Yorkshire Regiment, Green Howards, and Durham Light Infantry.

"Air reconnaissance had clearly indicated enemy preparations for attack, and in consequence our Air Forces opened a counter-offensive on the 21st with heavy attacks against enemy forward aerodromes. These attacks were continued each night and supplemented by low-flying dawn and dusk attacks by light bombers and fighters. The enemy paid us the compliment of trying to emulate our example on the three nights prior to his final advance on the 27th. He failed to achieve any success, and lost a number of aircraft to our fighters and anti-aircraft artillery. On the night 26th–27th May the German Afrika Korps carried out its part of the plan and passed to the south of Bir Hacheim, moving north with great rapidity towards Acroma, and also towards the old battlefields of El Duda and Sidi Rezegh, which were actually reached by some of its most forward troops. These were soon driven off by our armoured forces. Some Axis tanks actually reached the escarpment or cliff overlooking the coast road north of Acroma, but failed to interrupt communication between Tobruk and the South African troops holding our forward positions.

"It is now known that on the same night the enemy attempted a landing from the sea at this spot, presumably with the object of joining up with these tanks, but the hostile craft were driven off by our naval forces, acting in close co-operation with the Army.

"Long before they approached El Adem or Acroma the Axis armoured and motorised troops were brought to action by the 1st and 7th British Armoured Divisions, ably seconded by the British Heavy Tank Brigades which were in the area.

"The full brunt of the enemy initial advance to the east of Bir Hacheim was taken by the 3rd Indian Motor Brigade Group, which was overborne by sheer weight of metal, but not until after it had inflicted heavy losses on the enemy and seriously impeded his advance. In addition, his columns were subjected to repeated attacks by our fighters and bombers. Meanwhile the attack on Bir Hacheim by the Italian Mobile Corps had been beaten off by the Free or Fighting French troops, with heavy loss, and the northward advance of this force seems to have been seriously delayed in consequence.

"The third part of the enemy's plan, namely, the attacks against the northern front of our main positions south of Gazala, materialised on the 27th. They achieved little or nothing. Nevertheless, they seem to have cost the enemy a number of casualties. An attempt to break through our defences along the coast road by the Gazala inlet was easily stopped by 1st South African Division.

"Throughout the 28th, 29th and 30th May there was very heavy and continuous fighting between our armoured divisions and brigades, and the German Afrika Korps backed up by the Italian Mobile Corps. The battle swayed backwards and forwards over a wide area, from Acroma in the North to Bir Hacheim, 40 miles to the South, and from El Adem, which is near Tobruk, to our minefields 30 miles to the westward. Our troops gave the enemy no rest, and, finding himself running short of supplies and water, he had to make gaps in our minefields, one along the general line of the Capuzzo Road and another 10 miles to the South. These two gaps lay on either side of the defended area held by a brigade of infantry from the North of England. This brigade strenuously resisted the enemy's attempts to pass his transport through their ranks, and on the 28th Air Vice-Marshal Cunningham decided to direct his whole air force on to low attack against the enemy armour and motor transport in this region. These attacks were maintained with maximum intensity throughout the following three days, reaching their peak as the enemy endeavoured to pass through the gaps. It is still difficult to give a firm estimate of the number of vehicles and tanks knocked out or disabled by these attacks, but there has been ample confirmation that the effect was very great.

"Meantime each night our night bombers were attacking enemy forward airfields and his communications.

The End of the Beginning

"By nightfall on 31st May the enemy had succeeded in withdrawing many of his tanks and much transport into one or other of the gaps, which he then proceeded to protect from our attack from the East by bringing many of his anti-tank guns into action, with which he is well equipped. A large number of his tanks and many transport vehicles, however, remained on the wrong side of this barrier, and these are still being ceaselessly harried and destroyed by our troops, vigorously aided by the bombers and fighters of our air forces. The latest reports show that the enemy may have withdrawn some of his tanks from the gap areas and a good deal of transport as far back as 20 miles West of our forward positions, but this is unconfirmed. The country to the East of Bir Hacheim which is in our area is being mopped-up by our troops, which have destroyed many tanks and vehicles in this area; and captured two large workshops.

"Fierce fighting is still proceeding, and the battle is by no means over. Further heavy fighting is to be expected, but whatever may be the result, there is no shadow of doubt that Rommel's plans for his initial offensive have gone completely awry, and that this failure has cost him dear in men and material.

"The Axis air forces have been very active throughout the operations and have made continuous attacks on our troops and communications, but they too have lost heavily at the hands of our air forces and our anti-aircraft guns. The speed and effectiveness with which air support has been given have shown once again the intimate co-operation which has been achieved between the two Services in this theatre.

"There has not been time to assess the damage inflicted on the enemy, but a conservative estimate gives the number of his tanks destroyed or captured as about 260, and there is no doubt at all that the number of his transport vehicles destroyed or captured is very large. We have also had our losses, and it is inevitable that in a battle of this kind between armoured forces the casualties of both sides in tanks should be high. Our recovery organisation is, however, working very well, and whereas we have retained control of the battlefield and so can salve our tanks, the enemy cannot recover many of his, which should be permanently lost to him.

"Owing to the three days' concentration on low attack and the consequent desperate attempts by the enemy fighters to protect their land forces, their ground forces, our air losses have not been light, though in a number of instances our pilots have returned safe and our aircraft are being recovered."

General Auchinleck ends by repeating that the battle is not yet over, and the issue still remains to be decided, but he says that the spirit and morale of our men in Libya, both Army and Air Force, whether they come from India, South Africa, the United Kingdom or elsewhere in the British Commonwealth, and that of our most gallant Allies, the Free French, are magnificent.

In a further telegram the Commander-in-Chief adds:

"The skill, determination and pertinacity shown by General Ritchie and his Corps Commanders, Lieutenant-Generals Norrie and Gott, throughout this difficult and strenuous week of hard and continuous fighting, have been of the highest order."

He further dwells upon the excellent performance of the American Grant tanks, with which all users are well pleased, and says that our new heavy anti-tank gun has done great execution.

That finishes the message from General Auchinleck. From all the above it is clear that we have every reason to be satisfied, and more than satisfied, with the course which the battle has so far taken, and that we should watch its further development with earnest attention.

I ought not to sit down without referring to the mammoth air raid delivered by the Royal Air Force on the Cologne region during the night of 30th–31st May. In this triumph of skill, daring and diligence against the enemy, all previous records of night bombing have been doubled and excelled. On that occasion no fewer than 1,130 British-manned aircraft operated across the sea. The results have been of a devastating character, but accurate photography has so far been hampered by the pall of smoke which hung over the smitten area. Last night also, 1,036 machines of the Royal Air Force visited the Continent. Nearly all of these operated on the Essen region, and first reports received indicate numerous and widespread conflagrations. From this second large-scale raid 35 of our bombers are missing.

I do not wish it to be supposed that all our raids in the immediate future will be above the four-figure scale. Methods of attack will be continually varied according to circumstances. On the other hand, these two great night-bombing raids mark the introduction of a new phase in the British air offensive against Germany, and this will increase markedly in scale when we are joined, as we soon shall be, by the Air Force of the United States. In fact, I may say that as the year advances German cities, harbours and centres of war production will be subjected to an ordeal the like of which has never been experienced by any country in continuity, severity or magnitude.

I am sure the House will wish me to express its compliments to Air Marshal Harris and the officers, non-commissioned officers and men of the Bomber Command, including the efficient and devoted maintenance staffs, upon the work which they are doing and the results achieved. Congratulations upon this encouraging event are also due to my right hon. Friend the Secretary of State for Air, to the Chief of the Air Staff, and to the Air Ministry, for the activities of those committed to their charge.

The Anglo-Soviet Treaty

[June 11, 1942

N OW that we have bound ourselves to be allies and friends for twenty years, I take occasion to send you my sincere good wishes and to assure you of the confidence which I feel that victory will be ours. It has been a great pleasure to meet M. Molotov, and we have done a great beating-down of barriers between our two countries. I am very glad he is coming back this way, for there will be more good work to be done.

Fewer Gifts from America

[June 14, 1942

FOR a long time I have watched with grateful admiration the vast stream of gifts which from the first days of the War has been flowing from America to Great Britain for the relief of suffering and the succour of distress, and in a volume which has barely lessened as a result of the advent of war to America, though a considerable diminution of it was well to be expected. The generosity of these gifts, each one of which represents a personal sacrifice by an individual, is overwhelming and without precedent. I am therefore anxious in the first place to express to you, Mr. President, the profound gratitude of the British people, and I shall be glad if there is some way in which you may see fit to pass my feelings along to the American public.

My second purpose in addressing you to-day is, unhappily, one of informing you that we now feel under the necessity of asking that this brotherly flow of material shall be diminished. It is not that the gifts are not desired — indeed, they have constantly been ingeniously devised to meet our real needs, and the parcels from America have become a familiar and welcome feature in all the misfortunes which have overtaken our civilian population. The request which I am now compelled to make is due to additional demands on shipping resulting from the enormously increased flow of war materials for which ocean transport has to be provided. We shall have, therefore, to assign to goods of a more warlike character the shipping space which has hitherto been available for the relief of our people — a sacrifice which we shall make here without complaint, but not without very great regret.

As to the method of procedure, we have a committee here — the American Gifts Committee — which hitherto has endeavoured to ensure that gifts from America shall only be of a character that will meet some real need. The committee will now have to extend its activities and try to control the actual volume of gifts. A statement will shortly be issued to the Press indicating the lines along which it is hoped to proceed.

I cannot conclude this letter, Mr. President, without affirming once again our gratitude for the comfort in days of suffering and of trial that was brought to us by the people of America, and our desire to make known our thanks.

United Nations Day

A MESSAGE ISSUED ON JUNE 14, 1942

[June 14, 1942

IN a Proclamation to the people of the United States our great friend, President Franklin D. Roosevelt, has reminded them that for many years it has been the American custom to set aside June 14 in honour of their flag, the emblem of their freedom, their strength, and their unity as an independent nation under God. He has told them that as a nation they are fighting not alone, but shoulder to shoulder with the valiant peoples of the United Nations, the massed angered forces of common humanity; and he has asked them that on their Flag Day, June 14, they should honour not only their own Colours but also the flags, and, through the flags, the peoples of the United Nations.

Outside the United Kingdom these are the peoples whose names to-day make up that great Roll of Honour: — The United States of America, the Union of Soviet Socialist Republics, China, Australia, Belgium, Canada, Costa Rica, Cuba, Czechoslovakia, the Dominican Republic, El Salvador, Free France, Greece, Guatemala, Haiti, Honduras, India, Luxembourg, Mexico, the Netherlands, New Zealand, Nicaragua, Norway, Panama, Poland, the Union of South Africa, and Yugoslavia.

I join my voice to his in honouring to-day the forces of the United Nations. Let us pay this tribute to the valour and sacrifice of those who have fallen and to the courage and endurance of those who fight to-day. Let us remember every one, man, woman, and child, who in the oppressed and tortured countries works for the day of liberation that is coming.

In this ceremony we pledge to each other not merely support and succour till victory comes, but that wider understanding, that quickened sense of human sympathy, that recognition of the common purpose of humanity, without which the suffering and striving of the United Nations would not achieve its full reward.

All Possible Help to the Soviet Union

A MESSAGE TO M. STALIN ON THE ANNIVERSARY
OF THE GERMAN ATTACK ON THE SOVIET UNION
JUNE 22, 1942

[June 22, 1942

As the Soviet Union enters the second year of the War I, as Prime Minister of Great Britain, which in a few months' time will enter on its fourth year of war, send to you, the leader of the great allied Soviet peoples, a renewed expression of our admiration for the magnificent defence of your armed forces, guerrilla bands, and civilian workers during the past year, and of our firm conviction that those achievements will be equalled and surpassed in the coming months. The fighting alliance of our two countries and of our other allies, to whom there have now been joined the vast resources of the United States, will surely bring our enemies to their knees. You can count on us to assist you by every means in our power.

During the year which has passed since Hitler fell upon your country without warning, friendly relations between our two countries and peoples have been progressively strengthened. We have thought not only of the present, but of the future, and our Treaty of Alliance in the war against Hitlerite Germany and of collaboration and mutual assistance in the post-war period, concluded during M. Molotov's recent visit to this country, has been welcomed as sincerely by the British people as I know it has been welcomed by the Soviet people. That treaty is a pledge that we shall confound our enemies and, when the War is over, build a sure peace for all freedom-loving peoples.

The United States Army

A SPEECH TO AMERICAN TROOPS DURING A VISIT TO A
SOUTHERN ARMY CAMP IN THE UNITED STATES
JUNE, 1942

[June, 1942

I AM enormously impressed by the thoroughness and precision with which the formation of the great war-time army of the United States is proceeding. The day will come when the British and American armies will march into countries, not as invaders, but as liberators, helping the people who have been held under the cruel barbarian yoke.

That day may seem long to those whose period of training spreads across the weeks and months. But when it comes, it will make amends for all the toil and discipline that has been undergone. Also, it will open the world to larger freedom and to life, liberty, and the pursuit of happiness, as the grand words of your Declaration of Independence put it.

The War Outlook

A STATEMENT ISSUED JOINTLY BY MR. WINSTON CHURCHILL AND MR. ROOSEVELT ON THE PRIME MINISTER'S RETURN TO LONDON FROM WASHINGTON AFTER HIS THIRD CONFERENCE WITH THE PRESIDENT

JUNE 27, 1942

[*June 27, 1942*

THE week of conferences between the President and the Prime Minister covered very fully all of the major problems of the war which is conducted by the United Nations on every continent and in every sea. We have taken full cognizance of our disadvantages as well as our advantages. We do not underrate the task. We have conducted our conferences with the full knowledge of the power and resourcefulness of our enemies. In the matter of the production of munitions of all kinds, the survey gives on the whole an optimistic picture. The previously planned monthly output has not reached the maximum, but is fast approaching it on schedule.

Because of the wide extension of the War to all parts of the world, transportation of the fighting forces, together with the transportation of munitions of war and supplies, still constitutes the major problem of the United Nations. While submarine warfare on the part of the Axis continues to take a heavy toll of cargo ships, the actual production of new tonnage is greatly increasing month by month. It is hoped that as a result of the steps planned at this conference, our respective navies will further reduce the toll of merchant shipping.

The United Nations have never been in such hearty and detailed agreement on plans for winning the War as they are to-day. We recognise and applaud the Russian resistance to the main attack being made by Germany, and we rejoice in the magnificent resistance of the Chinese Army. Detailed discussions were held with our military advisers on methods to be adopted against

Japan and for the relief of China. While our plans, for obvious reasons, cannot be disclosed, it can be said that the coming operations which were discussed in detail at our Washington conferences, between ourselves and our respective military advisers, will divert German strength from the attack on Russia.

The Prime Minister and the President have met twice before, first in August, 1941, and again in December, 1941. There is no doubt in their minds that the overall picture is more favourable to victory than it was either in August or December of last year.

General Auchinleck Takes Command

A STATEMENT TO THE HOUSE OF COMMONS
JUNE 30, 1942

[June 30, 1942

I DO not propose to make any statement to-day about the momentous battle now being fought in Egypt, but I feel that the House would wish to know that on 25th June General Auchinleck decided to assume command of the Eighth Army personally, in succession to General Ritchie. As soon as General Auchinleck informed His Majesty's Government of the decision he had taken, he was at once told that it had our approval.

Answers to Questions in the House of Commons

[*June 30, 1942*

A Member of Parliament asked the Prime Minister on what date he expected to make a report to the House on his request to General Wavell that an officer should collect information regarding the loss of Malaya and Singapore. The Prime Minister replied: —

THE various papers received from General Wavell as the result of the collection of material which he was directed to make are not suitable for publication in wartime. I certainly never contemplated being committed to the publication of these documents, which were collected for the instruction and further information of the military authorities, and whether they should be made public or not could only be decided after they had been seen. It clearly would cause a great deal of ill-will throughout the British Empire.

Replying to a Member of Parliament who asked that there should be some public recognition of the hospitality accorded by the people of South Africa to His Majesty's forces who disembarked, in transit, at South African ports, the Prime Minister said: —

I am glad to have this opportunity of giving public expression to the appreciation which is felt by His Majesty's Government in the United Kingdom for the kindness and hospitality which have invariably been extended to all members of the Fighting Services passing through South Africa. We are all deeply grateful.

The Central Direction of the War

SPEECHES IN THE DEBATE ON THE MOTION OF
"NO-CONFIDENCE," HOUSE OF COMMONS
JULY 1 AND 2, 1942

June 3. *Rommel, foiled in his attempt to take Tobruk, regrouped his forces for a new attack.*
  Japanese aircraft raided Dutch Harbour, United States naval base in Alaska.

June 4. *Officially announced in Germany that Heydrich had died from wounds received in the bomb attack. Germans began reprisals against the civilian population of Czechoslovakia.*

June 5. *First news of Pacific naval battle off Midway Island, in which the Japanese lost three battleships and seven other warships.*

June 6. *British launched counter-attack against Rommel in Libya.*

June 9. *Mr. Churchill and President Roosevelt announced the formation of a combined Production and Resources Board and a Combined Food Board.*

June 11. *Announced that a 20-years Treaty of Alliance between Britain and Soviet Russia had been signed during a visit to London by M. Molotov.*

June 13. *Libya battle reached critical stage with big offensive movement by Rommel.*

June 15. *President Roosevelt declared that United Nations reservoir of resources was now approaching flood stage.*

June 18. *Revealed that Mr. Churchill was in Washington for consultation with President Roosevelt.*

June 19. *British army in Libya forced back on fortified positions along the Egyptian frontier.*

June 20. *Rommel captured Tobruk and claimed 25,000 prisoners.*

Announced that United States troops were now
stationed in Great Britain as well as Northern Ireland.

June 22. Mr. Harry Hopkins, President Roosevelt's personal assistant, predicted a mighty offensive against
Hitler "with a second, third and fourth front."

June 25. Rommel's armoured columns thrust over the
Egyptian frontier.

President Roosevelt and Mr. Churchill met
leaders of Congress at the White House and gave
a full review of the world situation.

Another 1,000-bomber raid by the R.A.F. on
Germany, with Bremen as the main objective, was
the most concentrated ever made, the bombing
lasting only 75 minutes.

June 27. Mr. Churchill returned from the United States
by plane, and a statement issued in London and
Washington said that coming operations would
take the strain off the Soviet Armies.

June 29. Rommel captured Mersa Matruh as the British retreat into Egypt continued.

June 30. Mr. Churchill announced that General Auchinleck had assumed personal command of the Eighth
Army in succession to General Ritchie.

July 1. Germans captured Sebastopol.

Sir John Wardlaw-Milne introduced a "no-
confidence" motion in the House of Commons.

July 2. In Egypt a fierce battle by the main armoured
forces of both sides raged west of El Alamein, 65
miles from Alexandria.

[*July 1, 1942*

On July 1, 1942, Sir John Wardlaw-Milne, Conservative Member of Parliament for Kidderminster, moved: —

"That this House, while paying tribute to the heroism and
endurance of the Armed Forces of the Crown in circumstances
of exceptional difficulty, has no confidence in the central direction of the War."

The Central Direction of the War, July 2, 1942

Before the debate opened Commander King-Hall rose to ask Sir John Wardlaw-Milne to defer moving his motion until the conclusion of the battle then raging in Libya. Sir John replied that if the Government had desired postponement on the ground of national interest he would have immediately acquiesced, but no such suggestion had come from the Government. Mr. Churchill then made this statement: —

I HAVE carefully considered this matter, and I have had at no time any doubt that if an appeal were made on the grounds of the urgency and seriousness of the situation the Debate would be postponed. But, after all, this Vote of Censure has been on the Order Paper for some time, and it has been flashed all over the world. When I was in the United States, I can testify to the lively excitement which was created by its appearance, and, although we in this country may have our own knowledge of the stability of our institutions and of the strength of the Government of the day, yet that is by no means the opinion which is shared or felt in other countries. Now that this has gone so far, and this matter has been for more than a week the subject of comment in every part of the world, it would be, in my opinion, even more injurious to delay a decision than to go forward with this issue.

[July 2, 1942

A two-day debate on Sir John Wardlaw-Milne's Motion was concluded by this speech by Mr. Churchill: —

THIS long Debate has now reached its final stage. What a remarkable example it has been of the unbridled freedom of our Parliamentary institutions in time of war! Everything that could be thought of or raked up has been used to weaken confidence in the Government, has been used to prove that Ministers are incompetent and to weaken their confidence in themselves, to make the Army distrust the backing it is getting from the civil power, to make the workmen lose confidence in the weapons they are striving so hard to make, to represent the Government as a set of nonentities over whom the Prime Minister towers, and then to undermine him in his own heart and, if possible, before the eyes of the nation. All this poured out by cable and radio to all parts of the world, to the distress of all our friends and to the delight of all our foes. I am in favour of this freedom, which no other country would use, or dare to use, in times of mortal peril such as those through which we are passing. But the story must not end there, and I make now my appeal to the House of Commons to make sure that it does not end there.

Although I have done my best, my utmost, to prepare a full and considered statement for the House, I must confess that I have found it very difficult, even during the bitter animosity of the diatribe of the hon. Member for Ebbw Vale (Mr. Bevan), with all its carefully aimed and calculated hostility, to concentrate my thoughts upon this Debate and to withdraw them from the tremendous and most critical battle now raging in Egypt. At any moment we may receive news of grave importance. But the right hon. Gentleman the Member for Devonport (Mr. Hore-Belisha) has devoted a large part of his speech, not to this immediate campaign and struggle in Egypt, but to the offensive started in Libya nearly eight months ago, and he, as did the mover of the Motion of Censure, accused me of making misstatements in saying that, for the first time, our men met the Germans on equal terms in the matter of modern weapons. This offensive was not a failure. Our Armies took 40,000 prisoners. They drove the enemy back 400 miles. They took the great fortified positions on which he had rested so long. They drove him to the very edge of Cyrenaica, and it was only when his tanks had been reduced to 70 or perhaps 80 that, by a brilliant tactical resurgence, the German general set in motion a series of events which led to a retirement I think to a point 150 miles more to the West than that from which our offensive had started. Ten thousand Germans were taken prisoner among those in that fight. I am not at all prepared to regard it as anything but a highly creditable and highly profitable transaction for the Army of the Western Desert. I do not understand why this point should

be made now, when, in all conscience, there are newer and far graver matters which fill our minds.

The military misfortunes of the last fortnight in Cyrenaica and Egypt have completely transformed the situation, not only in that theatre, but throughout the Mediterranean. We have lost upwards of 50,000 men, by far the larger proportion of whom are prisoners, a great mass of material, and, in spite of carefully-organised demolitions, large quantities of stores have fallen into the enemy's hands. Rommel has advanced nearly 400 miles through the desert, and is now approaching the fertile Delta of the Nile. The evil effects of these events, in Turkey, in Spain, in France and in French North Africa, cannot yet be measured. We are at this moment in the presence of a recession of our hopes and prospects in the Middle East and in the Mediterranean unequalled since the fall of France. If there are any would-be profiteers of disaster who feel able to paint the picture in darker colours, they are certainly at liberty to do so.

A painful feature of this melancholy scene was its suddenness. The fall of Tobruk, with its garrison of about 25,000 men, in a single day, was utterly unexpected. Not only was it unexpected by the House and the public at large, but by the War Cabinet, by the Chiefs of the Staff, and by the General Staff of the Army. It was also unexpected by General Auchinleck and the High Command in the Middle East. On the night before its capture, we received a telegram from General Auchinleck that he had allotted what he believed to be an adequate garrison, that the defences were in good order, and that 90 days' supplies were available for the troops. It was hoped that we could hold the very strong frontier positions which had been built up by the Germans and improved by ourselves, from Sollum to Halfaya Pass, from Capuzzo to Fort Maddalena. From this position our newly-built railroad ran backwards at right angles, and we were no longer formed to a flank — as the expression goes — with our backs to the sea, as we had been in the earlier stages of the new Libyan battle. General Auchinleck expected to maintain these positions until the powerful reinforcements which were approaching, and have in part arrived, enabled him to make a much stronger bid to seize the initiative for a counter-offensive.

The question of whether Tobruk could have been held or not

The End of the Beginning

is difficult and disputable. It is one of those questions which are more easy to decide after the event than before it. It is one of those questions which could be decided only with full knowledge of the approaching reinforcements. The critics have a great advantage in these matters. As the racing saying goes, they "stand on velvet." If we had decided to evacuate the place, they could have gone into action on "the pusillanimous and cowardly scuttle from Tobruk," which would have made quite a promising line of advance. But those who are responsible for carrying on the war have no such easy options open. They have to decide beforehand. The decision to hold Tobruk and the dispositions made for that purpose were taken by General Auchinleck, but I should like to say that we, the War Cabinet and our professional advisers, thoroughly agreed with General Auchinleck beforehand, and, although in tactical matters the commander-in-chief in any war theatre is supreme and his decision is final, we consider that, if he was wrong, we were wrong too, and I am very ready on behalf of His Majesty's Government to take my full share of responsibility. The hon. Member for Kidderminster (Sir J. Wardlaw-Milne) asked where the order for the capitulation of Tobruk came from. Did it come from the battlefield, from Cairo, from London or from Washington? In what a strange world of thought he is living, if he imagines I sent from Washington an order for the capitulation of Tobruk! The decision was taken to the best of my knowledge by the Commander of the Forces, and certainly it was most unexpected to the Higher Command in the Middle East.

When I left this country for the United States on the night of 17th June, the feeling which I had, which was fully shared by the Chief of the Imperial General Staff, was that the struggle in the Western Desert had entered upon a wearing-down phase, or a long battle of exhaustion, similar to that which took place in the autumn. Although I was disappointed that we had not been able to make a counter-stroke after the enemy's first onslaught had been, I will not say repulsed, but rebuffed and largely broken, this was a situation with which we had no reason to be discontented. Our resources were much larger than those of the enemy, and so were our approaching reinforcements. This desert warfare proceeds among much confusion and interruption of communications, and it was only gradually that the very grievous and disproportionate losses which our armour sustained in the fighting around and south of Knightsbridge became apparent.

Here I will make a short digression on a somewhat less serious plane. Complaint has been made that the newspapers have been full of information of a very rosy character. Several hon. Members have referred to that in the Debate, and remarked that the Government have declared themselves less fully informed than the newspapers. Surely this is very natural while a battle of this kind is going on? There never has been in this war a battle in which so much liberty has been given to war correspondents. They have been allowed to roam all over the battlefield, taking their chance of getting killed, and sending home their very full messages whenever they can reach a telegraph office. This is what the Press have always asked for, and it is what they got. These war correspondents, moving about amid the troops and sharing their perils, have also shared their hopes and have been inspired by their buoyant spirit. They have sympathised with the fighting men whose deeds they have been recording, and they have, no doubt, been extremely anxious not to write anything which would spread discouragement or add to their burdens.

I have a second observation to make on this minor point. The war correspondents have nothing to do except to collect information, write their dispatches and get them through the censor. On the other hand, the generals who are conducting the battle have other preoccupations. They have to fight the enemy. Although we have always asked that they should keep us informed as much as possible, our policy has been not to worry them but to leave them alone to do their job. Now and then I send messages of encouragement and sometimes a query or a suggestion, but it is absolutely impossible to fight battles from Westminster or Whitehall. The less one interferes the better, and certainly I do not want generals in close battle — and these desert battles are close, prolonged and often peculiarly indeterminate — to burden themselves by writing full stories on matters upon which, in the nature of things, the home Government are not called upon to give any decision. After all, there is nothing

The End of the Beginning

we can do about it here while it is going on, or only at very rare intervals. Therefore, the Government are more accurately, but less speedily, less fully and less colourfully informed than the newspapers. That is the explanation. It is not proposed to make any change in this procedure.

To return to my general theme; when on the morning of Sunday, the 21st, I went into the President's room, I was greatly shocked to be confronted with a report that Tobruk had fallen. I found it difficult to believe, but a few minutes later my own telegram, forwarded from London, arrived. I hope the House will realise what a bitter pang this was to me. What made it worse was being on an important mission in the country of one of our great Allies. Some people assume too readily that, because a Government keeps cool and has steady nerves under reverses, its members do not feel the public misfortunes as keenly as do independent critics. On the contrary, I doubt whether anyone feels greater sorrow or pain than those who are responsible for the general conduct of our affairs. It was an aggravation in the days that followed to read distorted accounts of the feeling in Britain and in the House of Commons. The House can have no idea how its proceedings are represented across the ocean. Questions are asked, comments are made by individual members or by independents who represent no organised grouping of political power, which are cabled verbatim, and often quite honestly taken to be the opinion of the House of Commons. Lobby gossip, echoes from the smoking-room and talk in Fleet Street, are worked up into serious articles seeming to represent that the whole basis of British political life is shaken, or is tottering. A flood of expectation and speculation is let loose. Thus I read streamer headlines like this: "Commons demand Churchill return face accusers," or "Churchill returns to supreme political crisis." Such an atmosphere is naturally injurious to a British representative engaged in negotiating great matters of State upon which the larger issues of the war depend. That these rumours coming from home did not prejudice the work I had to do was due solely to the fact that our American friends are not fair-weather friends. They never expected that this war would be short or easy, or that its course would not be chequered by lamentable misfortunes. On the contrary, I will admit that I believe

166

in this particular case the bonds of comradeship between all the men at the top were actually strengthened.

All the same, I must say I do not think any public man charged with a high mission from this country ever seemed to be barracked from his home land in his absence — unintentionally, I can well believe — to the extent that befell me while on this visit to the United States; and only my unshakable confidence in the ties which bind me to the mass of the British people upheld me through those days of trial. I naturally explained to my hosts that those who were voluble in Parliament in no way represented the House of Commons, just as the small handful of correspondents who make it their business to pour out damaging tales about our affairs to the United States, and I must add to Australia, in no way represent the honourable profession of journalism. I also explained that all this would be put to the proof when I returned by the House of Commons as a whole expressing a responsible, measured and deliberate opinion, and that is what I am going to ask it to do to-day.

I noticed that it was stipulated that I should not be allowed to refer in any way in the statement I am now making, or in a statement about Libya, to the results of my mission in the United States. I suppose it was not wished that I should be able to plead any extenuating and correlative circumstances. But I must make it clear that I accept no fetters on my liberty of debate except those imposed by the rules of Order or by the public interest. I have a worthier reason, however, for not speaking at length about my American mission further than the published statement agreed upon between the President and me. Here is the reason. Our conversations were concerned with nothing, or almost nothing, but the movement of troops, ships, guns and aircraft, and with the measures to be taken to combat the losses at sea and to replace, and more than replace, the sunken tonnage.

Here I will turn aside to meet a complaint which I have noticed that the Minister of Defence should have been in Washington when the disaster at Tobruk occurred. But Washington was the very place where he should have been. It was there that the most urgent future business of the war was being transacted, not only in regard to the general scene but also in regard to the

The End of the Beginning

particular matters that were passing. Almost everything I arranged in the United States with the President and his advisers is secret, in the sense that it must be kept from the enemy, and I have therefore nothing to tell about it, except this — that the two great English-speaking nations were never closer together, and that there never was a more earnest desire between Allies to engage the enemy or a more whole-hearted resolve to run all risks and make all sacrifices in order to wage this hard war with vigour and carry it to a successful conclusion. That assurance, at least, I can give the House.

I hope there will be no disparagement of the United States shipbuilding programme. We are making considerable shipbuilding efforts ourselves. We could only increase our output at the expense of other indispensable munitions and services. But the United States is building in the present calendar year about four times as much gross tonnage — not dead weight but gross tonnage — as we are building, and I am assured that she will launch between eight and ten times as much as we are building in the calendar year 1943. Shipping losses have been very heavy lately, and the bulk has been upon the Eastern shores of America. The most strenuous measures are being taken to curtail this loss, and I do not doubt that it will be substantially reduced as the masses of escort vessels now under construction come into service, and the convoy system and other methods of defence come into full and effective operation. These measures, combined with the great shipbuilding effort of the United States and the British Empire, should result in a substantial gain in tonnage at the end of 1943 over and above that which we now possess, even if, as I cannot believe, the rate of loss is not substantially reduced. This we shall owe largely to the prodigious exertions of the Government and people of the United States, who share with us, fully and freely, according to our respective needs and duties, in this as in all other parts of our war programme.

I have not trespassed very long on the United States aspect, although that is the most vital sphere, and I return to the Desert and to the Nile. I hope the House will realise that I have a certain difficulty in defending His Majesty's Government from the various attacks which have been made upon them in respect of materials and preparation, because I do not want to say anything that can be shifted, even by the utmost ingenuity of malice, into a reflection upon our commanders in the field, still less upon the gallant men they lead. Yet I must say that one of the most painful parts of this battle is that in its opening stages we were defeated under conditions which gave a good and reasonable expectation of success. During the whole of the spring we had been desirous that the Army of the Western Desert should begin an offensive against the enemy. The regathering and reinforcement of our Army was considered to be a necessary reason for delay, but of course this delay helped the enemy also.

At the end of March and during the whole of April, he concentrated a very powerful air force in Sicily and delivered a tremendous attack upon Malta, of which the House was made aware at the time by me. This attack exposed the heroic garrison and inhabitants of Malta to an ordeal of extreme severity. For several weeks hundreds of German and Italian aircraft — it is estimated more than 600, of which the great majority were German — streamed over in endless waves in the hopes of overpowering the defences of the island fortress. There had never been any case in this war of a successful defence against a superior air power being made by aircraft which have only two or three airfields to work from. Malta is the first exception. At one time they were worn down to no more than a dozen fighters, yet, aided by their powerful batteries, by the ingenuity of the defence, and by the fortitude of the people, they maintained an unbroken resistance. We continued to reinforce them from the Western Mediterranean as well as from Egypt by repeated operations of difficulty and hazard, and maintained a continuous stream of Spitfire aircraft in order to keep them alive, in spite of the enormous wastage, not only in the air but also in the limited airfields on the ground. As part of this, hundreds of fighter aircraft have been flown in from aircraft-carriers by the Royal Navy, and we were assisted by the United States Navy, whose carrier *Wasp* rendered notable service on more than one occasion, enabling me to send them the message of thanks, "Who says a wasp cannot sting twice?" By all these exertions, Malta lived through this prodigious and prolonged bombardment, until at last, at the beginning of May, the bulk of the German aircraft, already weakened by most serious losses, had to be withdrawn for the belated German offensive on the Russian front.

Malta had come through its fearful ordeal triumphant, and is now stronger in aircraft than ever before. But during the period when this assault was at its height, it was practically impossible for the fortress to do much to impede the reinforcements which were being sent to Tripoli and Benghazi. This, no doubt, was part of the purpose, though not the whole purpose, of the extraordinary concentration of air power which the enemy had thought fit to devote to the attack. The enemy did not get Malta, but they got a lot of stuff across to Africa. Remember that it takes four months to send a weapon round the Cape, and perhaps a week or even less to send it across the Mediterranean — provided it gets across. Remember also that the great number of these desertised Spitfires, if not involved in very severe fighting at Malta, would have been available to strengthen our Spitfire force in the battle which has been proceeding. Thus it may well be that we were relatively no better off in the middle of May than we had been in March or April.

However, the armies drew up in the Desert in the middle of May about 100,000 a side. We had 100,000 men, and the enemy 90,000, of whom 50,000 were Germans. We had a superiority in the numbers of tanks — I am coming to the question of quality later — of perhaps seven to five. We had a superiority in artillery of nearly eight to five. Included in our artillery were several regiments of the latest form of gun howitzer which throws a 55-pound shell 20,000 yards. There were other artillery weapons, of which I cannot speak, also available. It is not true, therefore, as I have seen it stated, that we had to face 50-pounder guns of the enemy with only 25-pounder guns. The 25-pounder, I may say, is one of the finest guns in Europe, and a perfectly new weapon which has only begun to flow out since the war began. It is true that the enemy, by the tactical uses which he made of his 88-mm. anti-aircraft guns, converting them to a different purpose, and of his anti-tank weapons, gained a decided advantage. But this became apparent only as the battle proceeded. Our Army enjoyed throughout the battle and enjoys to-day superiority in the air. The dive bombers of the enemy played a prominent part at Bir Hakeim and Tobruk, but it is not true that they should be regarded as a decisive or even as a massive factor in this battle. Lastly, we had better and shorter lines of communication than the enemy, our railway being already beyond Fort Capuzzo, and a separate line of communications running by the sea to the well-supplied base and depot of Tobruk.

We were, therefore, entitled to feel good confidence in the result of an offensive undertaken by us, and this would have been undertaken in the early days of June if the enemy had not struck first. When his preparations for an offensive became plainly visible, it was decided, and I think rightly, to await the attack in our fortified positions and then to deliver a counter-stroke in the greatest possible strength.

Here, then, were these armies face to face in the most forbidding and desolate region in the world, under conditions of extreme artificiality, able to reach each other only through a peculiar use of the appliances of modern war. The enemy's army had come across a disputed sea, paying a heavy toll to our submarines, and, except for the period when Malta was neutralised, to the Malta Air Force. The imperial Forces had almost all come 12,000 miles through submarines which beset the British shores, and round the Cape to Suez or from South Africa or India. One may say that the forces assembled on both sides in this extraordinary situation represented a war effort which in other theatres would have amounted to three or four times their numbers.

Such was the position when, on 26th May, Rommel made his first onslaught. It is not possible for me to give any final account of the battle. Events move with such rapidity that there is no time to disentangle the past: one tale is good till another is told. Any hasty judgment would be more exciting than true. The main features may, however, be discerned. Rommel had expected to take Tobruk in the first few days, but the reception which he got deranged his plan. Very heavy losses in armour were sustained by both sides. However, he held tenaciously to the inroad he had made, and we were so mauled in the struggle that no effective counter-stroke could be delivered. On 4th June an attempt was made, but was repulsed by a counter-attack with heavy loss by artillery. The battle then centred upon Bir Hakeim, where the Free French resisted with the utmost gallantry. Around this the struggle surged for eight or nine days. Finally it was decided to withdraw the garrison, and this was successfully accomplished, though with heavy losses.

Here, no doubt, was a turning-point in the battle. Whether anything more could have been done we cannot tell. Certainly very large numbers of troops remained on fronts which were not engaged, and certainly Rommel and his Germans punched on unflaggingly day after day. After the fall of Bir Hakeim another five days of fighting occurred round the Knightsbridge and Acroma positions. Up till 13th June the battle was equal. Our recovery process had worked well. Both sides lost, I will not say evenly, but proportionately, because our numbers were greater, and we could expect to lose more while keeping even. But on the 13th there came a change. On that morning we had about 300 tanks in action, and by nightfall no more than 70 remained, excluding the light Stuart tanks; and all this happened without any corresponding loss having been inflicted on the enemy. [Editor's note: This statement was corrected on September 8th, 1942. See footnote to this speech.] I do not know what actually happened in the fighting of that day. I am only concerned to give the facts to the House, and it is for the House to decide whether these facts result from the faulty central direction of the war, for which of course I take responsibility, or whether they resulted from the terrible hazards and unforeseeable accidents of battle. With this disproportionate destruction of our armour Rommel became decisively the stronger. The battlefield passed into the hands of the enemy, and the enemy's wounded tanks could be repaired by his organisation, while all our wounded tanks were lost to us.

Many evil consequences followed inevitably from this one day's fighting. There came the decision to withdraw from the Gazala position. The South African Division was withdrawn into Tobruk, and moved through Tobruk farther East, without heavy loss. The main part of the 50th English Division extricated itself by a 120-mile journey round the Southern flank of the enemy. In the desert, everything is mobile and mechanised, and when the troops move they can move enormous distances forward or back. The old conceptions and measurements of war do not apply at all. One hundred miles may be lost or won in a day or a night. There followed the decision to hold Tobruk together with the Halfaya-Sollum-Capuzzo-Maddalena line, which I have already mentioned, and then the fall of Tobruk after only one single day of fighting.

This entailed withdrawal from the Sollum-Halfaya line to the Mersa Matruh position, which placed 125 miles of waterless desert between the 8th Army and its foes. Most authorities expected that ten days or a fortnight would be gained by this. However, on the fifth day, on 26th June, Rommel presented himself with his armoured and motorised forces in front of this new position. Battle was joined on the 27th along the whole front, and for the first time I am glad to say our whole Army, which had been heavily reinforced with new and fresh troops, was engaged all together at one time. Although we consider we inflicted very heavy damage upon the enemy, the advance of the German Light Division together with the remainder of the Panzer Corps, 100 to 150 heavily armed tanks, which is about what it amounted to, led to our further retirement owing to the destruction of our armour. Naturally, I am not in a position to tell the House about the reinforcements which have reached the Army or which are approaching, except that they are very considerable, and after the lecture I have been read by the right hon. Gentleman apparently it is wrong even to say that we shall hold Egypt. I suppose one ought to say we are going to lose Egypt. But I will go so far as to say that we do not regard the struggle as in any way decided.

Although I am not mentioning reinforcements, there is one reinforcement which has come, which has been in close contact with the enemy, and which he knows all about. I mean the New Zealand Division. The Government of New Zealand, themselves under potential menace of invasion, authorised the fullest use being made of their troops, whom they have not withdrawn or weakened in any way. They have sent them into the battle, where, under the command of the heroic Freyberg, again wounded, they have acquitted themselves in a manner equal to all their former records. They are fighting hard at the moment.

Although the Army in Libya has been so far overpowered and driven back, I must make it clear, on behalf of the challenged central direction of the war, that this was not due to any conscious or wilful grudging of reinforcements in men or material. Of course, the emergency of the Japanese war had led to the removal of a part of the Australian Forces to defend their homeland, and very rightly. In fact, it was I who suggested to them that they should not consider themselves bound in the matter, having regard to their own danger. Several important units of British troops had to go to India, which, a little while ago, seemed threatened by invasion. Other forces in India which were due to proceed to the Middle East had to be retained there. But extreme exertions have been made by the home Government for the last two years to strengthen and maintain the Armies in the Middle East. During that time, apart altogether from reinforcements to other theatres, there have gone to the Middle East from this country, from the Empire overseas, and to a lesser extent from the United States, more than 950,000 men, 4,500 tanks, 6,000 aircraft, nearly 5,000 pieces of artillery, 50,000 machine guns and over 100,000 mechanical vehicles. We have done this in a period, let the House remember before they dismiss our efforts and our desires as inadequate to the occasion, when for a large part of the time we were threatened with imminent invasion here at home and during the rest of it were sending large supplies to Russia. So far as the central direction of the war is concerned, I can plead with some confidence that we have not failed in the exertions we have made or in the skill we have shown.

Now I come to the question of the quality of some of our material, to the design and armour of our tanks, and to our anti-tank artillery. This was dealt with at some length yesterday by my right hon. Friend the Minister of Production (Mr. Oliver Lyttelton), and by Lord Beaverbrook in another place. I agree with the hon. Member for Ebbw Vale that the House should read carefully these extremely masterly, intricate and authoritative statements of facts upon these matters. I do not attempt to go into them in detail here, as I should keep the House beyond the time they have so generously accorded me, but I must ask the House to allow me to place the salient points of the tank story before them.

The idea of the tank was a British conception. The use of armoured forces as they are now being used was largely French, as General de Gaulle's book shows. It was left to the Germans to convert those ideas to their own use. For three or four years before the war they were busily at work with their usual thoroughness upon the design and manufacture of tanks, and also upon the study and practice of armoured warfare. One would have thought that even if the Secretary of State for War of those days could not get the money for large scale manufacture he would at any rate have had full-size working models made and tested out exhaustively, and the factories chosen and the jigs and gauges supplied, so that he could go into mass production of tanks and anti-tank weapons when the war began.

When what I may call the Belisha period ended, we were left with some 250 armoured vehicles, very few of which carried even a 2-pounder gun. Most of these were captured or destroyed in France. After the war began the designs were settled and orders on a large scale were placed by the right hon. Gentleman. For more than a year, until Hitler attacked Russia, the threat of invasion hung over us, imminent, potentially mortal. There was no time to make improvements at the expense of supply. We had to concentrate upon numbers, upon quantity instead of quality. That was a major decision to which I have no doubt we were rightly guided.

We had, at the time after Dunkirk, to concentrate upon numbers. We had to make thousands of armoured vehicles with which our troops could beat the enemy off the beaches when they landed and fight them in the lanes and fields of Kent or Norfolk.

When the first new tanks came out they had grievous defects, the correction of which caused delay, and this would have been avoided if the preliminary experiments on the scale of 12 inches to the foot — full scale — had been carried out at an earlier period. Is that a very serious charge? Undoubtedly delay would have been saved if we had had the model there and worked it. How do you make a tank? People design it, they argue about it, they plan it and make it, and then you take the tank and test and re-test it. When you have got it absolutely settled then, and only then, you go into production. But we have never been able to indulge in the luxury of that precise and leisurely process. We have had to take it straight off the drawing-board and go into full production, and take the chance of the many errors which the construction will show coming out after hundreds and thousands of them have been made.

The End of the Beginning

At the present moment I am only dealing with the Matildas, Cruisers and Valentines, which I may say belong to the Belisha group. In spite of the fact that there was this undoubted delay through no preliminary work having been carried as far as it should have been, it would be wrong in my opinion to write off as useless the Matilda, the Cruiser and the Valentine tanks. They have rendered great services, and they are to-day of real value. In Russia the Valentine is highly rated. Has the House any idea of the number of tanks we have sent to Russia? As I said, we have sent 4,500 altogether to the Nile Valley. We have sent over 2,000 tanks to Russia, and the Russians are using them against the German armour, with vigour and effect. Therefore, I am not prepared to say that it is right to dismiss these weapons — although their appearance was retarded by the circumstances which I have mentioned — as not effective and powerful weapons of war.

Shortly after the present National Government was formed, in June, 1940, to be exact, I called a meeting of all the authorities to design and make a new tank, capable of speedy mass production and adapted to the war conditions to be foreseen in 1942. In 1942 that was the test. Of course I do not attempt to settle the technical details of tank design, any more than I interfere with the purely tactical decisions of generals in the field. All the highest expert authorities were brought together several times and made to hammer out a strong and heavy tank, adapted primarily for the defense of this Island against invasion, but capable of other employment in various theatres. This tank, the A.22, was ordered off the drawing-board, and large numbers went into production very quickly. As might be expected, it had many defects and teething troubles, and when these became apparent the tank was appropriately rechristened the "Churchill." These defects have now been largely overcome. I am sure that this tank will prove, in the end, a powerful, massive and serviceable weapon of war. A later tank, possessing greater speed, was designed about a year after, and plans have been made to put it into production at the earliest moment.

Neither of these types has yet been in employ against the enemy. He has not come here, and, although I sent the earliest two that were made out to Egypt to be tested and made desert-worthy, none has yet reached a stage where it can be employed at that distance.

It must be remembered that to get a tank from this country, or a gun, into the hands of troops in the Nile Valley or in the desert takes about six months. Hon. Members will see that the date on which this battle began was a date before we could have got the new and improved weapon into the hands of the troops. For this battle we tried to make up by numbers for an admitted inferiority in quality.

I have been asked by the hon. Gentleman who opened the Debate to speak about dive bombers and transport aircraft. I can only say that the highest technical authorities still hold very strong opinions on either side of this question. Of course, you cannot judge whether we ought to have had dive bombers at any particular date without also considering what we should have had to give up if we had had them. Most of the air-marshals, the leading men in the Air Force, think little of dive bombers, and they persist in their opinion. They are entitled to respect for their view, because it was from the same source that the 8-gun fighter was designed which destroyed so many hundreds of the dive bombers in the Battle of Britain and has enabled us to preserve ourselves free and uninvaded.

If we had made dive bombers instead of 8-gun fighter aircraft, we might not have had the 8-gun fighter aircraft to shoot down the JU.87's when they came over. Now there is no doubt whatever that the Army desire to have dive bombers, and nearly two years ago orders were placed for them. They have not come to hand in any number yet. That is a detailed story which I certainly do not wish to press, lest it should be thought in any way that we were throwing any blame off our shoulders on to those of the United States. On the point of priority, the case is clear, when you have, as you had then in the United States, an immense market, an immense productive sphere, and no priority questions had arisen. The rate at which the product was evolved was not influenced by the priority position. It was influenced by various incidents — changes of design and so forth — which caused delay.

The dive bomber against ships at sea appears to me to be a still more dangerous weapon. I say that because this is my own opinion on the matter, but as to transport aircraft I wish, indeed, we had 1,000 transport aircraft; but if we had built 1,000 of these unarmed transport aircraft, it would have cut down our already far from adequate bomber force. I know there is a tendency to deride and disparage the bomber effort against Germany, but I think that is a very great mistake. There is no doubt that this bomber offensive is one of the most powerful means we have of carrying on an offensive war against Germany. We did not like it when the blitz was on, but we bore it. Everyone knows that it was the main preoccupation of the Government and the municipal authorities of that day, with factories being delayed in their work, ports congested, and so forth. We, at any rate, had hope. We felt that we were on the rising tide. More was coming to us, and, moreover, we were buoyed up by the sympathy of the world — "London can take it," and so on. No such consolations are available in Germany. Nobody speaks with admiration and says, "Cologne can take it." They say, "Serve them right." That is the view of the civilised world. In addition to that, they know that this attack is not going to get weaker. It is going to get continually stronger until, in my view, it will play a great and perfectly definite part in abridging the course of this war, in taking the strain off our Russian Allies, and in reducing the building and construction of submarines and other weapons of war. Of course, one would like to have had both, but at this moment, much though we need transport aircraft, I am not at all sure, if I were offered a gift of 1,000 heavy bombers or 1,000 transports, which I should choose. I should take advice.

To return to the main argument which is before the House, I willingly accept, indeed I am bound to accept, what the Noble Lord (Earl Winterton) has called the "constitutional responsibility" for everything that has happened, and I consider that I discharged that responsibility by not interfering with the technical handling of armies in contact with the enemy. But before the battle began I urged General Auchinleck to take the command himself, because I was sure nothing was going to happen in the vast area of the Middle East in the next month or two comparable in importance to the fighting of this battle in the Western Desert, and I thought he was the man to handle the business. He gave me various good reasons for not doing so, and General Ritchie fought the battle. As I told the House on Tuesday, General Auchinleck, on 25th June, superseded General Ritchie and assumed the command himself. We at once approved his decision, but I must frankly confess that the matter was not one on which we could form any final judgment, so far as the superseded officer is concerned. I cannot pretend to form a judgment upon what has happened in this battle. I like commanders on land and sea and in the air to feel that between them and all forms of public criticism the Government stands like a strong bulkhead. They ought to have a fair chance, and more than one chance. Men may make mistakes and learn from their mistakes. Men may have bad luck, and their luck may change. But anyhow you will not get generals to run risks unless they feel they have behind them a strong Government. They will not run risks unless they feel that they need not look over their shoulders or worry about what is happening at home, unless they feel they can concentrate their gaze upon the enemy. And you will not, I may add, get a Government to run risks unless they feel that they have got behind them a loyal, solid majority. Look at the things we are being asked to do now, and imagine the kind of attack which would be made on us if we tried to do them and failed. In war time if you desire service you must give loyalty.

General Auchinleck is now in direct command of the battle. It is raging with great intensity. The communiqué which has been issued on the tape — I have not had any news myself — states that the attacks yesterday were repulsed. But the battle is of the most intense and serious character. We have assured General Auchinleck of our confidence, and I believe it will be found that this confidence has not been misplaced. I am not going to express any opinion about what is going to happen. I cannot tell the House — and the enemy — what reinforcements are at hand, or are approaching, or when they will arrive. I have never made any predictions, except things like saying that Singapore would hold out. What a fool and a knave I should have been to say that it would fall! I have not made any arrogant, confident, boasting predictions at all. On the contrary, I have stuck hard to my "blood, toil, tears and sweat," to which I have added muddle and mismanagement, and that, to some extent I must admit, is what you have got out of it.

I repudiate altogether the suggestion that I misled the House on 2nd June about the present campaign. All I said was that:

". . . it is clear that we have every reason to be satisfied, and more than satisfied, with the course which the battle has so far taken, and that we should watch its further development with earnest attention."

Nothing could be more guarded. I do not know what my critics would like me to say now. If I predict success and speak in buoyant terms, and misfortune continues, their tongues and pens will be able to dilate on my words. On the other hand, if I predict failure and paint the picture in the darkest hues — I have painted it in pretty dark hues — I might safeguard myself against one danger, but only at the expense of a struggling Army. Also I might be wrong. So I will say nothing about the future except to invite the House and the nation to face with courage whatever it may unfold.

I now ask the House to take a wider survey. Since Japan attacked us six months ago in the Far East we have suffered heavy losses there. A peace-loving nation like the United States, confined by two great oceans, naturally takes time to bring its gigantic forces to bear. I have never shared the view that this would be a short war, or that it would end in 1942. It is far more likely to be a long war. There is no reason to suppose that the war will stop when the final result has become obvious. The Battle of Gettysburg proclaimed the ultimate victory of the North, but far more blood was shed after the Battle of Gettysburg than before. At the same time, in spite of our losses in Asia, in spite of our defeats in Libya, in spite of the increased sinkings off the American coast, I affirm with confidence that the general strength and prospects of the United Nations have greatly improved since the turn of the year, when I last visited the President in the United States. The outstanding feature is of course the steady resistance of Russia to the invaders of her soil, and the fact that up to now at the beginning of July, more than half-way through the summer, no major offensive has been opened by Hitler upon Russia, unless he calls the present attacks on Kharkov and Kursk a major offensive. There is no doubt that the Russian Government and nation, wedded by the ties of blood, sacrifice and faith to the English-speaking democracies of the West, will continue to wage war, steadfast, stubborn, invincible. I make no forecast of the future. All I know is that the Russians have surprised Hitler before, and I believe they will surprise him again. Anyhow whatever happens they will fight on to death or victory. That is the cardinal fact at this time.

The second great fact is the growth of air power on the side of the Allies. That growth is proceeding with immense rapidity, and is bound to manifest itself as the months pass by. Hitler made a contract with the demon of the air, but the contract ran out before the job was done, and the demon has taken on an engagement with the rival firm. How truly it has been said that nations and people very often fall by the very means which they have used and built their hopes upon for their rising-up!

For the last six months our convoys to the East have grown. Every month about 50,000 men with the best equipment we can make have pierced through the U-boats and hostile aircraft which beset these islands, and have rounded the Cape of Good Hope. That this should have been done so far without loss constitutes an achievement prodigious and unexampled in history. As these successive Armies, for they are little less, round the Cape, we decide where they are to go. Some months ago Australia feared that an invasion was imminent. If so, our Forces would have gone to aid our kith and kin irrespective of the position in the Middle East. Personally, I have never thought that the homeland of Australia would be heavily invaded by Japan in the present year, and now that the Australian manhood is armed and in the field, and that a large American Army has arrived in Australia and on the island stepping-stones across the Pacific as a feature of the central direction of the war, I am confident that the mass invasion of Australia would be a most hazardous and unprofitable operation for Japan. On the contrary, throughout the whole of the South-West Pacific the watchword of the Allies is now "attack."

In March and April last we were deeply anxious about India, which, before Japan entered the war, had been stripped almost bare of trained troops and equipment for the sake of other theatres. India has now been strongly reinforced. A far larger Army, British and Indian, stands in India under the command of General Wavell than ever before in the history of the British connection. Ceylon, which at one time appeared to be in great jeopardy, is now strongly defended by naval, air and military forces. We have secured a protective naval base in Madagascar.

The End of the Beginning

When I remember reading an article by the right hon. Gentleman (Mr. Hore-Belisha) headed, "Take Madagascar Now" — I am not blaming the right hon. Gentleman, as he could not know that our troops had been some weeks on the sea — I really wonder whether he might not have found time to make some acknowledgment of the speed and efficiency with which his direction had been carried out.

All this improvement in the position of Australia, New Zealand and India has been effected in the main by the brilliant victories gained by the United States Navy and Air Force over the Japanese in the Coral Sea and at Midway Island. No fewer than four out of eight Japanese regular aircraft-carriers — vessels which take four years to make — have been sunk, as well as one of their converted auxiliary carriers. When the Japanese came into the Bay of Bengal at the beginning of April with five carriers, we experienced great anxiety, but the five are now at the bottom of the sea; and the Japanese, whose resources are strictly limited, are beginning to count their capital units on their fingers and toes. These splendid achievements have not received the attention they deserve in this Island. Superb acts of devotion have been performed by the American airmen. From some of their successful attacks on the Japanese aircraft, only one aircraft returned out of ten; in others, the loss was more than half. But the work has been done, and the position in the Pacific has been definitely altered in our favour. This relief has enabled important forces to be directed upon Egypt. The extraordinary valour and tenacity of the Russian defence of Sebastopol and General Timoshenko's massive strokes in the battles round Kharkov, together with the lateness of the season, have enabled us to concentrate our efforts on the destruction of Rommel's army. At this moment, the struggle in Egypt is gradually approaching its full intensity. The battle is now in the balance, and it is an action of the highest consequence. It has one object, and one object only, namely, the destruction of the enemy's army and armoured power. Important aid is now on the way, both from Britain and from the United States. A hard and deadly struggle lies before the Armies on the Nile. It remains for us at home to fortify and encourage their Commander by every means in our power.

I wish to speak a few words "of great truth and respect" — as they say in the diplomatic documents — and I hope I may be granted the fullest liberty of debate. This Parliament has a peculiar responsibility. It presided over the beginning of the evils which have come on the world. I owe much to the House, and it is my hope that it may see the end of them in triumph. This it can do only if, in the long period which may yet have to be travelled, the House affords a solid foundation to the responsible Executive Government, placed in power by its own choice. The House must be a steady, stabilising factor in the State, and not an instrument by which the disaffected sections of the Press can attempt to promote one crisis after another. If democracy and Parliamentary institutions are to triumph in this war, it is absolutely necessary that Governments resting upon them shall be able to act and dare, that the servants of the Crown shall not be harassed by nagging and snarling, that enemy propaganda shall not be fed needlessly out of our own hands, and our reputation disparaged and undermined throughout the world. On the contrary, the will of the whole House should be made manifest upon important occasions. It is important that not only those who speak, but those who watch and listen and judge, should also count as a factor in world affairs. After all, we are still fighting for our lives, and for causes dearer than life itself. We have no right to assume that victory is certain; it will be certain only if we do not fail in our duty. Sober and constructive criticism, or criticism in Secret Session, has its high virtue; but the duty of the House of Commons is to sustain the Government or to change the Government. If it cannot change it, it should sustain it. There is no working middle course in war-time. Much harm was done abroad by the two days' Debate in May. Only the hostile speeches are reported abroad, and much play is made with them by our enemy.

A Division, or the opportunity for a Division, should always follow a Debate on the war, and I trust, therefore, that the opinion of the overwhelming majority of the House will be made plain not only in the Division, but also in the days which follow, and that the weaker brethren, if I may so call them, will not be allowed to usurp and almost monopolise the privileges and proud authority of the House of Commons. The Majority of the House must do their duty. All I ask is a decision one way or another.

The End of the Beginning

There is an agitation in the Press, which has found its echo in a number of hostile speeches, to deprive me of the function which I exercise in the general conduct and supervision of the war. I do not propose to argue this to-day at any length, because it was much discussed in a recent Debate. Under the present arrangement the three Chiefs of the Staff, sitting almost continuously together, carry on the war from day to day, assisted not only by the machinery of the great Departments which serve them, but by the Combined General Staff, in making their decisions effective through the Navy, Army and Air Forces over which they exercise direct operational control. I supervise their activities, whether as Prime Minister or Minister of Defence. I work myself under the supervision and control of the War Cabinet, to whom all important matters are referred, and whom I have to carry with me in all major decisions. Nearly all my work has been done in writing, and a complete record exists of all the directions I have given, the inquiries I have made, and the telegrams I have drafted. I shall be perfectly content to be judged by them.

I ask no favours either for myself or for His Majesty's Government. I undertook the office of Prime Minister and Minister of Defence, after defending my predecessor to the best of my ability, in times when the life of the Empire hung upon a thread. I am your servant, and you have the right to dismiss me when you please. What you have no right to do is to ask me to bear responsibilities without the power of effective action, to bear the responsibilities of Prime Minister but clamped on each side by strong men, as the hon. Member said. If to-day, or at any future time, the House were to exercise its undoubted right, I could walk out with a good conscience and the feeling that I have done my duty according to such light as has been granted to me. There is only one thing I would ask of you in that event. It would be to give my successor the modest powers which would have been denied to me.

But there is a larger issue than the personal issue. The mover of this Vote of Censure has proposed that I should be stripped of my responsibilities for Defence in order that some military figure or some other unnamed personage should assume the general conduct of the war, that he should have complete control of the

Armed Forces of the Crown, that he should be the Chief of the Chiefs of the Staff, that he should nominate or dismiss the generals or the admirals, that he should always be ready to resign, that is to say, to match himself against his political colleagues, if colleagues they could be considered, if he did not get all he wanted, that he should have under him a Royal Duke as Commander-in-Chief of the Army, and finally, I presume, though this was not mentioned, that this unnamed personage should find an appendage in the Prime Minister to make the necessary explanations, excuses and apologies to Parliament when things go wrong, as they often do and often will. That is at any rate a policy. It is a system very different from the Parliamentary system under which we live. It might easily amount to or be converted into a dictatorship. I wish to make it perfectly clear that as far as I am concerned I shall take no part in such a system.

Sir J. Wardlaw-Milne here interjected: I hope that my right hon. Friend has not forgotten the original sentence, which was "subject to the War Cabinet"?

Mr. Churchill continued: —

Subject to the War Cabinet, against which this all-powerful potentate is not to hesitate to resign on every occasion if he could not get his way. It is a plan, but it is not a plan in which I should personally be interested to take part, and I do not think that it is one which would commend itself to this House. The setting down of this Vote of Censure by Members of all parties is a considerable event. Do not, I beg you, let the House underrate the gravity of what has been done. It has been trumpeted all round the world to our disparagement, and when every nation, friend and foe, is waiting to see what is the true resolve and conviction of the House of Commons, it must go forward to the end. All over the world, throughout the United States, as I can testify, in Russia, far away in China, and throughout every subjugated country, all our friends are waiting to know whether there is a strong, solid Government in Britain and whether its national leadership is to be challenged or not. Every vote counts. If those who have assailed us are reduced to contemptible proportions and their Vote of Censure on the National Government is converted to a vote of censure upon its authors, make no mistake, a cheer will go up from every friend of Britain and every faithful servant of our cause, and the knell of disappointment will ring in the ears of the tyrants we are striving to overthrow.

The House of Commons divided, and Sir John Wardlaw-Milne's Motion of "No Confidence" was defeated by 475 votes to 25.

NOTE

In the House of Commons on September 8, 1942, in reply to Capt. Anstruther-Gray, who asked the Prime Minister the number of British tanks that were destroyed by the Germans in Libya on 13th June, with a view to correcting public misconception on this matter; and who it was who informed him that some 230 British tanks were lost in that one day's fighting, Mr. Churchill replied: —

My statement that 230 tanks were lost on 13th June was based on a misreading of the terms of the telegram from the Middle East. According to the latest information, about 200 tanks were lost over a period of about a week. It is not possible to say exactly how many were lost on 13th June, but the bulk of the losses probably took place on that and the previous day.

The R. A. F. in Egypt

A MESSAGE SENT TO AIR CHIEF MARSHAL TEDDER, C.-IN-C.
OF THE R.A.F. IN THE MIDDLE EAST, JULY 4, 1942

[July 4, 1942

Here at home we are all watching with enthusiasm the brilliant, supreme exertions of the Royal Air Force in the battle now proceeding in Egypt. From every quarter the reports come in of the effect of the vital part which your officers and men are playing in the Homeric struggle for the Nile Valley. The days of the Battle of Britain are being repeated far from home. We are sure you will be to our glorious Army the friend that endureth to the end.

A Pledge to China

[July 5, 1942

F IVE years ago to-day Japan launched her treacherous attack on your country. For five years you have, in spite of suffering and disappointment, maintained a united front against aggression. The world has watched with admiration the mighty efforts made by China, not only on the field of battle but also in the sphere of internal reconstruction.

Both China and the British Commonwealth have known what it is to stand alone against the aggressor. To-day we are fighting side by side against our common enemies, and with us to-day we have the tremendous resources of the United States of America. Each of us has his part to play. The war in Europe and the Middle East is as much part of the defence of China as the war in the Far East is part of the defence of Britain. We are determined to extend to the Chinese people every material, moral, and spiritual help in our power.

Of ultimate victory we are sure. When it is won our present association will have laid the foundations of a lasting friendship based on mutual confidence and respect, which will secure peace and justice to all the peoples of the world.

Army and R. A. F. Co-operation

[*July 7, 1942*

Replying to a Member of Parliament who asked whether the aircraft allocated to General Auchinleck for the campaign being fought in the Middle East were under his direct command for operations, the Prime Minister said: —

ON October 7th, 1941, before the winter battle in Libya, I gave a ruling on this subject as follows:

"Upon the Military Commander-in-Chief in the Middle East announcing that a battle is in prospect, the Air Officer Commanding-in-Chief will give him all possible aid irrespective of other targets, however attractive. The Army Commander-in-Chief will specify to the Air Officer Commanding-in-Chief the targets and tasks which he requires to be performed, both in the preparatory attack on the rearward installations of the enemy and for air action during the progress of the battle. It will be for the Air Officer Commanding-in-Chief to use his maximum force for these objects in the manner most effective. This applies not only to any squadrons assigned to Army co-operation permanently, but also to the whole air force available in the theatre."

This direction is agreeable to both Services and has been in force ever since.

Replying to other questions concerning the joint training of the Army and the R.A.F., the Prime Minister said: —

The joint training of the Army and the Royal Air Force is already proceeding on a considerable scale and is being continually extended. The aircraft of Army Co-operation Command, which is itself being substantially expanded, are occupied solely on such training. Squadrons of Bomber and Fighter Command are also regularly used for this purpose.

*   *   *   *

We try to find the true and proper course between, on the one hand, not having aircraft attached to the infantry, which would be a misfortune, and, on the other hand, keeping large masses of aircraft which are required for major purposes standing by on specialised functions.

*   *   *   *

The whole question of air-borne troops, whether it concerns the gliders, which may be attached to machines with power, whether it concerns parachute troops themselves, or whether it concerns the aircraft which are power-driven and tow the gliders — all these matters are under one organisation and are being studied as a whole.

A Motto for Scouts

[July 16, 1942

I FIRST met B.P. many years before the birth of the Scout movement. He was a man of character, vision, and enthusiasm, and he passed these qualities on to the movement which has played, and is playing, an important part in moulding the character of our race. Sturdiness, neighbourliness, practical competence, love of country, and above all, in these times, indomitable resolve, daring, and enterprise in the face of the enemy, these are the hallmarks of a Scout. . . . "Be Prepared" to stand up faithfully for Right and Truth however the winds may blow.

Answers to Questions in the House of Commons

JULY 21, 1942

[July 21, 1942

Replying to a Member who asked for a statement regarding the holding of a General Election before the end of 1942, the Prime Minister said: —

IT would be most unusual and in my view contrary to the best precedents for any statement to be made forecasting the advice which in hypothetical circumstances should be tendered to the King in respect of a Dissolution of Parliament.

The Member (Mr. De la Bere) then asked: Is it not essential whilst perils press to reason calmly about holding a General Election? Would the Prime Minister impress on Lord Beaverbrook the necessity for calm reasoning? Mr. Churchill replied: —

I must embrace this opportunity of testifying my admiration for the principles of free speech and a free Press.

Replying to a Member who asked that a ruling should be given so that R.A.F. machines taking part in naval operations should come under the supreme control of the senior naval officer conducting the operations, the Prime Minister said: —

In the Middle East during active military operations the General, working in the closest association with the Air Commander, has the directing power. Aircraft co-operating with the Fleet conform strictly to naval requirements and movements. In the intervals between land or sea operations, ample opportunities for discussion and agreement between the three Commanders-in-Chief are provided by their meetings under the presidency of the Minister of State. Quite a different arrangement prevails at home, where, for the purposes of the North-Western Approaches and the narrow seas, the Admiralty is the predominant authority. In this case the Coastal Command is under the operational control of the Admiralty, and questions of the relative strength of the Coastal and Bomber Commands are decided by the Minister of Defence, or by the Defence Committee. In other theatres of war arrangements are made to meet the particular conditions there existing, having regard principally to the predominant character of the operations.

Replying to a Member who asked through what channels demands are submitted to the Ministry of Aircraft Production for aircraft for Army Co-operation Command and for the Fleet Air Arm, the Prime Minister said: —

The War Office place before the Air Ministry their requirements, and after discussion the most suitable types of aircraft are chosen. Orders for such aircraft are then given by the Air Ministry to the Ministry of Aircraft Production. Thereafter there is direct liaison between the War Office, Air Ministry and Ministry of Aircraft Production on matters of design, modification and production. Approved requirements for the Fleet Air Arm are made direct to the Ministry of Aircraft Production by the Admiralty.

In reply to a further question suggesting that the Air Ministry could hold up demands for Army aeroplanes, the Prime Minister said: —

They cannot do so at all. If any such action were taken it would immediately be brought to the notice, successively, of the Defence Committee, and the War Cabinet.

* * * *

The Minister of Defence and the Defence Committee, advised as necessary by the Chiefs of Staff, approve and from time to time review the aircraft programme, which lays down the number of aircraft of various types to be manufactured.

Retribution on Nazis

A MESSAGE TO A NEW YORK DEMONSTRATION BY JEWISH
SOCIETIES AGAINST GERMAN ATROCITIES
JULY 21, 1942

[July 21, 1942

YOU will recall that on October 25 last year President Roosevelt and I expressed the horror felt by all civilised peoples at Nazi butcheries and terrorism. Our resolve is to place retribution for those crimes among the major purposes of this war.

Defence of Iraq

[August 29, 1942

SIR KINAHAN CORNWALLIS will already have told Your Excellency how sorry I was not to have been able to break my recent journey at Bagdad. It would have given me great pleasure to meet His Royal Highness the Regent and yourself. I have followed with deep interest the march of events in Iraq during the last fifteen months. The steady improvement that has occurred under the wise guidance of the Regent and yourself is the cause of much satisfaction to all sincere friends of Iraq, and I deeply appreciate the manner in which the present Administration have fulfilled their obligations under the Anglo-Iraqui Treaty, and have co-operated with His Majesty's Government in the fight against Nazi tyranny and the forces of evil. The defence of Iraq against enemy attack is a matter of vital concern to the Allies, and I am sure that Your Excellency will have welcomed with special satisfaction the establishment of a new and independent command in Iraq and Persia, and the appointment of General Sir Henry Maitland-Wilson to this important post.

Answers to Questions in the House of Commons

SEPTEMBER 8 AND 29, 1942

[September 8, 1942

Replying to a Member who drew attention to the advantages to be derived from the friendship and co-operation of British and U.S. forces during short visits, apart from the appointment of permanent liaison officers, the Prime Minister said: —

VISITS of British naval officers and petty officers to American units in British waters have taken place. British Army officers and N.C.O.'s are attached to American Field Force formations and vice versa. Personnel from the American Forces attend nearly all the courses of instruction run by the British Army in this country. There is also a considerable interchange of Air Force personnel for purposes of mutual assistance.

Replying to a question concerning awards for gallantry to the Merchant Navy, the Prime Minister said: —

Officers of the Merchant Navy, serving as such, who receive the Order of the British Empire are appointed to the Civil Division, which is, of course, of equal status to the Military Division of the Order. It is not proposed to vary this arrangement, or to make any recommendation for the creation of further decorations. The personnel of the Merchant Navy serving under special agreement as part of the Royal Navy have hitherto been eligible for the naval gallantry awards other than the D.S.O. That position has now been rectified, and the D.S.O. is available for Merchant Navy officers serving in these circumstances.

The special services of the Merchant Navy generally were recognised several years ago by His Majesty's approval of officers and men in that service being eligible, under certain circumstances, for the award of the Victoria Cross and the Distinguished Service Cross. I am glad to be able to inform the House that His Majesty has been pleased to approve the addition of the Distinguished Service Order to the list of decorations open for award in the Merchant Navy.

[*September 29, 1942*

In reply to a Member who asked that Merchant Navy officers and men should be appointed to the Military Division of the Order of the British Empire for gallantry against the enemy, instead of to the Civil Division, the Prime Minister said: —

NAVAL awards are now available for the Merchant Navy for gallantry in action with the enemy. The conditions for appointment to the Order of the British Empire in the Royal Navy and the Merchant Navy are similar, whether the recommendation is made for services at sea or on shore, and whether for bravery not in the face of the enemy or for good service. There is no difference in standard between the Military and Civil Divisions, that is entirely a matter of occupation. It is not proposed to vary the long-standing custom that the appointments of civilians shall be in the Civil Division and of military personnel in the Military Division of the Order.

The Death of the Duke of Kent

A SPEECH TO THE HOUSE OF COMMONS
SEPTEMBER 8, 1942

[*September 8, 1942*

I BEG to move,

"That an humble Address be presented to His Majesty to express the deep concern of this House on the loss which His Majesty has sustained by the death on active service of Air Commodore His Royal Highness Prince George Alexander Edmund, Duke of Kent, and to condole with His Majesty on this melancholy occasion:

"and to assure His Majesty that this House shares the general feeling of sorrow for the heavy bereavement which His Majesty and His Majesty's Family have sustained by the death of a Prince who was regarded with universal affection and esteem by His Majesty's subjects, and will ever participate with the most affectionate and dutiful attachment in whatever may concern the feelings and interests of His Majesty."

I also propose to move a second Motion:

"That this House do condole with Her Royal Highness the Duchess of Kent on the great loss which Her Royal Highness has sustained by the death on active service of Air Commodore His Royal Highness the Duke of Kent."

The loss of this gallant and handsome Prince, in the prime of his life, has been a shock and a sorrow to the people of the British Empire, standing out lamentably even in these hard days of war. To His Majesty the King it is the loss of a dearly-loved brother, and it has affected him most poignantly. I knew the late Duke of Kent from his childhood, and had many opportunities of meeting him during the war, both at the Admiralty and there-

The Death of the Duke of Kent, September 8, 1942

after. His overpowering desire was to render useful service to his King and country in this period when we are all of us on trial.

There are difficulties which attend a King's brother of which those who are not of an exalted station can hardly be aware. But the Duke of Kent was ready to waive his rank, to put aside all ceremony, and to undergo any amount of discomfort and danger or, what is harder still, of monotonous routine conscientiously performed, in order to feel quite sure that he was making a real contribution to our national struggle for life and honour. The field he made his own was that of the welfare and comfort of the Royal Air Force, which entailed an immense amount of work and travelling, and yielded a continuous and useful result to which the personal qualities of the Duke contributed markedly. It was while performing these duties as an Air Commodore, he having given up his previous rank of Air Marshal, that the hazards of the air claimed their forfeit. He and all his companions save one were dashed instantaneously to death.

There is something about death on active service which makes it different from common or ordinary death in the normal course of nature. It is accepted without question by the fighting men. Those they leave behind them are also conscious of a light of sacrifice and honour which plays around the grave or the tomb of the warrior. They are, for the time being, uplifted. This adds to their fortitude, but it does not in any way lessen their pain. Nothing can fill the awful gap, nothing can assuage or comfort the loneliness and deprivation which fall upon wife and children when the prop and centre of their home is suddenly snatched away. Only faith in a life after death in a brighter world where dear ones will meet again — only that and the measured tramp of time can give consolation.

The Duke of Kent had a joyous union and a happy family. The British people are devoted believers in their ancient Monarchy, regarding it as one of the bulwarks of their liberties and one of the essential elements in their constitutional processes. They, therefore, always follow with solicitude the joys and sorrows of the Royal Family, and they rejoiced in the spectacle of this happy home. I speak here in this famous Assembly, the champion and the successful practiser of democratic government,

199

The End of the Beginning

August 17.	Announced that Mr. Churchill had visited Moscow and, together with Mr. Harriman (President Roosevelt's representative), had conferred with Premier Stalin.
August 18.	General Alexander succeeded General Auchinleck as Commander-in-Chief, Middle East.
August 19.	The greatest Combined Operations raid of the war carried out in the Dieppe area by British, Canadian, American and Fighting French troops, who stayed ashore nine hours. During the operation 82 enemy aircraft were destroyed for certain and more than 100 more were probably destroyed or damaged. Ninety-four British planes were lost.
August 21.	Japan admitted that an American landing had been made on Makin in the Gilbert Islands.
August 22.	Brazil declared war on Germany and Italy.
August 24.	Mr. Churchill arrived back in London from his visit to Moscow and the Middle East.
August 25.	The Duke of Kent was killed when a flying boat crashed in the North of Scotland.
August 27.	Japanese forces attempted to land at Milne Bay in the south-east of New Guinea and were strongly engaged by Allied troops.
August 29.	Officially announced that the United States forces' attack on the Solomons had resulted in six of the Islands being held firmly by the Americans.
August 31.	General MacArthur announced that the Japanese attack on Milne Bay had resulted in an Allied victory.
September 1.	Rommel's forces moved forward in a fierce attack on the British left flank in Libya, and a battle developed.
September 2.	German threat to Stalingrad grew as the invaders reached the Volga.

The War Situation, September 8, 1942

September 4. *Rommel's forces withdrew in Egypt, heavily pursued by the Eighth Army.*

September 6. *Big cuts in rail and road transport, including the removal of cheap day fares, were announced.*

September 7. *President Roosevelt, in a message to Congress, asked for legislation authorising him to stabilise the cost of living, and warned Congress that if necessary he would take action himself.*

[September 8, 1942

NINE weeks have passed since I spoke here on the Vote of Censure. I am most grateful to the House for the substantial majority which they then gave to me and to the Government. Every proof that is given to the world of the inflexible steadfastness of Parliament and of its sense of proportion strengthens the British war effort in a definite and recognisable manner. Most particularly are such manifestations of our national willpower a help to the head of the British Government in time of war. The Prime Minister of the day, as head of the Executive, has to be from time to time in contact and correspondence with the Heads of the Executives of the great Allied States. President Roosevelt and Premier Stalin are not only Heads of the Executive, but are Commanders-in-Chief of the Armed Forces. We work out affairs in a different way. The Prime Minister is the servant of the House, and is liable to dismissal at a moment's notice by a simple vote. It is only possible for him to do what is necessary, and what has got to be done on occasion by somebody or other, if he enjoys, as I do, the support of an absolutely loyal and united Cabinet, and if he is refreshed and fortified from time to time, and especially in bad times, as I have been, by massive and overwhelming Parliamentary majorities. Then your servant is able to transact the important business which has to be done with confidence and freedom, and is able to meet people at the heads of the Allied countries on more or less equal terms and on occasion to say "Yes" and "No" without delay upon some difficult questions. Thus we arrive, by our ancient constitutional methods, at practical working arrangements which show that Parliamentary democracy can adapt itself to all situations and can go out in all weathers. That is why I am especially grateful to the House for their unswerving support, and for the large majority with which they rejected a hostile vote on the last occasion we were together.

Since that day and since the House separated there have been several important operations of war. The first of these has been the carrying into Malta of a convoy of supplies sufficient to ensure the life and resistance of that heroic island fortress for a good many months to come. This operation was looked forward to with a certain amount of anxiety on account of the great dangers to which many of His Majesty's most valuable ships must be exposed. For this purpose a powerful battle squadron, supported by three aircraft-carriers, trained to work in combination, and by powerful cruiser squadrons and flotillas was set in motion through the Straits of Gibraltar. At the same time the Malta Air Force was raised to a very high level of strength by the flying-through of Spitfires from other carriers, so that an effective protective umbrella was spread around the island for a considerable distance, and the local command of the air was effectively assured. The convoy was thus able to force its way through the extraordinary dangers which beset its passage from Sardinia onwards. Three or four hundred German and Italian shore-based bombers, torpedo planes and long-range fighters were launched against our armada — an enormous concourse of ships — and in the narrows, which were mined, it was attacked by E-boats and U-boats. Severe losses were suffered both by the convoy and the escorting fleet. One aircraft-carrier, the *Eagle,* two cruisers and one destroyer were sunk, and others damaged. But this price, although heavy, was not excessive for the result obtained, for Malta is not only as bright a gem as shines in the King's Crown, but its effective action against the enemy's communications with Libya and Egypt is essential to the whole strategic position in the Middle East. In the same operation one eight-inch Italian cruiser and one six-inch Italian cruiser were torpedoed and badly damaged, and two U-boats were sunk. A most remarkable feature of this fighting was undoubtedly the defeat, by gunfire and by aircraft from the carriers, of the enemy's shore-based aircraft. Fifty-six Axis aircraft were shot down for certain, and 15 others were probably destroyed. Of these 39 were shot down by carrier-borne aircraft of the Fleet, and 17 by the "Ack-Ack" guns of the ships of the convoy and of the escort. In addition, at least 16 were destroyed by aircraft from Malta, and all this loss was sustained by these very powerful shore-based squadrons, operating from bases in comparatively close proximity, without their being able to inflict by air action any appreciable damage upon the ships of war or the supply ships of the convoy — a remarkable fact.

Although the loss of the *Eagle* at the outset of the operation affected the combination of the three carriers on which much store was set — which always seemed to me, personally, to be of the highest importance and a new feature — we must regard the whole episode as a further proof of the value of aircraft-carriers working together in combination at sea, and also of the increasing power of the gunnery of the Fleet and of the merchant vessels, which were all armed to the teeth and fought with customary determination. The whole operation was carried out with the utmost discipline and determination, reflecting the highest credit on all officers and men concerned, both of the Royal Navy and Mercantile Marine, and upon the skilful admirals in charge — Admiral Syfret, Admiral Burrough and Admiral Lyster.

The second important operation was the attack upon Dieppe. It is a mistake to speak or write of this as "a Commando raid," although some Commando troops distinguished themselves remarkably in it. The military credit for this most gallant affair goes to the Canadian troops, who formed five-sixths of the assaulting force, and to the Royal Navy, which carried them all there and which carried most of them back. The raid must be considered as a reconnaissance in force. It was a hard, savage clash such as will very likely become increasingly frequent as the war deepens. We had to get all the information necessary before launching operations on a much larger scale. This raid, apart from its reconnaissance value, brought about an extremely satisfactory air battle in the West which the Fighter Command wish they could repeat every week. It inflicted perhaps as much loss upon the enemy in killed and wounded as we suffered ourselves. I, personally, regarded the Dieppe assault, to which I gave my sanction, as an indispensable preliminary to full-scale operations. I do not intend to give any information about these operations, and I have only said as much as I have because the enemy can see by his daily reconnaissances of our ports many signs of movements that we are unable to conceal from his photography. He is also aware of the steady and rapid influx into this Island of United States divisions and other troops, but what he does not know is how, when, where and with what forces and in what fashion he will be smitten. And on this point it is desirable that he should be left to his own ruminations, unassisted by British or American advice or comment.

Since the successful action off Midway Island, our American Allies, with the very active support of Australian Forces, have been engaged with the Japanese in the South-west Pacific, and in the course of these operations they have taken the offensive and occupied the Islands of Guadalcanal and Tulagi and other islands in the Solomons. They have, moreover, according to the reports which have already been seen in the Press, frustrated Japanese activities in Milne Bay. The fighting ashore, in which United States marines were prominent, and the fighting at sea, have both been exceptionally bitter. In the fighting at sea His Majesty's Australian ship *Canberra* has been sunk, as has already been announced. His Majesty's Government considered that the Commonwealth Government should not bear this grievous loss, following the sinking of other gallant Australian ships. We have therefore decided to offer freely and unconditionally the transfer of His Majesty's eight-inch gun cruiser *Shropshire* to the Commonwealth Government. The offer has been most warmly received.

Since we were last together the tendencies of war have continued to move in our favour. Of the Russian Front, I will only at this moment say that it is 8th September. In other quarters the growing predominance of the Allied air power is continuous. From June onwards to the first week in September, just closed, we have discharged nearly double the bomb load upon Germany which was discharged in the corresponding period of last year, and that with much greater precision. A far larger proportion fell in built-up areas or hit the actual target. The United States daylight bombing is a new and increasingly important factor, and there is no doubt that both in accuracy of aim and in mutual defensive power new possibilities of air warfare are being opened by our American comrades and their Flying Fortresses. The losses at sea are still very heavy, but I am glad to say that the months of July, August, and September so far as it has run, are a definite improvement on those which preceded them. This is due largely to the continued development and completion of the convoy system off the American coast, and this improvement has been effected in spite of heavy losses in war operations, such as the Russian and Malta convoys.

During these same months, the line of new building of merchant ships of the United Nations has definitely crossed and maintained itself on the graph above the line of sinkings. Warfare — and this is even more important, because offence is more important than defence, however successful — warfare on U-boats has been more successful than at any former period in the war. In fact, very few days have passed without one or more being sunk or damaged by us or our Allies. One would, of course, expect the U-boats to suffer heavier losses as there are more of them about, and I cannot say that the sinkings of U-boats have nearly kept pace with the believed and planned new construction. On the other hand, our heavy and successful bombing of the German shipbuilding yards will have an increasing effect upon future output and assembly of U-boats, and the part which the Air is taking in the U-boat warfare grows more important with every week that passes.

We must regard the struggle at sea as the foundation of all the efforts of the United Nations. If they lost that, all else would be denied to them; but there is no reason to suppose that we have not the means of victory in our hands, provided that the utmost in human power is done here and in the United States.

Lastly, we may note that the ruthless unlimited German U-boat warfare, and the outrages to which this gave vent, have brought us a new Ally, and in the dawn of the fourth year of the War we welcome the accession of Brazil to the ranks of the

United Nations. We are entitled to regard this as a most helpful and encouraging event.

Continued efforts are made by us and our Allies to unify and concert the command and action of the United Nations, and particularly of their leading members. These efforts are made in spite of all the obvious difficulties which geography can interpose. During the month of July, President Roosevelt sent a most important mission to this country. No announcement of this was made at the time. The mission comprised General Marshall, the Head of the United States Army, Admiral King, the Head of the Navy, and Mr. Hopkins, the President's Personal Representative. These gentlemen met in numerous conferences; not only the British Chiefs of Staff, but the Members of the War Cabinet, and of the Defence Committee, which is a somewhat smaller grouping of it. During a period of ten days or more the whole field of the War was explored and every problem of importance in it was scrutinised and weighed. Decisions of importance were taken affecting the whole future general conduct of our operations not only in Europe but throughout the world. These decisions were in accordance with the wishes of President Roosevelt, and they received his final approval. Thus, by the end of July complete agreement on war policy and war plans had been reached between Great Britain and the United States. This agreement covers the whole field of the War in every part of the world, and also deals with the necessary productive and administrative measures required to enforce the combined policy and strategy which has been agreed upon.

Armed with this body of agreement between Great Britain and the United States, and invigorated by the goodwill of the House manifested at what was a particularly dark, unhappy and anxious moment, I took advantage of the Recess to visit the Army in the Middle East and to visit Premier Stalin in Moscow. Both these journeys seemed necessary in the public interest, and I believe that the results achieved, although now secret, will as they become apparent justify any trouble or expense incurred.

Travelling always in a Liberator bomber, it was possible for me to reach Cairo in an uncommonly short time. Before I left I had some reason to believe that the condition of the Desert Army and the troops in Egypt was not entirely satisfactory. The

The War Situation, September 8, 1942

Eighth Army, or the Army of the Western Desert, or the Desert Army, as I like to call it, had lost over 80,000 men. It had been driven back about 400 miles since May, with immense losses in munitions, supplies and transport. General Rommel's surprisingly rapid advance was only rendered possible because he used our captured stores and vehicles. In the battles around Gazala, in the stress of the retreat and the fighting at El Alamein, where General Auchinleck succeeded in stabilising the front, the structure of the Army had become much deranged. The divisional formations had been largely broken up, and a number of battle groups or other improvised formations had sprung into being piecemeal in the course of the hard fighting. Nevertheless, as I can myself testify, there was a universal conviction in officers and men of every rank that they could beat the Germans man to man and face to face. But this was coupled with a sense of being baffled and of not understanding why so many misfortunes had fallen upon the Army. The spirit of the troops was admirable, but it was clear to me that drastic changes were required in the High Command and that the Army must have a new start under new leaders. I was fortified in these conclusions by the advice of the Chief of the Imperial General Staff, who accompanied me, and also by the massive judgment of Field-Marshal Smuts, who flew from Cape Town to Cairo to meet me, and also, of course, to see the South African divisions which he has sent into the line.

I, therefore, after many heart-searchings, submitted proposals to the War Cabinet for changing and remodelling the High Command. In these proposals, General Alexander, fresh from his brilliant uphill campaign in Burma — a most testing ordeal for any man — succeeded General Auchinleck, and General Gott, who was greatly trusted by the troops, was to command the Eighth Army. The Cabinet was in the act of endorsing these telegraphed recommendations when General Gott was killed by the enemy. I felt this very much, because I met him only the day before; I spent a long time in his company, and he seemed a most splendid man. General Montgomery, who now commands the Eighth Army, is one of our most accomplished soldiers, and we had need of him for certain purposes here at home. However, the imminent threat of battle in the Western Desert left us no choice but to call upon him. I am satisfied that the combination of General Alexander as Commander-in-Chief and General Montgomery under him commanding the Eighth Army, with General McCreery, an officer deeply versed in the handling of tanks, as Chief of the General Staff, is a team well adapted to our needs, and the finest at our disposal at the present time. There were, of course, a number of other changes. It is always painful making such changes, but in wartime individual feelings cannot be spared, and whatever is thought to be the best arrangement must be made without regard to persons, and must be made quickly. I hope the House will not press me to argue these matters of merits in detail, as I certainly should not be able to comply with their wish without detriment to the public interest.

Of General Auchinleck I will only say that he is an officer of the greatest distinction, and of a character of singular elevation. He wrested victory for us at the battle of Sidi Rezegh in November, and in the early days of July he stemmed the adverse tide at El Alamein. He has at present, at his own request, gone on leave, and it is my hope that his services may be available later on in the war.

In spite of the heavy losses which I mentioned, the Army of the Western Desert is now stronger actually and relatively than it has ever been. In fact, so large have the new reinforcements which have reached this Army been, that what is to a large extent a new Army has been created while the fighting has actually been in progress. The principal measures which rendered this possible were taken before the disaster of Tobruk, and, indeed, before the opening of the battle at Gazala in May. They were part of the general preparations which, looking ahead, we made for the hazards and stresses of the Desert campaign of 1942. As far back as March last I asked President Roosevelt to lend me shipping to transport an additional 40,000 or 50,000 men to the Middle East so as to have something to veer and haul upon, so as to have a force which could be turned to the various theatres in which danger might develop. The President consented and placed at our disposal a number of American ships, and in consequence at the critical moment we had rounding the Cape a very large and well-equipped force which could be directed immediately to Egypt. It is to this that the improvement in our affairs, the maintenance of our affairs, in that region must largely be attributed. Besides this a broadening stream of drafts to replace casualties, of equipment, tanks, anti-tank guns, "Ack-Ack" guns and vehicles of all kinds has been flowing from this country and from the United States to the Middle East, and we now have in Egypt a very good, strong, well-equipped and resolute Army barring the further advance of the invader.

In the Debate on the Vote of Censure on Thursday, 2nd July, some of the Opposition speakers seemed to think that the fall of Cairo and Alexandria was only a matter of days. "Wait till Monday," "Wait till Tuesday," it was said, "and events will reinforce our criticisms." Well, we have waited, and now after more than two months I feel able to assure the House that they may be confident in our ability to maintain the successful defence of Egypt, not for days or for weeks, but for several months ahead. I say several months ahead, but I might say more. Suffice it to say that. I am strengthened in this view by the results of the heavy fighting of last week. Owing to the restraint and understatement which have been practised in the Middle East communiqués in deference to the taste of the House, the scale and intensity of these operations has not been realised, or has only now begun to be realised. General Rommel has been much hampered by the sinking of so many of his supply ships by our submarines, as well as by the British and United States air attacks renewed again from Malta and also from Egypt. Under the inconveniences resulting from their pressure, as we may suppose, he came round our Southern flank last Monday week in a major offensive with the whole German Afrika Korps, including the 90th Light Division, the two Panzer divisions, and a large part of the 20th Italian Motorised Corps. We have not been able to keep our left hand upon the Qattara depression, which dies away at this point to the Eastward, and there was plenty of room for Rommel to execute such a manœuvre. The Desert Army under its new command had, however, been reorganised in depth, and had been reinforced by every brigade, by every tank and by every gun that could be hurried forward from the Delta. I had the good fortune to visit the troops on exactly the ground where this battle took place, and I must say it seemed to me very obliging of General Rommel to have come on to us just where all the preparations had been made for his hearty reception.

This desert warfare has to be seen to be believed. Large armies, with their innumerable transport and tiny habitations, are dispersed and scattered as if from a pepper-pot over the vast indeterminate slopes and plains of the desert, broken here and there only by a sandy crease or tuck in the ground or an outcrop of rock. The ground in most places, especially on all commanding eminences, is rock with only an inch or two of sand on the top, and no cover can be obtained for guns or troops except by blasting. Scattered though the troops are, there is an elaborate system of signalling, the enormous development of which is incredible. The more improvements there are in our means of communication, the more people are required to serve the Signal Branch. But owing to this elaborate system of signalling, in which tens of thousands of people are engaged, this army, scattered over these vast areas, can be moved and brought into action with extraordinary rapidity, and enormous distances can be covered by either side in what would have seemed a few years ago to be an incredibly short space of time.

It did not seem to our commanders that General Rommel would dare to by-pass the Desert Army, with its formidable armoured striking power, and push on to Cairo, and in this they were right; but in order that the Desert Army should have the fullest freedom of manœuvre a new Army has been brought into being along the line of the Nile and the Delta, where conditions prevail totally different from those which exist in the desert. In fact, you could not have a greater contrast in every military condition than is presented at the point where cultivation begins and the desert ends. Rommel was not, however, disposed to run the risk of going round and by-passing the Army, and he strove instead to repeat the tactics he had used at Gazala. He was met not only by British armour but by British artillery used on a scale hitherto unprecedented. We had many hundreds of 25-pounders, as good a field gun as exists in the world, as well as many hundreds of 6-pounder high velocity anti-tank guns in action. We had a good superiority in armour, though we were not quite equal in the heaviest-gunned tanks, and we had once again undoubted mastery in the air. The attack of the Axis army, which had been reinforced up to 12 divisions and had also very powerful artillery, with some superiority in medium guns, and powerful armoured forces, was first brought to an abrupt standstill and then pressed slowly and steadily back with heavy losses of tanks and vehicles of all kinds. We are entitled to consider this last week's fighting as distinctly not unsatisfactory, especially when we compare it with what our position was 2½ months ago. As to the future, I can only say that the Desert Army will welcome every opportunity of fighting that is offered to it, and that further developments may be awaited with good heart by all who are watching events in that theatre.

The striking feature in this theatre is, of course, the outstanding strength and resiliency of our Air Force. Three quarters of the Air Force is British, but there are also some most gallant and efficient Australian and South African squadrons and powerful United States air groups working with the Royal Air Force. Co-operation between the Air and the Army had been brought to the very highest degree in the days of General Auchinleck, and it is now renewed between Air Chief Marshal Tedder and General Alexander and Air Vice-Marshal Conyngham and General Montgomery. The Army and Air commanders in the field live and camp together in the same moving headquarters, and the Air Force, instead of being divided among the troops, is used as a whole in characteristic fashion for their benefit and, as far as I could see, not only for their benefit but to their very great satisfaction. The Air Force has played a decisive part throughout this campaign. Without its superior power, no one can say whether we should have got thus far. But the story is only half told, and it would be inartistic to attempt to anticipate the further chapters which remain to be written.

Three times when I asked the question, "What do you think of the dive bombers?" — because I asked all sorts of questions of all sorts of people — I got the answer, "Which dive bombers?" from officers of different ranks. There is no doubt at all that our ground strafing aircraft and fighter bombers are achieving results at least equal to those of the Stukas, without being vulnerable as the Stukas are when caught unprotected by their fighter escort. The most intense exertions have been made by all the air squadrons, not only during the action but in the preparatory stages. I should not have thought it possible that such a high percentage of sorties could be maintained without detriment to health and efficiency. Nothing could exceed, however, the efficiency and ardour of all the airmen whom I saw, and nothing could exceed the admiration and good will in which the Air Force is held by its comrades in the Army. I took pains while I was there to visit and inspect almost every large formation, not only those at the front, but others which were preparing in the rear. I spent five days in this way, and was most kindly received by the troops, to whom I explained the extraordinary importance and significance of their task and its bearing upon the issues of the whole war. Their life in the fierce light of the desert, with its cool strong breezes, is hard but healthy. I have never seen an army which deserved victory more, and I await with confident hope the further unfolding of the scroll of fate.

Apart from the changes in the High Command, I reached the conclusion that the Middle East Command was too extensive in itself, and that General Auchinleck had been unduly burdened by having to consider the problems of Persia and Iraq, some 600 or 700 miles away, at the same time that he had Rommel on his hands within 50 miles of Alexandria. I therefore obtained permission from my colleagues for the detaching of Persia and Iraq from the Middle Eastern Command, and the making of a new and separate Command round the Tenth Army based on Basra and Baghdad. This sphere is given to Sir Henry Maitland-Wilson, who, from his command of the Ninth Army in Syria and Palestine, has already had opportunities of being thoroughly acquainted with the situation. The Tenth Army is being rapidly strengthened and, with the substantial Air Force which it will require, may eventually give support to the Russian left flank, and will in any case defend the soil of Persia.

During my visit to Cairo the Chief of the Imperial General Staff and I had the advantage of long consultations with General Wavell about India, with Lord Gort about Malta, and with General Platt about East Africa. In Cairo I was received by King Farouk and in Teheran by the Shah of Persia. Both these young rulers, who are also brothers-in-law, affirmed their loyalty to the cause of the United Nations, and the Shah of Persia was good enough to enter upon a most able exposition of the solid reasons which make the interests of Persia inseparable from the victory of Britain and her Allies.

The main purpose of my journey was, however, to visit Premier Stalin in Moscow. This was accomplished in two long flights with a break at Teheran. We flew across the two mountain systems, each about 300 miles wide, which lie South of the Caspian Sea and between which spread the plains and plateaus of Persia. Some of these peaks go up to 18,000 or 19,000 feet, but as we flew by day we had no need to go higher than 13,000 feet. We flew across long stretches of the Caspian Sea and up the Ural River towards Kuibyshev (formerly Samara), and reached Moscow in the afternoon.

In this part of my mission I was accompanied by Mr. Averell Harriman, President Roosevelt's Personal Representative. The House will see that it was a great advantage to me to have the support of this most able and forceful man, who spoke with the august authority of the President of the United States. We spent four days in conferences with Premier Stalin and M. Molotov, sitting sometimes for five and six hours at a time, and we went into everything with the utmost candour and thoroughness. At the same time, the Chief of the Imperial General Staff and General Wavell, who accompanied me, had further conferences with Marshals Voroshilov and Shaposhnikov, and dealt with the more technical aspects of our joint affairs. Naturally I should not give any account of the subjects we discussed, or still less of the conclusions which we reached. I have reported all these to the War Cabinet, and Mr. Harriman has reported them to President Roosevelt, but all must remain secret.

I may say, however, that the Russians do not think that we or the Americans have done enough so far to take the weight off them. This is not at all surprising, in view of the terrific onslaught which they are enduring and withstanding with such marvellous tenacity. No one in the last war would have deemed it possible that Russia could have stood up as she has been doing to the whole weight of the Teutonic armies. I say the whole weight, because, although there are 40 to 45 German divisions facing us in the West and holding down the subjugated countries, these numbers are more than made up against Russia by Finnish, Hungarian, Rumanian and Italian troops who have been dragged by Hitler into this frightful welter. It is a proof of the increased strength which Premier Stalin has given to Russia that this prodigious feat of the resistance of Russia alone to the equivalent of the whole of the Teutonic Army has been accomplished for so long and with so great a measure of success. It is difficult to make the Russians comprehend all the problems of the sea and of the ocean. We are sea animals, and the United States are to a large extent ocean animals. The Russians are land animals. Happily, we are all three air animals. It is difficult to explain fully all the different characteristics of the war effort of various countries, but I am sure that we made their leaders feel confidence in our loyal and sincere resolve to come to their aid as quickly as possible and in the most effective manner, without regard to the losses or sacrifices involved so long as the contribution was towards victory.

It was an experience of great interest to me to meet Premier Stalin. The main object of my visit was to establish the same relations of easy confidence and of perfect openness which I have built up with President Roosevelt. I think that, in spite of the accident of the Tower of Babel which persists as a very serious barrier in numerous spheres, I have succeeded to a considerable extent. It is very fortunate for Russia in her agony to have this great rugged war chief at her head. He is a man of massive outstanding personality, suited to the sombre and stormy times in which his life has been cast; a man of inexhaustible courage and will-power, and a man direct and even blunt in speech, which, having been brought up in the House of Commons, I do not mind at all, especially when I have something to say of my own. Above all, he is a man with that saving sense of humour which is of high importance to all men and all nations, but particularly to great men and great nations. Stalin also left upon me the impression of a deep, cool wisdom and a complete absence of illusions of any kind. I believe I made him feel that we were good and faithful comrades in this war — but that, after all, is a matter which deeds, not words, will prove.

One thing stands out in my mind above all others from this visit to Moscow — the inexorable, inflexible resolve of Soviet Russia to fight Hitlerism to the end until it is finally beaten down. Premier Stalin said to me that the Russian people are naturally a

The War Situation, September 8, 1942

peaceful people, but the atrocious cruelties inflicted upon them by the Germans have roused them to such a fury of indignation that their whole nature is transformed.

As I flew back to Cairo across the vast spaces, back across the Caspian Sea and the mountain ranges and deserts, I bore with me the conviction that in the British Empire, the United States and the Soviet Union, Hitler has forged an alliance of partnership which is strong enough to beat him to the ground and steadfast enough to persevere, not only until his wickedness has been punished, but until some at least of the ruin he has wrought has been repaired.

We have recently been reminded that the third anniversary of the War has come and gone, and that we are now entered upon the fourth year. We are indeed entitled, nay, bound, to be thankful for the inestimable and measureless improvements in our position which have marked the last two years. From being all alone, the sole champion left in arms against Nazi tyranny, we are now among the leaders of a majestic company of States and nations, including the greatest nations of the world, the United States and Russia, all moving forward together until absolute victory is won, and not only won but established upon unshakable foundations. In spite of all the disappointing episodes, disasters and sufferings through which we have passed, our strength has grown without halt or pause, and we can see each day that not only our own power but the weight of the United States becomes increasingly effective in the struggle.

Apart from the physical and moral dangers of the War through which we have made our way so far without serious injury, there was a political danger which at one time seemed to me, at any rate, to be a formidable threat. After the collapse of France, when the German armies strode on irresistibly in triumph and conquest, there seemed to be a possibility that Hitler might establish himself as a kind of Charlemagne in Europe, and would unite many countries under German sway, while at the same time pointing to our island as the author of the blockade and the cause of all their woes. That danger, such as it was, and I certainly did not think it negligible, has rolled away. The German is now more hated in every country in Europe than any race has been since human records began. In a dozen countries

The End of the Beginning

Hitler's firing-parties are at work every morning, and a dark stream of blood flows between the Germans and almost all their fellow men. The cruelties, the massacres of hostages, the brutal persecutions in which the Germans have indulged in every land into which their armies have broken have recently received an addition in the most bestial, the most squalid and the most senseless of all their offences, namely, the mass deportation of Jews from France, with the pitiful horrors attendant upon the calculated and final scattering of families. This tragedy fills one with astonishment as well as with indignation, and it illustrates as nothing else can the utter degradation of the Nazi nature and theme, and the degradation of all who lend themselves to its unnatural and perverted passions.

When the hour of liberation strikes in Europe, as strike it will, it will also be the hour of retribution. I wish most particularly to identify His Majesty's Government and the House of Commons with the solemn words which were used lately by the President of the United States, namely, that those who are guilty of the Nazi crimes will have to stand up before tribunals in every land where their atrocities have been committed in order that an indelible warning may be given to future ages, and that successive generations of men may say, "So perish all who do the like again."

Airgraphs to South Africa

[September 9, 1942

LAST May, when the novel means of communication by air-graph was first instituted for correspondence from the Union of South Africa to the United Kingdom, you most kindly sent me a letter by the first dispatch. Now that a two-way service is being inaugurated, I hasten to send you by the same means this message of heartfelt greeting.

I am most gratified that it has been possible in this way to overcome the handicaps of time and space which war conditions have accentuated. May the service long remain to promote mutual knowledge and friendship between our countries as a sure basis for co-operation both in war and in peace.

The Situation in India

[*September 10, 1942*

THE course of events in India has been improving, and is, on the whole, reassuring. The broad principles of the declaration made by His Majesty's Government which formed the basis of the Mission of the Lord Privy Seal to India must be taken as representing the settled policy of the British Crown and Parliament. These principles stand in their full scope and integrity. No one can add anything to them, and no one can take anything away. The good offices of the Lord Privy Seal were rejected by the Indian Congress Party. This, however, does not end the matter. The Indian Congress Party does not represent all India. It does not represent the majority of the people of India. It does not even represent the Hindu masses. It is a political organisation built around a party machine and sustained by certain manufacturing and financial interests. Outside that party and fundamentally opposed to it are the 90,000,000 Moslems in British India who have their rights of self-expression; the 50,-000,000 Depressed Classes, or the Untouchables as they are called because they are supposed to defile their Hindu co-religionists by their presence or by their shadow; and the 95,000,000 subjects of the Princes of India with whom we are bound by treaties; in all 235,000,000 in these three large groupings alone, out of about 390,000,000 in all India. This takes no account of large elements among the Hindus, Sikhs and Christians in British India who deplore the present policy of the Congress Party. It is necessary that these main facts should not be overlooked here or abroad, because no comprehension of the Indian problem or of the relations between Britain and India is possible without the recognition of these basic data.

The Congress Party has now abandoned in many respects the policy of non-violence which Mr. Gandhi has so long inculcated in theory, and has come into the open as a revolutionary movement designed to paralyse the communications by rail and telegraph and generally to promote disorder, the looting of shops and sporadic attacks upon the Indian police, accompanied from time to time by revolting atrocities — the whole having the intention or at any rate the effect of hampering the defence of India against the Japanese invader who stands on the frontiers of Assam and also upon the eastern side of the Bay of Bengal. It may well be that these activities of the Congress Party have been aided by Japanese fifth-column work on a widely-extended scale and with special direction to strategic points. It is noteworthy, for instance, that the communications of the Indian forces defending Bengal on the Assam frontier have been specially attacked.

In these circumstances the Viceroy and Government of India, with the unanimous support of the Viceroy's Council, the great majority of which are Indians, patriotic and wise men, have felt it necessary to proclaim and suppress the central and provincial organs of this association which has become committed to hostile and criminal courses. Mr. Gandhi and other principal leaders have been interned under conditions of the highest comfort and consideration, and will be kept out of harm's way till the troubles subside.

It is fortunate, indeed, that the Congress Party has no influence whatever with the martial races, on whom the defence of India apart from British Forces largely depends. Many of these races are divided by unbridgeable religious gulfs from the Hindu Congress, and would never consent to be ruled by them. Nor shall they ever be against their will so subjugated. There is no compulsory service in India, but upwards of a million Indians have volunteered to serve the cause of the United Nations in this world struggle. The bravery of the Indian troops has been distinguished in many theatres of war, and it is satisfactory to note that in these last two months, when the Congress has been measuring its strength against the Government of India, more than 140,000 new volunteers for the Army have come forward in loyal allegiance to the King-Emperor, thus surpassing all records in order to defend their native land. So far as matters have gone up to the present, they have revealed the impotence of the Congress Party either to seduce or even sway the Indian Army, to draw from their duty the enormous body of Indian officials, or still less to stir the vast Indian masses.

India is a continent, almost as large as and actually more populous than Europe, and divided by racial and above all by religious differences far deeper than any that have separated Europeans. The whole administration of the government of the 390,000,000 who live in India is carried on by Indians, there being under 600 British members of the Indian Civil Service. All the public services are working. In five provinces, including two of the greatest and comprising 110,000,000 people, provincial ministers responsible to their Legislatures stand at their posts. In many places, both in town and country, the population has rallied to the support of the civil power. The Congress conspiracy against the communications is breaking down. Acts of pillage and arson are being repressed and punished with incredibly small loss of life. Less than 500 persons have been killed over this mighty area of territory and population and it has only been necessary to move a few brigades of British troops here and there in support of the civil power. In most cases the rioters have been successfully dealt with by the Indian police. I am sure the House would wish me to pay a tribute to the loyalty and steadfastness of these brave Indian police, as well as of the Indian official classes generally, whose behaviour has been deserving of the highest praise.

To sum up, the outstanding fact which has so far emerged from the violent action of the Congress Party has been their non-representative character and their powerlessness to throw into confusion the normal peaceful life of India. It is the intention of His Majesty's Government to give all necessary support to the Viceroy and his Executive in the firm but tempered measures by which they are protecting the life of the Indian community and leaving the British and Indian Armies free to defend the soil of India against the Japanese.

I may add that large reinforcements have reached India, and that the numbers of white soldiers now in that country, though very small compared with its size and population, are larger than at any time in the British connection. I, therefore, feel entitled to report to the House that the situation in India at this moment gives no occasion for undue despondency or alarm.

The Pen and the Sword

[September 10, 1942

I CONGRATULATE you on the striking turn-out of this remarkable battalion. Philosophers have argued about whether the pen is mightier than the sword. But here we have both. I wish to compliment you on the public spirit which has enabled you by continuous sacrifice of your leisure and by attention to drill and training to produce a military unit which can take part in any game which may happen to be tried. The security of our Island from invasion cannot be achieved without the part played by those 1,750,000 men who do their regular work and, at the same time, are available at the shortest notice to defend their hearths and homes. I am sure that however the winds may blow we shall see in this Island that we are in no need to ask favours of the enemy.

Madagascar Operations Resumed

A STATEMENT TO THE HOUSE OF COMMONS
SEPTEMBER 11, 1942

[September 11, 1942

THE House will already have learned that His Majesty's Government recently decided to resume operations in Madagascar, and to seize key points on the West coast of the island from which enemy submarines might operate against our shipping in the Mozambique Channel. Majunga, Morondava and Nosi Be were assaulted in the early hours of yesterday morning and captured with little opposition and light casualties. The town of Majunga surrendered during the course of the day, and the operations against Morondava and Nosi Be were also completely successful. The operations, in which all three Services co-operated, were carried out precisely according to plan. British, Union of South Africa, East African troops and South African Air Forces took part in the operations.

China's Inspiration

[*September 16, 1942*

I AM deeply grateful for your Excellency's message on the occasion of the third anniversary of the outbreak of war between this country and Germany. I welcome your tribute all the more, coming as it does from the leader of a courageous and steadfast people, who have already withstood the onslaught of the Japanese aggressor for more than five long years. Their resistance owes much, as the British people well know, to your Excellency's resolution and unswerving loyalty to the cause of freedom, to which we have both consecrated all our energies. With such a cause to inspire us, victory is certain, and when that day dawns, as dawn it will, the British people will be proud to acclaim the Chinese as fellow-architects of victory.

Five Hundred Victory Ships in a Year

A MESSAGE IN PRAISE OF THE SHIPBUILDERS OF THE UNITED
STATES, SENT TO MR. J. G. WINANT, THE AMERICAN AMBAS-
SADOR TO GREAT BRITAIN, AND READ BY HIM IN A BROADCAST
TO HIS COUNTRYMEN
SEPTEMBER 27, 1942

[*September 27, 1942*

THE extreme measures demanded of the United Nations in
our effort to stem the tide of Axis aggression throughout the
world have produced many wonderful examples of courage, resourcefulness, and industry. One of the most remarkable is the
American shipbuilding programme. The completion of nearly
500 large ocean-going cargo vessels in the short space of the past
twelve months since the launching of the *Patrick Henry*, the first
Liberty ship, is almost unbelievable. It is a record beyond
compare.

It is an achievement far beyond even the most optimistic hopes
and expectations. Your countrymen have placed in service in the
intense sea battle a total of nearly 5,300,000 deadweight tons of
shipping during the year ending to-day. You know well, and so
do the Nazis, what this added tonnage means to the armed forces
of the United Nations who are engaging the enemy on every
battlefront of the world.

You know well what it means to the enslaved peoples of Europe
who are depending on these armed forces to free them from the
yoke of Nazi tyranny. I am glad to join in this United Nations
salute to the Victory Fleet, to the men who are building these
ships, and the men who are sailing them on the seven seas.

The faithful effort of everyone engaged in this vital programme
will take an honourable place in history, and will be remembered
through the years as a master stroke in freedom's cause.

Madagascar Operations Reviewed

A STATEMENT TO THE HOUSE OF COMMONS
SEPTEMBER 29, 1942

September 10.   *British Forces began operations to bring the whole of Madagascar under Allied control.*

September 14.   *Admiralty announced that a strong combined attack by land, sea and air had been made on Tobruk.*

September 17.   *Officially revealed that the R.A.F. were now dropping four-ton bombs on Germany.*

September 19.   *Soviet armies launched attacks at twelve points on the Russian front in effort to relieve pressure on Stalingrad.*

September 25.   *Revealed that at least forty German aircraft and two U-boats had been destroyed in an attack on a huge British convoy which had just reached Russia.*

     R.A.F. bombed an Oslo meeting as it was being addressed by Quisling.

September 27.   *General Wavell, in a speech reviewing the War, said the Germans appeared to be considerably behind their time table.*

[September 29, 1942

THE success of the initial landings and the fact that they were accomplished with only the lightest casualties to both sides were due in great measure to the efficiency of the Royal Navy and the speed with which they ferried the troops on to the beaches at the right time.

After British troops had secured the port of Majunga, motorised units of the King's African Rifles disembarked for their advance on the capital 300 miles to the south. Their first objective was the

The End of the Beginning

1,600 feet long suspension bridge over the Betsiboka River, 140 miles from Majunga. They reached this point at 9.30 A.M. on the second day, and found that the Vichy French had cut the suspension cables. Although the centre span had collapsed into the water, the infantry crossed and secured a bridgehead against slight opposition. Very shortly afterwards, the advance on the capital was resumed.

On the 16th September M. Annet, the Vichy French Governor of the island, broadcast an appeal for an armistice. One of our planes was sent to Tananarive to bring his plenipotentiaries to Majunga, where Lieut.-General Sir William Platt received them on the 17th. The French were unable to accept our terms, however, and the delegates left the next morning. Earlier on that same morning our seaborne forces appeared off the east coast port of Tamatave and called upon the town to surrender. The commandant refused and fired on our envoys, but after a brief bombardment by His Majesty's ships, the white flag was hoisted over the town at 8 A.M. Our troops landed without incident and pursued the retiring French forces to Brickaville, the principal town on the railway from Tamatave to the capital, which they captured on the 19th.

At this time, our column from Majunga had reached a point some 40 miles north of Tananarive and here they met their first serious opposition. This was overcome in two sharp engagements on the 21st and 22nd, and our forces entered the capital at midday on the 23rd. They were received with strong demonstrations of good will and even enthusiasm. Operations against the remaining Vichy French forces south of the capital are proceeding. Resistance in the northern part of the island between Diego Suarez and Majunga has collapsed, and all is now quiet in this area.

I should mention that I received news this morning that Tulear, an important port in the southern portion of the island, surrendered to an ultimatum without any bombardment being necessary.

The Prime Minister added, in reply to a question: —

I think the resistance was mainly symbolic.

Answers in the House of Commons

[September 29, 1942

When asked by a Member to make a "categorical denunciation" of Laval for his Vichy Government Policy of brutality and treachery, the Prime Minister replied:

I AM afraid I have rather exhausted the possibilities of the English language.

In reply to a Member who asked whether the Prime Minister could now assure the House that there was no lack of harmony and reciprocity in Allied war planning, or of machinery to maintain the same, Mr. Churchill said: —

Reciprocity cannot be accepted as a principle, when all concerned should do their utmost. Harmony, on the other hand, is our constant aim, and there is certainly no lack of machinery to achieve it.

In reply to a Member who asked how many times we had attacked targets on the mainland of Italy, the Prime Minister said: —

Military targets on the mainland of Italy have been attacked 104 times by the Royal Air Force. In addition there have been a number of naval bombardments, including that of Genoa on 9th February, 1941, and on the night of 10th–11th February, 1941, British parachute troops were landed in Southern Italy.

Captain Cunningham-Reid asked the Prime Minister why we have not bombed Rome.

THE PRIME MINISTER: I have nothing to add to previous statements on this subject.

The End of the Beginning

Captain Cunningham-Reid: Has the fact that we have not yet bombed this Nazi capital anything to do with Catholic susceptibilities?

THE PRIME MINISTER: I think my answer is conclusive.

Commander Locker-Lampson: Would not the bombing of Rome unite Italians and not split them?

THE PRIME MINISTER: I cannot answer hypothetical questions.

Mr. Ivor Thomas: Is the right hon. Gentleman aware that there are no military objectives in Rome?

THE PRIME MINISTER: I certainly could not accept any limiting views.

In reply to a Member who asked the Prime Minister to urge on all persons with access to inside information the need to exercise restraint in public statements or published speculations about Second Front possibilities, Mr. Churchill said: —

I welcome this opportunity of again emphasising the undesirability of public statements or speculations as to the time and place of future Allied offensive operations, even though such statements or speculations are based on inferences and not, as the question would seem to imply, on inside information.

[September 30, 1942

Replying to a Member who asked whether, in view of the visit to China of a Parliamentary deputation, both Houses of Parliament should pass a resolution of sympathy and goodwill to China, the Prime Minister said: —

THE suggestion was carefully considered. It was felt, however, that as the Lord Chancellor and the Speaker had been asked to select the personnel of the delegation it would be appropriate if the delegation were supplied with a joint letter signed by the

Answers in the House of Commons, September 30, 1942

Lord Chancellor and the Speaker to General Chiang Kai-shek expressing the admiration and sympathy felt by the British Parliament and the British people both for the Chinese people and for General Chiang Kai-shek in particular as China's leader. I think we should not in any way depart from precedent in entrusting our representations in these matters to the highest authorities in both Houses of Parliament.

When a Member interjected: Does not the right hon. Gentleman remember the record of the Lord Chancellor? the Prime Minister replied: —

If I were to try to remember everyone's record, I should be fully occupied.

[THE DIEPPE ASSAULT]

AIR SUPPORT

During the course of the operation the Military Force Commander made a signal which included the statement that air support was "faultless." The problem of air support for the Army is under constant examination.

TANKS

I understand that they were held up by the altogether unexpected strength of blocks at the ends of the streets, which it had not been anticipated they would not be able to destroy by the fire of their guns. They were, I believe, Churchill tanks, which no doubt explains the friendly interest in their performances, but I have not heard that they acquitted themselves with any marked lack of propriety.

CHURCHILL TANKS' GUN MOUNTINGS

They are under the most constant study, change and improvement. A very large number in this country are being tested in every way, but the point will, I am sure, attract the attention of the Service Departments concerned.

CASUALTIES

In my Statement of 8th September, I was referring to the assaulting force as a whole, the greater part of which were brought

231

back by the Royal Navy. There is no inconsistency with the statement of the Canadian Minister of National Defence, who was
referring only to casualties among the Canadian troops who
took part.

I do not know whether we need be so very meticulous in giving
the exact figures. The enemy have made their statement, and they
do not know how many we got back safe. I do not think there will
be any advantage in it, but the losses were very heavy and went
up to nearly one half.

*Here a Member interjected: The losses were five-sixths of the
Canadian Force, therefore the total force was 6,000, and the casualties appear to be more than half. The Prime Minister continued: —*

There seems to be some discrepancy in the arithmetic, but
the facts that I have given are correct. When I say five-sixths, I
am bound to say it might have been four-fifths. I did not myself
divide the figures. It may be that between five-sixths and a half
there might be some small discrepancy. If so, I greatly regret it.

*In reply to a Member who asked whether, in view of raids by
armed parties from Eire on Northern Ireland, an effective boundary under military control would be established, and whether
the censorship and control of travel at present in force between
two portions of the United Kingdom would be transferred to
traffic and mail between the United Kingdom and Eire, the Prime
Minister said: —*

The primary responsibility for dealing with criminal outrages,
including those in which the criminals use arms, rests on the
civil authorities, who can call for the assistance of the military
authorities if need arises. Appropriate arrangements have been
made in Northern Ireland for the provision of such assistance
if required. I understand the Government of Northern Ireland
are satisfied that the situation is well in hand. As regards control of the land boundary, careful examination has shown that
any such scheme as is suggested would not be the best method
of preventing leakage of information. For this purpose other
measures are taken which I am advised are more appropriate and

effective. It would not be practicable to adopt the proposal to dispense with the existing control over traffic and communications from Great Britain.

In reply to further questions regarding dangers of attack on the frontier and the murder of constables in Northern Ireland, the Prime Minister said: —

I have never pretended to regard the situation as satisfactory, but the arrangements made go a considerable way to mitigate the danger.

I see no reason to withdraw my trust from the regular processes of British justice.

[October 6, 1942

Replying to questions concerning Premier Stalin's statements to an American journalist about a Second Front, the Prime Minister said: —

I HAVE, of course, read and considered the statement, and we are quite clear that no statement from His Majesty's Government is called for at the present time, further than those which have already been made on this particular subject.

I would strongly advise the House not to press these matters unduly at a period which is certainly significant.

Planning for Victory

A MESSAGE TO THE CENTRAL COUNCIL OF THE NATIONAL
UNION OF CONSERVATIVE AND UNIONIST ASSOCIATIONS AT
CAXTON HALL, WESTMINSTER
OCTOBER 1, 1942

September 30.   *Hitler, in a Berlin speech, adopted a less
boastful tone and made no promises of a
speedy victory or the immediate crushing of
Russia.*

[*October 1, 1942*

I MUCH regret that the many demands upon my time will
make it impossible for me to attend the forthcoming meeting of
the Central Council, which I understand will be devoted mainly
to discussions initiated by members of the Post-War Problems
Committee.

Nothing must ever be permitted to divert our energies from
the urgent war duties that are imposed upon us, if we are to avert
from ourselves the fate that has overtaken so many forlorn countries. Neither, however, must we be taken unawares when victory
on the field of battle has at length been won. It is right and
desirable that informed forethought should be given to the complex problems of rehabilitation and reconstruction that will await
solution when the perils that now threaten us daily are over-
past.

The need to be prepared to put in hand plans of reconstruction when the moment arrives has never been absent from the
minds of H.M. Government, as is shown by the fact that certain
Ministers have been charged with this specific responsibility. But
this does not absolve the organisation of our party from pursuing its own survey, in the light of the new conditions that may
be expected to obtain when peace comes, and from making its
contribution to the common pool.

Planning for Victory, October 1, 1942

The War has brought about a tremendous disturbance, not only in our physical lives, but in the minds and hearts of men, and the work that is being steadfastly undertaken by the Central Committee and sub-committees considering these questions will provide a valuable stimulus to thought on the new political problems that peace will bring.

Being confident that these Committees share to the full my conviction that the whole-hearted prosecution of the War to its victorious conclusion is the first and greatest of our tasks, I wish them success in their labours.

" *Keep Right on to the End* "

A SPEECH IN THE USHER HALL, EDINBURGH, WHEN THE
PRIME MINISTER RECEIVED THE FREEDOM OF THE CITY
OCTOBER 12, 1942

October 4.   *In a statement on the Second Front, Premier
Stalin said he hoped the Allies would fulfil
their obligations fully and on time.*

October 7.   *As a sequel to a British landing party's raid on
Sark, the Germans announced that they would
put into chains prisoners taken in the Dieppe
raid, alleging that Germans taken prisoner on
Sark were ill treated. The British War Office
branded the German allegations as lies.*

October 10.   *It was announced that 1,376 German prisoners
would be chained as a reply to the chaining
of British prisoners by the Germans.*

[*October 12, 1942*

I HAVE never before been made a Freeman of any city, and though, during the War, I have been complimented by a number of invitations which I greatly value, your Freedom is the only one I have felt myself so far able to receive in the hard press of events. It seemed to me that Edinburgh, the ancient capital of Scotland, enshrined in the affections of the Scottish race all over the world, rich in memories and tradition, immortal in its collective personality, stands by itself; and therefore I am here to-day to be refreshed by your very great kindness and inspiration, and to receive the all too flattering tribute from my old friend, Willie Y. Darling, your Lord Provost.

The old quarrels, the age-old feuds which rent our island, have been ended centuries ago by the Union of the Crowns, and by the happy fulfilment of the prophecy that wherever the Stone of Scone shall rest the Scottish race shall reign.

"Keep Right on to the End," October 12, 1942

The whole British Empire, and, most of all, the United Kingdom of Great Britain and Northern Ireland, owes an inestimable debt to our King and Queen. In these years of trial and storm they have shared to the full the perils, the labours, the sorrows and the hopes of the British nation. I have seen the King, gay, buoyant and confident, when the stones and rubble of Buckingham Palace lay newly scattered in heaps upon its lawns. We even to-day are mourning the King's brother, who was killed on active service on a Highland hillside. You here in Scotland and in Edinburgh must especially rejoice in the charm and grace of a Scottish Queen whom Scotland has given to us all for this time of crisis.

I could not, as First Minister, come to Edinburgh, a city which has always been proud of its Royal connection, without expressing your sentiments of loyalty and devotion to our beloved Sovereign and his Consort, and paying them the tribute which their virtues and their actions alike deserve.

I come to you straight from a visit to the Fleet. I have spent the last few days going over a great many of our ships, some great, some small, some fresh from action in the Mediterranean, others from fighting their way through with the Russian convoys. I could not imagine a greater contrast between this Fleet in a harbour somewhere in Scotland and the Desert Army which I was visiting for two or three days some seven weeks ago. The scene, the light, the colour, the elements, the uniforms, the weapons, all were utterly different, but there was one feature which was not different — the spirit was the same. The Desert Army was confident that it would stand an unbreakable barrier between Rommel and the Nile Valley, and the Fleet is sure that once again it will stand between a Continental tyrant and the dominion of the world.

I have myself some ties with Scotland which are to me of great significance — ties precious and lasting. First of all, I decided to be born on St. Andrew's Day — and it was to Scotland I went to find my wife, who is deeply grieved not to be here to-day through temporary indisposition. I commanded a Scottish battalion of the famous 21st Regiment for five months in the line in France in the last war. I sat for 15 years as the representative of "Bonnie Dundee," and I might be sitting for it still if the matter had rested entirely with me. But although I have found

The End of the Beginning

what I trust is a permanent happy home in the glades of Epping Forest, I still preserve affectionate memories of the banks of the Tay. Well, here you will admit are some ties to unite me to Scotland, and now to-day you have given me a new one which I shall value as long as I live.

We call ourselves in our grand alliance the United Nations. Here, indeed, in Scotland is an example of national unity. Our present Secretary of State, our good and faithful friend, Tom Johnston, has inaugurated a notable experiment in forming an unofficial All-Party Council of State of which every living ex-Secretary of State for Scotland is a member. Such brotherhood and comradeship have yielded excellent results.

From every quarter come reports that the people of Scotland are in good heart. They are also, I am glad to learn, in good health. Here, in the fourth year of the world war, more people in Scotland are getting three square meals than ever before was known. In Glasgow, the school medical authorities report that in the last year, 1941, the latest for which we have received the figures, the average net increase in the weight of school entrants above the figures for the five years 1935–1939 was 1 lb. And boys of 13 years of age were nearly 3 lbs. heavier than those in the same period before the war.

The whole country is pulling together as it has never done before in its history. Cruel blows like the loss of the original 51st Division in France have been borne with fortitude and silent dignity. A new 51st Division has been born, and will sustain the reputation and avenge the fortunes of its forerunner. The air bombing was endured with courage and resource. In all the Services, air and land and sea, in the merchant ships, in all the many forms of service which this great struggle has called forth, Scotsmen have gained distinction. You may indeed repeat with assurance the poet's lines:

> Gin dangers dare we'll thole our share,
>   Gie's but the weapons, we've the will
> Beyont the main to prove again
>   Auld Scotland counts for something still.

Let us then for a moment cross the main and take a wider view. Our enemies have been more talkative lately. Ribbentrop, Göring and Hitler have all been making speeches which are of

238

interest because they reveal with considerable frankness their state of mind.

There is one note which rings through all these speeches; it can be clearly heard above their customary boastings and threats — the dull, low, whining note of fear. They are all speeches of men conscious of their guilt and conscious also of the law. How different from the tone of 1940 when France was struck down, when Western Europe was subjugated, when Mussolini hastened to stab us in the back, when Britain stood all alone, the sole champion in arms for the freedom and inheritance of mankind! How different are these plaintive speeches and expostulations from what we used to hear in those days!

Evidently something has happened in these two years to make these evildoers feel that aggression, war, bloodshed, the trampling down of the weak, may not be after all the whole story. There may be another side to the account. It is a long account, and it is becoming pretty clear that the day is coming when it will have to be settled. The most striking and curious part of Hitler's speech was his complaint that no one pays sufficient attention to his victories.

"Look at all the victories I have won," he exclaims in effect. "Look at all the countries I have invaded and struck down. Look at the thousands of kilometers that I have advanced into the lands of other people. Look at the booty I have gathered, and all the men I have killed and captured. Contrast these exploits with the performances of the Allies. Why are they not down-hearted and dismayed? How do they dare to keep up their spirits in the face of my great successes and their many misfortunes?"

I have not quoted his actual words. I have given their meaning and their sense. That is his complaint. That is the question which puzzles him and angers him. It strikes a chill into his marrow, because in his heart he knows that with all his tremendous victories and vast conquests his fortunes have declined, his prospects have darkened to an immeasurable degree in the last two years, while at the same time Britain, the United States, Russia, and China have moved forward through tribulation and sorrow, steadily forward, steadily onward, from strength to strength. He sees with chagrin and amazement that our defeats are but stepping-stones to victory, and that his victories are only the stepping-stones to ruin.

far — I always say so far — of his second vast campaign against Russia.

The heroic defence of Stalingrad — the fact that the splendid Russian armies are everywhere intact, unbeaten, and unbroken, nay, counterattacking with amazing energy along the whole front from Leningrad to the Caucasus Mountains, the fearful losses suffered by the German troops, the near approach of another Russian winter — all these grim facts, which cannot be concealed, cast their freezing shadow upon the German people already wincing under the increasing impact of British bombing. The German people turn with a stony gaze upon the leader who has brought all this upon them, and dumbly, for they dare not speak aloud, they put the terrible question — "Why did you go there? Why did you invade Russia?"

Already Field-Marshal Göring has made haste to point out that this decision was Hitler's alone, that Hitler alone conducts the war, and that the Generals of the German Army are only assistants who carry out his orders. Already Himmler, the police butcher, has been decorated, honoured and promoted in token not only of tho importance of hio work in ohooting and hanging thousands of Russian prisoners of war and in torturing Poles, Czechoslovaks, Yugoslavs and Greeks, but of the increasing need for his devilish arts to be employed in the homeland of Germany itself. Evidently in such a plight it would be natural for Hitler to raise a stir in some other quarter, and what could be more attractive to such a being than to mishandle captives who are powerless in his hands? There are other matters which should cause Hitler and his guilty but somewhat ridiculous confederate, Mussolini, to ask themselves uncomfortable questions.

The U-boat warfare still remains the greatest problem of the United Nations, but there is no reason whatever why it should not be solved by the prodigious measures of offence, of defence, and of replacement on which Britain, Canada and, above all, the United States, are now engaged. The months of August and September have been, I will not say the best, but the least bad months since January. These months have seen the new building of merchant ships which substantially outweigh the losses.

They have seen the greatest tonnage of British bombs dropped upon Germany. They have covered the most numerous safe arrivals of United States troops in the British Isles. They have marked a definite growth of Allied air superiority over Germany, Italy and Japan.

In these same months, far away in the Pacific, the Australians, with our American Allies, have made a good advance in New Guinea. It is not my habit to encourage light or vain expectations, but these are solid and remarkable facts.

Surveying both sides of the account — the good and the bad, with equal composure and coolness — we must see that we have reached a stern and sombre moment in the war, one which calls in a high degree for firmness of spirit and constancy of soul.

The excitement and the emotion of those great days when we stood alone and unaided against what seemed overwhelming odds and, singlehanded, saved the future of the world are not present now. We are surrounded by a concourse of Governments and nations, all of us bound together in solemn unbreakable alliance, bound together by ties not only of honour but of self-preservation. We are able to plan our slow but sure march onward. Deadly dangers still beset us. Weariness, complacency, or discord, squabbles over petty matters, would mar our prospects.

We must all drive ourselves to the utmost limit of our strength. We must preserve and refine our sense of proportion. We must strive to combine the virtues of wisdom and of daring. We must move forward together, united and inexorable.

Thus, with God's blessing, the hopes which are now justified, which we are now entitled to feel, will not fail or wither. The light is broadening on the track, and the light is brighter too. Among the qualities for which Scotland is renowned, steadfastness holds perhaps the highest place.

Be steadfast, then, that is the message which I bring to you, that is my invocation to the Scottish people, here in this ancient capital city, one of whose burgesses I now have the honour to be. Let me use the words of your famous minstrel — he is here to-day — words which have given comfort and renewed strength to many a burdened heart:

> Keep right on to the end of the road,
> Keep right on to the end.

Defence of a City

[*October 12, 1942*

THIS fine sample — for it is no more than a sample — of your Air Raid Precautions, and those engaged in them, give one confidence that should the enemy renew his attacks upon our cities — as he may do in the future — Edinburgh will be prepared to meet whatever his malice may bring. I saw a statement made the other day that the attack which may be expected this winter would make all previous attacks look like a picnic. I don't agree with that. The power of the enemy is less than it was — very much less than it was, comparatively to our power and methods of dealing with enemy night raids. At the same time it seems to me possible that, having failed in other quarters, he may attempt to make some small return for the good services which we are rendering him in the continuous bombing of German towns, which will go forward on an increasing scale from now until the end of the war. But you must be ready here — and you are ready — to meet any emergency that may come, with the customary efficiency and management for which the Scottish administration and people are distinguished. I thank you.

Chaining of Prisoners of War

[October 13, 1942

His Majesty's Government have never countenanced any general order for the tying-up of prisoners on the field of battle. Such a process, however, may be necessary from time to time under stress of circumstances, and may indeed be in the best interest of the safety of the prisoners themselves. The Geneva Convention upon the treatment of prisoners of war does not attempt to regulate what happens in the actual fighting. It is confined solely to the treatment of prisoners who have been securely captured and are in the responsible charge of the hostile Government. Both His Majesty's Government and the German Government are bound by this Convention. The German Government, by throwing into chains 1,376 British prisoners of war for whose proper treatment they are responsible, have violated Article 2 of the aforesaid Convention. They are thus attempting to use prisoners of war as if they were hostages upon whom reprisals can be taken for occurrences on the field of battle with which the said prisoners can have had nothing to do. This action of the German Government affronts the sanctity of the Geneva Convention, which His Majesty's Government have always been anxious to observe punctiliously.

His Majesty's Government have therefore approached the protecting Power and invited that Power to lay before the German Government our solemn protest against this breach of the Geneva Convention and to urge them to desist from it, in which case the counter measures of a similar character which His Majesty's Government felt themselves forced to take in order to protect their prisoners of war in enemy hands will immediately be withdrawn.

Until we learn from the protecting Power the result of this

protest, I have no further statement to make upon the subject, and I should strongly deprecate any discussion which might be prejudicial to the action of the protecting Power and consequently to the interests of the prisoners of war of both belligerent countries.

Books for the Forces

AN APPEAL ISSUED ON OCTOBER 13, 1942

[October 13, 1942

F OR the men and women of the forces at home and abroad I make an appeal to which every family in the Kingdom can respond. I do not ask for money. I ask only for books, magazines, and periodicals.

If you had seen, as I have seen on my many visits to the forces, and particularly in the Middle East, the need for something to read during the long hours off duty and the pleasure and relief when that need is met, you would gladly look, and look again, through your bookshelves and give what you can. If you hesitate to part with a book which has become an old friend, you can be sure that it will be a new friend to men on active service.

The procedure is quite simple. Almost any post office will take your books and magazines if handed in unwrapped, unstamped, and unaddressed. They will then be distributed to all the services where most required. Malta, the Middle East, Iceland, and a dozen other places abroad will welcome your gifts, and there are lonely stations at home to be supplied.

Will you contribute from your shelves, and remember when you buy a book or a magazine that there are many waiting to read it after you?

General Smuts's Visit

[October 15, 1942

FIELD–MARSHAL SMUTS, Prime Minister of the Union of South Africa and a member of the United Kingdom War Cabinet in the last War, has arrived in London. We were sure that Parliament would like to have an opportunity of meeting this illustrious statesman and soldier while in this country. He has kindly consented to address members of both Houses on an early occasion. The date, hour and place will be imparted to the House in secret session in a few minutes by the Lord Privy Seal. I hope that all members will make arrangements to be present.

" *Be Prepared* "

A MESSAGE SENT TO A PARADE OF CIVIL DEFENCE WORKERS
AT WEMBLEY AND READ BY MR. HERBERT MORRISON, HOME
SECRETARY AND MINISTER OF HOME SECURITY
OCTOBER 18, 1942

[October 18, 1942

U NDOUBTEDLY the Allies are overtaking the Germans in air power. But none of us must rest upon his laurels or remain unthinkingly content with the methods of 1940–41. We cannot know with certainty the total weight of attack which the Germans may be able, or may decide, to bring to bear upon any particular city. It may well be heavy and menacing enough to call for everything that Civil Defence can produce in order to defeat it. It is our duty to be prepared every day and at all points. This is the assumption which the national interest demands that we make.

Tribute to General Smuts

A SPEECH OF THANKS AFTER GENERAL SMUTS HAD
ADDRESSED AN ASSEMBLY OF BOTH HOUSES OF
PARLIAMENT IN LONDON
OCTOBER 21, 1942

[*October 21, 1942*

WHEN I met General Smuts in Cairo I laboured to persuade him to come and visit us here in England. I laboured because I saw that I was struggling for a great prize. I felt that his arrival in this country at a time when the war hangs heavily upon us and is tense in many respects would be a great reinforcement to our councils and our spirits. The wisdom which he brings, the knowledge which he has of all those matters upon which he has touched in his broad survey, are invaluable to those who are charged with executive responsibility, and his presence among us, as you have felt for yourselves this afternoon, is a comfort and an inspiration.

I will not detract from anything that he has said by entering upon the topics which he has covered. All that he has said arises from profound reflection — calm, quiet, profound reflection — full knowledge, and resolute, unflinching, inflexible conviction and courage.

I feel that you will allow me in your name to express to him our most profound acknowledgments, our gratitude, our thanks, for all he has done in the long years of his life, and also for the impressive statement which he has delivered to us this afternoon on what is in many ways an unprecedented occasion. I ask you all to signify your feelings by rising and giving him the acclamation which his character and his life work equally deserve.

Messages

[*October 28, 1942*

[TO THE GREEK PEOPLE ON THE SECOND ANNIVERSARY OF THE ITALIAN ATTACK ON GREECE]

A YEAR ago to-day I expressed our gratitude for what the people of Greece had done and were then doing for the Allied cause. Another year has passed during which the invaders of your land have tried by brute force and starvation to subdue the fires of Greek independence. They have failed, and your courage and spirit in adversity remain a lively inspiration to the United Nations.

Outside their own country the armed forces of Greece, the navy, army, and air force, are once again in the field already testing their growing strength in the face of the enemy, and anxious for the day, not far off now, when they will be with you and avenging your sufferings.

The British people greet you in admiration and sympathy, and in the firm confidence that the day of freedom will surely dawn.

[*October 29, 1942*

[TO A MEETING HELD AT THE ROYAL ALBERT HALL, LONDON, TO PROTEST AGAINST GERMAN ATROCITIES]

THE systematic cruelties to which the Jewish people — men, women, and children — have been exposed under the Nazi regime are amongst the most terrible events of history, and place an indelible stain upon all who perpetrate and instigate them.

Free men and women denounce these evil crimes, and when this world struggle ends with the enthronement of human rights, racial persecution will be ended.

[October 30, 1942

[TO THE SCOTTISH UNIONISTS' CONFERENCE
AT GLASGOW]

WE are refraining from the normal activities of party politics while all parties are co-operating together in the bitter struggle to win the war. Victory in the war is essential to our life as a nation and as free individuals, and every effort from every man and woman in the country is required for its achievement. Nevertheless our future depends also upon a democratic system which operates through Parliament, and people who believe in the same principle and have the same object in view must co-operate to achieve their purpose.

Coal and War

SPEECH TO THE CONFERENCE OF DELEGATES OF COAL-
OWNERS AND MINERS, HELD AT THE WESTMINSTER
CENTRAL HALL
OCTOBER 31, 1942

[*October 31, 1942*

WAR is made with steel, and steel is made with coal. This is the first and only industry I have addressed as an industry during the time of my responsibility. I am doing so because coal is the foundation and, to a very large extent, the measure of our whole war effort. I thought it would be a good thing if we met in private. The Press are our good friends, they play their part in the battle, a valuable part and an indispensable part, but the difficulty about making reported speeches is — look at all the ears that listen, look at the different audiences that have to be considered! So, if you will allow me to say so, I thought it would be a compliment to the coal industry if I, in my position, and the other Ministers who are here, came and had a talk in private with you about our great affairs. Of course, I cannot see the whole of the coal industry, but I have come here to give you first-hand guidance, and I am going to ask you to go back to your pits as the ambassadors of His Majesty's Government, to tell them the impressions you have formed and assist to the utmost in promoting the common cause.

I am very glad indeed to see the success Gwilym is making of his extremely hard job. He bears a name which is a household word, and he is adding the distinction which a second generation can impart to such a name: the distinction of great services rendered by the father, sustained and carried forward by the son. I am told that in the few months since he has been Minister of Fuel, Power and Light, out of 1,600 Pit Production Committees he has actually visited and addressed 714. No one can say that he is sparing himself, and no one can say that his exertions have gone without response. The output has improved in recent weeks, and I well know what an effort that must require because of the adverse circumstances which war-time conditions impose upon production, but still it is not enough. As he told you just now, the great munition plants are coming into production. Factories, plants and mills begun two years ago are now completed. The population has been assembled, the workers are there, and the great wheels are turning, turning out the apparatus of war, and they are consuming in many cases 40 per cent more fuel, largely in the form of gas, than was the case last year. This comes to us at a time of special necessity. We are making the utmost economies compatible with the health and welfare of the people in the consumption of fuel, but such economies as we can make cannot achieve the results necessary to bridge the gap between the growing consuming power of the great war plants and the existing supply. Besides, I do not want to cut the cottage homes too sharply. The people must have warmth for their spirits and for their war efficiency, and one can easily go too far in that direction.

The White Paper has placed the coal industry upon the basis of national service for the duration of the war, and for a further period until Parliament has reviewed the scheme in the light of the experience gained. I therefore come here to-day to call upon everyone in that industry, managements and miners alike, hand in hand, to sweep away all remaining obstacles to maximum production. That is the object with which this meeting is called, but here let me say this. I am very sorry that we have had to debar so many miners from going to the war in the Armed Forces. I respect their feelings, but we cannot afford it; we cannot allow it. Besides the need for their services in the pits, there is danger in the pits too, and where there is danger there is honour. "Act well thy part, there all the honour lies," and that is the motto I want to give out to all those who in an infinite variety of ways are playing an equally worthy part in the consummation of our high purpose.

But I have not come to address you mainly about coal. I have come to talk mainly about war, and that is why I brought the Field-Marshal [Smuts] with me. It was a surprise, but also a prize. He and I are old comrades. I cannot say there has never been a kick in our gallop. I was examined by him when I was a prisoner of war, and I escaped; but we made an honourable and generous peace on both sides, and for the last forty years we have been comrades working together. I was very glad to entice him over here. He has great duties to discharge in South Africa. He holds that gateway to our brothers in Australia and New Zealand and the Middle East. He holds that gateway faithfully and surely, for — to quote his own famous phrase, although not everybody knows it is his own phrase — for the British Commonwealth of Nations, and, as you all feel he may justly say, for purposes which are wider and larger and longer even than the British Commonwealth of Nations.

You, Major Lloyd George, have spoken about the past, about the crisis of 1940, and we ought from time to time to look back to that astonishing experience in our lives. Unprepared, almost unarmed, left alone, this country never flinched. With one voice it defied the tyrant. That was indeed our finest hour, and it was from that hour that our deliverance came. We had in this small Island, this Island lost in the northern mists, rendered a service to the whole world which will be acknowledged even when a thousand years have passed.

This brings me to a point which I will venture to mention. I do not think the British have any need to apologise for being alive. When I see critics in other countries, and not only in other countries, and a stream of criticism which would suggest that we were an unworthy nation; that we were an exploiting nation; that our contribution to world progress has been wanting, nothing is less true. Well was it for Europe, well was it for the world, that the light shone out which the British people had carefully nourished, that a light shone out from this Island to guide them all forward upon their paths. Therefore, I am not going to apologise, and I have to pick my words carefully here, for the fact that we are alive, still alive and kicking. But, Mr. Chairman, I frankly admit that we owe much to the mistakes of our enemies. We have made mistakes, we have made miscalculations; but we are being saved from the consequences of our shortcomings by the incomparably greater mistakes and blunders which these all-wise glittering dictators have perpetrated. Look at the mistake that Hitler made in not trying invasion in 1940. Mind you, he tried, tentatively, but the Royal Air Force crushed him. He did attempt to destroy our air fields, our air organisation and our aircraft factories; he tried; but I have often asked myself what would have happened if he had in fact put three-quarters of a million men on board all the barges and boats and let them stream across and taken the chance of losing three-quarters of them. There would have been a terrible shambles in this country, because we had hardly a weapon; we had not at that time fifty tanks, whereas we now have 10,000 or 12,000. We had not at that time fifty tanks; we had a couple of hundred field guns, some of them brought out of the museums; we had lost all our equipment at Dunkirk and in France; and indeed we were spared an agonising trial. Of course, we should have gone on fighting, but modern weapons, the weapons made, forged and shaped by modern science and industry, give a terrible advantage against people almost entirely without them, however brave they may be, however ready to give their lives, however proud to give their lives they may be. Well, at any rate, without entering into an attempt to pass final judgment on whether he would have succeeded or not, I am quite content that he did not try, or that he did not try more than he did. But what about the next mistake? I am bound to say I thought it very likely in the early Summer that he would attack Turkey and try to by-pass Russia, but it soon became clear, some weeks before, that he intended to invade Russia in order to steal the larger part of the Russian cornlands and factories and to make it into a great slave area ruled over by the *Herrenvolk;* but he reckoned without his host. He invaded Russia to find a nation of people ready to fight and die with a valour and steadfastness which none can excel. That was a great mistake. Another mistake was his forgetting about the Russian Winter. You know, it gets cold there, very cold indeed. The snow falls down and lies on the ground, and an icy wind blows in across the Steppes. He overlooked that point, and I expect he has overlooked it again, now that his second campaign against Russia is ending in frustration. Another mistake of our foes was made by Japan when they attacked the United States at Pearl Harbour instead of attacking us alone who were already busy with Italy and Germany in Europe. It was most fortunate that, led away by their dark conspiracies and schemes, dizzy and dazzled from poring over plans, they sprang out upon a peaceful nation with whom they were at that time in peaceful parley, and were led away and tottered over the edge and, for the sake of sinking half a dozen ships of war and beating up a naval port, brought out against them the implacable energies and the measureless power of the 130 million educated people who live in the United States. We have much to be thankful for.

I sometimes have a feeling, in fact I have it very strongly, a feeling of interference. I want to stress that. I have a feeling sometimes that some guiding hand has interfered. I have the feeling that we have a guardian because we serve a great cause, and that we shall have that guardian so long as we serve that cause faithfully. And what a cause it is! One has only to look at the overwhelming evidence which pours in day by day of the bestial cruelties of the Nazis and the fearful misery of Europe in all the lands into which they have penetrated; the people ground down, exploited, spied upon, terrorised, shot by platoons of soldiers, day after day the executions, and every kind of petty vexation added to those dark and bloody acts of terrorism. Think what they would do to us if they got here. Think what they would do to us, we who have barred their way to the loot of the whole world, we whom they hate the most because they dread and envy us the most. Think what they would do to us.

I said just now that we have had to forbid miners to go into the Armed Forces, and how much I feel we owe you an apology for that, but I must now say that, with my responsibilities, I cannot let miners who have been trained as soldiers leave the Army in large numbers. The miners are amongst the best fighting men we have. The Army needs them, and you would wreck every platoon and every section if you pulled out those men who have made their friends and made their comradeships and know the work and have been trained for over two years in many cases. I have to think of the strength and efficiency of the Army. First, we have to ward off invasion. That for the moment is not a danger, but the danger may come back. First we had to ward off invasion all through the Summer and Winter of 1940 and through the Spring and Summer of 1941, and then, after the attack began on Russia, we were easier in that respect, but we had to be ready for it; and now we are again thinking about invasion, but invasion the other way round, invasion not to conquer and pillage, invasion to liberate and rescue. That is what is in our minds. All Europe is seething under the Nazi yoke. The Army must be ready. It must be ready when the opportunity comes, as come it will, so some must stay in the pits and others must stay in the Army. Both are needed, both are equally needed, and for both there is equal credit.

Now let me speak about the dangers which lie ahead. The first of all our dangers is the U-boat peril. That is a very great danger. Our food, our means of making war, our life, all depend upon the passage of ships across the sea. The whole power of the United States to manifest itself in this war depends upon the power to move ships across the sea. Their mighty power is restricted, it is restricted by those very oceans which have protected them. The oceans which were their shield have now become a bar, a prison house, through which they are struggling to bring armies, fleets and air forces to bear upon the great common problems we have to face. Now we see our way through. I say that with all solemnity and sobriety. We see our way through. Although it is true that there will be many more U-boats working next year than there are now, and there may be 300 to 400 at work now, yet we have a vast construction of escort vessels, submarine-hunting vessels, afoot, as well as replacements of merchant ships; and in the United States, which has resources in steel far greater than ours and which is not so closely and deeply involved at present, a programme on astronomical lines has been developed and is being carried forward in the construction both of escort vessels and of merchant ships. But what a terrible waste it is to think of all these great ships that are sunk, full of priceless cargoes, and how necessary it is to make that extra intensification of effort which will enable us to get ahead and to establish more complete mastery and so save these ships from being sunk, as well as adding new ones to the Fleet, by which alone the victory of the good cause can be achieved.

There is a second danger. You must never underrate the power of the German machine. It is the most terrible machine that has been created. After the last war they kept the brains of the

German Army together. They kept their Great Staff together. Although their weapons were taken away, this tremendous association of people who think about nothing but war, studying war, ruthless scientific war, was held together, thousands of them, and they were able to train and build up an Army which, as you saw, in a few weeks shattered to pieces the once famous Army of France, and which has marched into country after country and laid it low, and laid low every form of opposition, and only now in the vast spaces of Russia is confronted with this immense and valiant race which has stood against them; only now has the resistance of superior numbers made them pay the terrible toll of probably over 4,000,000 lives or men disabled; only now; but do not let us delude ourselves. Hitler lies in the centre, and across all the great railway lines of Europe he can move very rapidly forces from one side to the other. He may close down on one front and open up on another. He has now, across in France and the Low Countries, a German Army as large as we have in this country, apart of course from the Home Guard. That is our great standby against parachute invasion. When I see the number of Divisions there are in France and realise that he can bring back in a few months, at any time in the Spring, 60 or 70 more Divisions, while perhaps lying quiescent or adopting a defensive attitude or perhaps giving some ground on the Russian front, I cannot feel that the danger of invasion can be put out of our minds. After all, if these men can strike us and strike us at the heart, the world is theirs. We are the target. We are the prize. We have sent and are sending many troops away. We are fighting very hard in Egypt now. That battle has only just begun. It is going to be a fight through to a finish. We have sent half a million men from this country to Egypt, to India, to the great regions which lie south of the Caspian Sea, during this present year alone. We must be ready. We must be ready here at the centre, not only to take advantage of any weakness on their part, but to be prepared to ward off any counter-stroke which they may cast upon us. Do not let people suggest to you that the major dangers of this war are past. We got through one supreme crisis where we might have been snuffed out, and now I do not think such a crisis can recur only because we are armed, because we are ready, because we are organised, because we have the weapons, because we have great numbers of trained men. But do not let us suppose that the dangers are past, even though mortal danger was warded off two years ago.

There is a third danger, and it presents itself in a less precisely defined form. The last hope of the guilty Huns is a stalemate. Their idea has been made very plain in a series of speeches all delivered in the last month by Hitler, Göring, Goebbels and others, all defining and describing one conception, the idea of making a vast fortress of the greater part of Europe, with the Russian cornfields worked by slaves from the subjugated nations and by the prisoners of war, of whom they have several million, of organising a great European arsenal out of all the factories of the conquered countries, of starving and disciplining everyone in this great fortress area in order to feed the master race, and so hold out for years and years hoping that we shall get tired and fall out amongst ourselves and make a compromise peace, which means, and can only mean, that they will begin again. That is the third danger, and in some ways I think you will admit it is the most insidious of all.

How, then, are we to make sure of shortening the War? It is said we ought to concert our war plans. Well, everyone would agree to that. There is an obstacle, however, which should not escape attention — geography. You remember that thing we used to learn at school — all those maps; geography. We do the best we can to get over geography. The Field-Marshal and I fly to and fro wherever we have to go, for no other purpose than to bring into the closest possible concert the plans of the principal different nations on whom our alliance depends, and one of these fine days — mark my words — you will see whether we have been idle and whether we are quite incapable of design and action.

My Lords and Gentlemen, we have great Allies. We are no longer alone. Thirty nations march with us. Russia has come in, the United States have come in, there is another great ally on the way — supremacy in the air. We have got that supremacy in Egypt now. Presently we shall have it everywhere. Already we are blasting their war industries, already they are receiving what they gave, with interest — with compound interest. Soon they will get a bonus. Help us in all this. I know you will. All depends upon inflexible willpower based on the conviction shared by a whole people that the cause is good and righteous. Let it be the glory of our country to lead this world out of the dark valley into the broader and more genial sunshine. In the crisis of 1940, it is no more than the sober truth to say, we saved the freedom of mankind. We gave Russia time to arm, and the United States to organise; but now it is a long cold strain we have to bear, harder perhaps for the British to bear than the shocks which they know so well how to take. We must not cast away our great deliverance; we must carry our work to its final conclusion. We shall not fail, and then some day, when children ask "What did you do to win this inheritance for us, and to make our name so respected among men?" one will say: "I was a fighter pilot"; another will say: "I was in the Submarine Service"; another: "I marched with the Eighth Army"; a fourth will say: "None of you could have lived without the convoys and the Merchant Seamen"; and you in your turn will say, with equal pride and with equal right: "We cut the coal."

* * * *

In the name of His Majesty's Government, representing all Parties, and personally, from the bottom of my heart, I thank you most profoundly.

Messages

[November 4, 1942

[FOR THE FIRST ISSUE TO BE PRINTED IN ENGLAND
OF THE UNITED STATES ARMY MAGAZINE *YANK*]

FIVE months ago your Commander-in-Chief in his message
to the first issue of *Yank* described you as the delegates of freedom.
Since then the people of Great Britain have seen with pride and
confidence the ever-increasing numbers of American troops arriving in this country. Now in this first issue of *Yank* to be printed
in London, I myself should like to welcome to these Islands all
of you who are taking part in the European theatre of operations.

I hope that when you and your British comrades in arms will
have brought freedom to the enslaved continent of Europe, some
of you will return to this country from America in the happier
days of peace to renew the friendships which you are making now.
In the meantime, I am sure that you will find this London edition
of *Yank* a welcome link with your families at home as well as
with your comrades serving in the other theatres of war. May its
fortunes and yours prosper.

[November 5, 1942

[TO MR. JOHN CURTIN, THE PRIME MINISTER
OF AUSTRALIA]

I SEND you my warmest congratulations upon the fresh distinction gained by the 9th Australian Division under General
Morshead in the memorable Battle of Egypt. They have played
a glorious part in what may well become a decisive victory.

Messages, November 7, 1942

(Similar messages were sent to Mr. Peter Fraser, Prime Minister of New Zealand, praising the 2nd New Zealand Division, under General Freyberg, and to Mr. Hofmeyr, Acting Prime Minister of South Africa, praising the S. A. Division, under General Pinaar.)

[November 7, 1942

[TO GENERAL PLATT ON THE SUCCESSFUL CONCLU-
SION OF THE CAMPAIGN IN MADAGASCAR]

I OFFER you my most cordial congratulations upon the success of your Madagascar task. Exceptional zeal and enterprise were shown by you and the naval authorities in undertaking this campaign in spite of very great reductions which, on account of other needs, you had to suffer in the forces available. The thoroughness with which the operations were prepared and the speed and vigour with which they were carried through are highly creditable to all ranks, in particular to Major-General Smallwood and your staff, and, above all, to yourself.

" *The End of the Beginning* "

A SPEECH AT THE LORD MAYOR'S DAY LUNCHEON
AT THE MANSION HOUSE, LONDON
NOVEMBER 10, 1942

October 13.	*Reported that six Japanese warships had been sunk in a battle off the Solomons.*
	General Smuts arrived in London for war conferences.
October 16.	*After attacking Malta for six days, the Axis losses totalled 103 planes.*
October 17.	*It was announced that U.S. troops had arrived in Liberia and that R.A.F. patrols against U-boats were operating from Liberian bases.*
October 20.	*News was released that H.M.S. Anson and H.M.S. Howe, new battleships of the King George V class, had joined the Fleet. Mr. Alexander, First Lord of the Admiralty, stated that since the war began more than 530 Axis submarines had been destroyed or damaged.*
October 21.	*General Smuts, addressing Members of both Houses of Parliament, said: "The stage is now set for the last, the offensive phase of the War."*
October 23.	*Mrs. Roosevelt arrived in London after flying the Atlantic.*
October 24.	*Britain launched a great attack in Egypt by land, sea and air — the start of the great North African offensive.*
	R.A.F. bombed Milan in daylight.
October 30.	*Japanese Fleet withdrew from the Battle of the Solomons after losing several big ships.*
November 4.	*General Alexander announced a great British*

> *victory in Egypt after eleven days of fierce fighting, Axis forces being in full and disordered retreat. British troops captured General von Thoma, Commander of the German Afrika Korps, and destroyed 260 tanks and 600 planes.*

November 6.   *Officially announced that hostilities had ceased in Madagascar and an armistice been signed.*

November 7.   *Opening of a great new front. British and American forces, under the command of the U.S. General Eisenhower, and supported by the Royal Navy and the R.A.F., landed at many points in French North Africa and quickly occupied Algiers, Oran, Casablanca and other important cities. At the other end of North Africa the retreat of the Axis forces became a complete rout.*

[November 9, 1942

I NOTICE, my Lord Mayor, by your speech that you had reached the conclusion that the news from the various fronts has been somewhat better lately. In our wars the episodes are largely adverse, but the final results have hitherto been satisfactory. Away we dash over the currents that may swirl around us, but the tide bears us forward on its broad, resistless flood. In the last war the way was uphill almost to the end. We met with continual disappointments, and with disasters far more bloody than anything we have experienced so far in this one. But in the end all the oppositions fell together, and all our foes submitted themselves to our will.

We have not so far in this war taken as many German prisoners as they have taken British, but these German prisoners will no doubt come in in droves at the end just as they did last time. I have never promised anything but blood, tears, toil, and sweat. Now, however, we have a new experience. We have victory — a remarkable and definite victory. The bright gleam has caught the helmets of our soldiers, and warmed and cheered all our hearts. The late M. Venizelos observed that in all her wars England — he should have said Britain, of course — always wins one battle — the last. It would seem to have begun rather earlier this time. General Alexander, with his brilliant comrade and lieutenant, General Montgomery, has gained a glorious and decisive victory in what I think should be called the Battle of Egypt. Rommel's army has been defeated. It has been routed. It has been very largely destroyed as a fighting force.

This battle was not fought for the sake of gaining positions or so many square miles of desert territory. General Alexander and General Montgomery fought it with one single idea. They meant to destroy the armed force of the enemy, and to destroy it at the place where the disaster would be most far-reaching and irrecoverable.

All the various elements in our line of battle played their parts — Indian troops, Fighting French, the Greeks, the representatives of Czechoslovakia and the others who took part. The Americans rendered powerful and invaluable service in the air. But as it happened as the course of the battle turned — it has been fought throughout almost entirely by men of British blood from home and from the Dominions on the one hand, and by Germans on the other. The Italians were left to perish in the waterless desert or surrender as they are doing.

The fight between the British and the Germans was intense and fierce in the extreme. It was a deadly grapple. The Germans have been outmatched and outfought with the very kind of weapons with which they had beaten down so many small peoples, and also large unprepared peoples. They have been beaten by the very technical apparatus on which they counted to gain them the domination of the world. Especially is this true of the air and of the tanks and of the artillery, which has come back into its own on the battlefield. The Germans have received back again that measure of fire and steel which they have so often meted out to others.

Now this is not the end. It is not even the beginning of the end. But it is, perhaps, the end of the beginning. Henceforth Hitler's Nazis will meet equally well armed, and perhaps better armed troops. Henceforth they will have to face in many theatres of war that superiority in the air which they have so often used without mercy against others, of which they boasted all round the world, and which they intended to use as an instrument for convincing all other peoples that all resistance to them was hopeless. When I read of the coastal road crammed with fleeing German vehicles under the blasting attacks of the Royal Air Force, I could not but remember those roads of France and Flanders, crowded, not with fighting men, but with helpless refugees — women and children — fleeing with their pitiful barrows and household goods, upon whom such merciless havoc was wreaked. I have, I trust, a humane disposition, but I must say I could not help feeling that what was happening, however grievous, was only justice grimly reclaiming her rights.

It will be my duty in the near future to give to Parliament a full and particular account of these operations. All I will say of them at present is that the victory which has already been gained gives good prospect of becoming decisive and final so far as the defence of Egypt is concerned.

But this Battle of Egypt, in itself so important, was designed and timed as a prelude and counterpart of the momentous enterprise undertaken by the United States at the western end of the Mediterranean — an enterprise under United States command in which our Army, Air Force, and, above all, our Navy, are bearing an honourable and important share. Very full accounts have been published of all that is happening in Morocco, Algeria, and Tunis. The President of the United States, who is Commander-in-Chief of the armed forces of America, is the author of this mighty undertaking, and in all of it I have been his active and ardent lieutenant.

You have no doubt read the declaration of President Roosevelt, solemnly endorsed by His Majesty's Government, of the strict respect which will be paid to the rights and interests of Spain and Portugal, both by America and Great Britain. Towards those countries our only policy is that they shall be independent and free, prosperous and at peace. Britain and the United States will do all that they can to enrich the economic life of the Iberian Peninsula. The Spaniards especially, after all their troubles, require and deserve peace and recuperation.

At this time our thoughts turn towards France, groaning in

bondage under the German heel. Many ask themselves the question: Is France finished? Is that long and famous history, adorned by so many manifestations of genius and valour, bearing with it so much that is precious to culture and civilisation, and above all to the liberties of mankind — is all that now to sink for ever into the ocean of the past, or will France rise again and resume her rightful place in the structure of what may one day be again the family of Europe? I declare to you here, on this considerable occasion, even now when misguided or suborned Frenchmen are firing upon their rescuers, I declare to you my faith that France will rise again. While there are men like General de Gaulle and all those who follow him — and they are legion throughout France — and men like General Giraud, that gallant warrior whom no prison can hold, while there are men like those to stand forward in the name and in the cause of France, my confidence in the future of France is sure.

For ourselves we have no wish but to see France free and strong, with her Empire gathered round her and with Alsace-Lorraine restored. We covet no French possession; we have no acquisitive appetites or ambitions in North Africa or any other part of the world. We have not entered this war for profit or expansion, but only for honour and to do our duty in defending the right.

Let me, however, make this clear, in case there should be any mistake about it in any quarter. We mean to hold our own. I have not become the King's First Minister in order to preside over the liquidation of the British Empire. For that task, if ever it were prescribed, someone else would have to be found, and, under democracy, I suppose the nation would have to be consulted. I am proud to be a member of that vast commonwealth and society of nations and communities gathered in and around the ancient British monarchy, without which the good cause might well have perished from the face of the earth. Here we are, and here we stand, a veritable rock of salvation in this drifting world.

There was a time, not long ago, when for a whole year we stood all alone. Those days, thank God, have gone. We now move forward in a great and gallant company. For our record we have nothing to fear, we have no need to make excuses or apologies.

"*The End of the Beginning*," *November 10, 1942*

Our record pleads for us, and will gain gratitude in the breasts of free men and women in every part of the world.

As I have said, in this war we desire no territorial gains and no commercial favours; we wish to alter no sovereignty or frontier for our own benefit or profit. We have come into North Africa shoulder to shoulder with our American friends and Allies for one purpose, and one purpose only — namely, to gain a vantage ground from which to open a new front against Hitler and Hitlerism, to cleanse the shores of Africa from the stain of Nazi and Fascist tyranny, to open the Mediterranean to Allied sea power and air power, and thus effect the liberation of the peoples of Europe from the pit of misery into which they have been cast by their own improvidence and by the brutal violence of the enemy.

These two African undertakings, in the east and in the west, were part of a single strategic and political conception which we have laboured long to bring to fruition, and about which we are now justified in entertaining good and reasonable confidence. Thus, taken together, they were two aspects of a grand design, vast in its scope, honourable in its motive, noble in its aim. The British and American affairs continue to prosper in the Mediterranean, and the whole event will be a new bond between the English-speaking peoples and a new hope for the whole world.

I recall to you some lines of Byron, which seem to me to fit the event, the hour, and the theme: —

> Millions of tongues record thee, and anew
> Their children's lips shall echo them, and say —
> "Here, where the sword united nations drew,
> Our countrymen were warring on that day!"
> And this is much, and all which will not pass away.

Armistice in Madagascar

A STATEMENT TO THE HOUSE OF COMMONS
NOVEMBER 10, 1942

[*November 10, 1942*

Since my last statement on the Madagascar operations our forces have continued to advance southwards, hampered by road blocks and obstructions. On 2nd October there was a sharp engagement approximately seventy miles south of the capital, as a result of which Antsirabe was occupied. The local populace gave our troops an enthusiastic welcome. The Vichy resistance was next encountered about 130 miles south of Tananarive, but as a result of vigorous action by our Forces, Ambositra and Ivato were occupied on 19th October. The last organised resistance north of Fianarantsoa, which is the chief town in the south of the island and is approximately 180 miles south of the capital, was overcome on 29th October, and the town was occupied on the evening of the same day. Upwards of 1,000 prisoners were taken during this period.

The advance southwards continued, but a French emissary arrived at our forward brigade headquarters on 5th November and asked for an armistice. At 2 o'clock in the afternoon hostilities ceased. The armistice was signed at midnight on 5th–6th November, and everything is proceeding very smoothly.

Between 10th September — when further operations in Madagascar began with the assault on Majunda — and 17th October we lost only 17 killed and 45 wounded. Since 17th October our casualties have been extremely light, but details are not known.

The War Situation

A SPEECH TO THE HOUSE OF COMMONS
NOVEMBER 11, 1942

November 11. Admiral Darlan threw in his lot with the Allied forces in North Africa and ordered all French forces to surrender.

Axis forces marched into Unoccupied France and also flew troops to seize Bizerta, Tunis and other points in Tunisia.

The King opened a new session of Parliament.

[*November 11, 1942*

THE custom has always been to compliment the Mover and Seconder of the Address upon the speeches which they have delivered, and very often those compliments have been well founded. I am sure that the House, without distinction of party, will feel that that is the case to-day. My hon. Friend the Member for South Bristol (Mr. Walkden) speaks as the representative of one of the great trade unions of the country, those institutions which lie so near the heart and core of our social life and progress, and have proved that stability and progress can be combined. He speaks in that capacity, and my hon. and gallant Friend the Member for Stafford (Major Thornycroft), who has not been very long in this House, has already begun to find his feet here, and the speech which he has made to-day gives every assurance that he will play a valuable and increasing part in our Debates. I should like to express to both hon. Members my acknowledgments of the extremely kind and complimentary remarks which they have made about me. Really their whole outlook has been one of extreme benevolence to the Government, to its head, to our fortunes in war, and also to the admirable constituencies which they represent. I thank them both for the part which they have played.

We meet in a time of great stress, when events are moving very fast, and when final views cannot easily or lightly be taken. I have, however, to tell the House about the great Battle of Egypt, which is a British victory of the first order, and also about the other half of the combination, namely, the United States and British intervention in North Africa.

There are three points which must be duly examined in matters of this magnitude and violence. First, the time required for preparation. Secondly, the need of combination and concert. And thirdly, the importance of surprise. I will address myself to these points in the course of my statement. Here let me say that the pressure at present is extreme, and I must ask for the indulgence of the House if, in any part of my statement, I should lack full historical precision. I have not had the time to give the mature consideration to the exact balance between the different elements and forces involved that would be possible in ordinary times. I do the best I can.

Taking first the question of time, it is not generally realised how much time these great operations take to mount. For instance, the British divisions which have reinforced the Eighth Army for this battle left England in May or early June. Most of the 6-pounders we have been and are now using in so many hundreds were dispatched before the fall of Tobruk. This also applies to the more heavily armoured and more heavily gunned British tanks. As for the American tanks — the admirable Shermans — they came to us in the following way.

On that dark day when the news of the fall of Tobruk came in, I was with President Roosevelt in his room at the White House. The House knows how bitter a blow this was. But nothing could have exceeded the delicacy and kindness of our American friends and Allies. They had no thought but to help. Their very best tanks — the Shermans — were just coming out of the factories. The first batch had been newly placed in the hands of the divisions who had been waiting for them and looking forward to receiving them. The President took a large number of these tanks back from the troops to whom they had just been given. They were placed on board ship in the early days of July, and they sailed direct to Suez, under American escort for a considerable part of the voyage. The President also sent us a large number of self-propelled 105 mm. guns, which are most useful weapons for contending with the 88 mm. high velocity guns of which the Germans have made so much use. One ship in this convoy — this precious convoy — was sunk by a U-boat, but immediately, without being asked, the United States replaced it with another ship carrying an equal number of these weapons. All these tanks and high velocity guns played a recognisable part, indeed an important part, in General Alexander's battle.

When I was in Egypt in the early days of August I visited myself every unit which was to be armed with these tanks and guns, some of them the most seasoned regiments we have, including the Yeomanry Division. But, alas, they had no weapons adequate for the fight, and even those they had had been taken away from them in the stress of General Auchinleck's battle. I was able to tell those troops that the very finest weapons that existed would soon be in their possession; that these came direct from the President, and that, meanwhile, they must prepare themselves by every form of exercise and training for their use when they were delivered. That was at the beginning of August. But none of these units was ready to fight in the repulse of Rommel's attack in the second battle of Alamein, although all of them were ready for action by 23rd October when we began what I call the Battle of Egypt. Thus, you will see that the decision taken by the President on 20th June took four months to be operative, although the utmost energy and speed were used at each stage. Records were broken at every point in the unloading and fitting-up of the weapons and in their issue to the troops, but it was indispensable that the men should also have reasonable training in handling them. One may say, in fact, that between taking the decision for reinforcing the Middle East for a great operation and the reinforcements coming into action, a period of five months or even more has been required.

Thus, before the Vote of Censure in the early days of July, all measures in our power had already been taken, first to repel the enemy's further assaults, and, secondly, to take decisive offensive action against him. See, then, how silly it is for people to imagine that Governments can act on impulse or in immediate response to pressure in these large-scale offensives. There must be planning, design and forethought, and after that a long period of silence, which looks — I can quite understand it — to the ordinary spectator as if it were simply apathy or inertia, but which is, in fact, steady indispensable preparation for the blow. Moreover, you have first to get sufficient ascendancy even to prepare to strike such a blow.

I am certainly not one of those who need to be prodded. In fact, if anything, I am a prod. My difficulties rather lie in finding the patience and self-restraint to wait through many anxious weeks for the results to be achieved. And because a Government cannot at every moment give an explanation of what it is doing and what is going on, it would be, and it will be, a great mistake to assume that nothing is being done. In my view, everything in human power was done, making allowance for the fallibility of human judgment. We re-created and revivified our war-battered Army, we placed a new Army at its side, and rearmed it on a gigantic scale. By these means we repaired the disaster which fell upon us, and converted the defence of Egypt into a successful attack.

Of course, if we had not had the disaster, the measures taken in the hopes of better fortune would have carried us by now far on the road to Tripoli; but what was prepared to lead on to success came in as a means of retrieving failure. The failure has delayed our operations. Our position, in time, has been set back. Still, there are consolations. The losses to the enemy in all this Egyptian fighting have been very heavy. He could not have found a worse place to lose a battle. The cost to him of maintaining this African campaign has been exorbitant. One in every three of his ships, with their sorely-needed cargoes, has gone to the bottom of the sea, through our submarines and our Air Force, and the resources of German and Italian shipping are most severely strained. Now, in this battle, the enemy's losses have been mortal so far as this theatre is concerned, and he has had to employ a great part of his air force, including one-third of his transport and long-range reconnaissance planes, merely to keep his army supplied with food, ammunition and fuel. His air effort against Russia was definitely affected during all these last three months. His U-boat activities in the Mediterranean have been considerably reduced. Great as has been the cost and the burden to us of the African campaign, many as have been its disappointments and mistakes, it has, from first to last, been an immense drain upon German and Italian resources, and the most effective means we have yet had of drawing a portion of the enemy's strength and wrath away from Russia upon ourselves.

Another important point to remember is the need of combining and concerting the operations of the various Allies and making them fit together into a general design, and of doing this in spite of all the hard accidents of war and the incalculable interruptions of the enemy. One great obstacle to the constant unity of the Allies is geography. We stand around the circumference of the circle. The main enemy lies in the centre. A vast void separates us from the other war, in which we are equally interested, proceeding in the Pacific theatre. Hitler can summon quite easily a conference in Berlin or anywhere he chooses in Central Europe, and can bring together, apart from Japan, all those concerned in the war effort of the Axis Powers, without these representative authorities being subject to any serious inconvenience, or being even temporarily detached from the tasks each of them has in hand. For us, through geography, joint consultation is far more difficult. President Roosevelt has not found it possible to leave the United States, nor Premier Stalin to leave Russia. Therefore, I have had to make journeys in each direction, carrying with me to and fro many important military authorities and other experts, and to labour, so far as possible, to bring all our plans into concert and harmony. We have brought them, for the time being, into some harmony.

So far as Russia is concerned, her course and position were fixed. The Soviets had to repel the terrific onslaught of Germany. They have been completely absorbed in their own defence, and, in defending themselves, they have rendered an incomparable service to the common cause. They have rendered this service by killing or permanently putting out of action far more millions than Germany lost during the whole of the last war. I recognise the force of all that Premier Stalin said in his last speech about the enormous weight that has been thrown on Russia. My heart has bled for Russia. I have felt what almost every one in this House must have felt, that intense desire that we should be suffering with her and that we should take some of the weight off her. Everything that he said about the burden thrown on them, the disproportionate burden, is perfectly true. It is evident however that Russia is at least three times as strong a living organism as she was in the last war. The idea that Russia could withstand the whole of the German Army in the last war was never for a moment entertained. Then she had only a small fraction of the German power to meet, but now she has the whole weight of it, and as for any that is employed on this side, or in the conquered countries, that is more than made up for by the horde of divisions provided by Finland, Rumania, Hungary, and others of the Nazi-ridden or Fascist-ridden States. The Russians have borne the burden and the heat of the day, and I think it absolutely natural on their part, and fully within their rights, to make the very strong and stark assertions which they have made. Our need was to help them, but to help them in a manner effective and suitable. It might have been a relief to our feelings — at least in the early stages — if we had delivered a premature attack across the Channel, if we had had, for instance, a dozen Dieppes on one day and a couple of Dunklrks a week or two later. But a disaster of that character would have been of no help to Russia. It would have been the greatest disservice to Russia.

But the attack which will be made in due course across the Channel or the North Sea requires an immense degree of preparation, vast numbers of special landing craft, and a great Army trained, division by division, in amphibious warfare. All this is proceeding, but it takes time. Of course, should the enemy become demoralised at any moment, the same careful preparations would not be needed. Risks could be run on a large scale. But this is certainly not the case at the present time. There is a German Army in France as large, apart from the Home Guard, as ours in Great Britain. It is not so well equipped as the British or American troops, but it contains many veteran German soldiers, many experienced officers who have taken part in the overthrow and massacre of a dozen countries. It has ample weapons of the latest type; it has the aid of the immense fortifications erected along the Channel and North Sea coasts. There are also the extraordinary and peculiar difficulties attendant on all landings across the sea in the teeth of opposition — the chances of

weather in this somewhat variable Northern climate, the difficulty of reconciling tides and the moon, of catching at one moment high visibility from the air and smooth waters for the
landing craft. There are many other factors. I could speak for
an hour upon them, but I do not intend to labour the matter,
certainly not in Public Session, because a great many of these
difficulties it will be our duty to overcome.

But all of them constitute a problem which makes the process
of moving an Army across the Channel from one side to the
other — it cuts both ways — a problem which, happily for us, has
never yet been solved in war. It would have been most improvident for us to attempt such an enterprise before all our preparations were ready. They have very greatly advanced. Enormous installations have been and are being brought into existence at
all our suitable ports, but no one would have been justified, nor
indeed would it have been physically possible, in attempting an
invasion of the Continent during the summer or autumn of
1942. Here let me say a word about pressure. No amount of
pressure by public opinion or from any other quarter would
make me, as the person chiefly responsible, consent to an operation which our military advisers had convinced me would lead
to a great disaster. I should think it extremely dishonourable
and indeed an act of treason to the nation to allow any unin-
structed pressure, however well meant, or sentimental feelings,
however honourable, to drive me into such reckless or wanton
courses. Again and again, with the full assent of my colleagues
in the War Cabinet, I have instructed the Chiefs of the Staff that
in endeavouring to solve their problems they should disregard
public clamour, and they know that His Majesty's Government,
resting securely upon this steady House of Commons, is quite
strong enough to stand like a bulkhead between the military
authorities and the well-meaning impulses which stir so many
breasts. It is not for me to claim the whole responsibility for
what has not been done, but I should be quite ready and well
content to bear it.

Why, then, it will be said, did you allow false hopes to be
raised in Russian breasts? Why then did you agree with the
United States and Russia upon a communiqué which spoke of a
second front in Europe in 1942? I must say, quite frankly, that

The End of the Beginning

I hold it perfectly justifiable to deceive the enemy, even if at the same time your own people are for a while misled. There is one thing, however, which you must never do, and that is to mislead your Ally. You must never make a promise which you do not fulfil. I hope we shall show that we have lived up to that standard. All British promises to Russia have been made in writing or given across the table in recorded conversations with the Soviet representative. In June I gave the Russian Government a written document making it perfectly clear that, while we were preparing to make a landing in 1942, we could not promise to do so. Meanwhile, whether or not we were going to attack the Continent in August, September or October, it was of the utmost consequence to Russia that the enemy should believe that we were so prepared and so resolved. Only in this way could we draw and keep the largest possible number of Germans pinned in the Pas de Calais, along the coast of France and in the Low Countries. We have drawn and kept at least 33 German divisions in the West, and one-third of the German bomber air force is there, and this bomber force is not being used to bomb us to any extent. Why? It was being saved up for these very landings, should they occur, on the beaches, and they have remained, playing no effective military part for a considerable time. We ourselves are also engaging, including the Middle East and Malta fighting, more than half of the whole fighter strength of Germany. In addition, there are ten German divisions in Norway. The main part of the German fleet has been for some months tied to the Northern fjords. There are about 350 of their best aircraft gathered up in the Far North to impede our convoys to Russia. Here is another front we have found it very costly to maintain. Let me tell you about that.

Of the 19 convoys we have sent to Russia, every one has been an important fleet operation, because the enemy's main fleet was close at hand. The latest one required the use of 77 ships of war, apart altogether from the supply ships. The Foreign Secretary, if he is well enough — my right hon. Friend has a temporary indisposition to-day — or if not, the Under-Secretary of State for Foreign Affairs, will recount in some detail later on in the Debate the immense output of munitions which we have sent to Russia during a period when we ourselves were being vehemently re-

278

proached, and naturally reproached, for the comparative ill-equipment of our own troops. Indeed, I think that the effort and achievement of this country, industrial, naval, and military, during the year 1942 should be a source of pride and thanksgiving, not only to all in these Islands, but to our Allies both in the East and in the West.

Now I come to the great enterprise which has just been unfolded. On my first visit to Washington after the United States was attacked by Japan, Germany and Italy, President Roosevelt favoured the idea that French North Africa was specially suitable for American intervention in the Western theatre. This view was fully shared by us. However, it was clearly the duty both of Britain and of the United States to exhaust every possibility of carrying more direct aid to Russia by means of a liberating descent upon France. Both plans were, therefore, studied by the Staffs with the utmost attention, and preparations were made for both possibilities, either alternatively or simultaneously. Personally, I have always considered the Western front as one. We hold a very powerful enemy army pinned on the French shores, and every week our preparations to strike it will increase and develop. At the same time we make this wide encircling movement in the Mediterranean, having for its primary purpose the recovery of the command of that vital sea, but also having for its object the exposure of the under-belly of the Axis, especially Italy, to heavy attack. That seemed from the beginning of this year to be the correct strategy. The establishment of a Mediterranean as well as an Atlantic or Channel front would obviously give us wide freedom of manœuvre. Our sea power and the gradual development of our amphibious power enabled both operations to be contemplated on a very large scale. The 18th and 19th century battles were fought on fronts of six or seven miles, but the same principles apply on fronts which nowadays extend for 2,000 miles or more.

As the year advanced, it became clear that the provision of landing craft would not be on a sufficiently large scale to enable a heavy intervention to take place across the Channel in the favourable-weather months of 1942. General Marshall, the Head of the American Army, with which is included the American Air Force, paid two visits to this country, the first in April, the second in July; and on the second occasion he was accompanied by Admiral King, the Commander-in-Chief of the American Navy. It was decided on this second occasion to hold the enemy on the French shore, and to strike at his Southern flank in the Mediterranean through North Africa. In this decision the British and American Staffs were wholly united, and their views were shared and adopted by the President and the British War Cabinet. Orders were issued accordingly with extreme urgency at the end of July. Here I should like to say that in the planning of this joint operation the American and British staff officers, of whom many scores have been employed night and day, have worked together like a band of brothers. The comprehension which exists, the give and take, the desire to be first in giving quick service, are very marked, and will be an invaluable ingredient in our future tasks and our future achievements. Orders for the North African expedition were accordingly issued at the end of July.

As a very important part of this North African operation, it was necessary to bring the British Eighth Army into a condition to regain the initiative and to resume the offensive in Egypt. At that time there was very great anxiety about our ability even to hold the front at Alamein. However, General Auchinleck, that fine officer, succeeded in stemming the enemy's advance. The powerful reinforcements, which I have mentioned, of men and material had arrived or were on the water close at hand, and the troops were being equipped with all the latest material which was pouring in, and were rapidly fitting themselves for a renewal of the conflict on a great scale. As I was far from satisfied with the conditions reported to prevail in the Eighth Army, and was concerned about its confidence in the higher command, I thought it my duty to visit this Army, taking with me the Chief of the Imperial General Staff, Sir Alan Brooke, in whose judgment I have the greatest confidence, in order that together we might see the situation on the spot and take any decisions which might be found necessary.

There was an even greater need for such a journey. Although, as I have said, we had told the Soviet Government that we could make no promise to attack across the Channel in 1942, but only that we would do our utmost to overcome the difficulties of such an operation, yet now that we had settled not to make the attempt in the autumn of 1942, but, on the other hand, to make an enveloping attack on North Africa, it was necessary to explain the whole position to Premier Stalin. I thought it better — and my colleagues pressed this view upon me — that I should deal with this matter personally, face to face, rather than leave it to the ordinary diplomatic channels. It was a very serious conversation which I had to undertake. I therefore sought and obtained the approval of the War Cabinet to make the journey which I described to the House when I came back about six weeks ago. I am sure that the course adopted prevented a great deal of friction and ill feeling between us and our Russian Allies, and I was very glad to read Mr. Stalin's statement when he said:

"There followed another important step, the visit to Moscow of the British Prime Minister, Mr. Churchill, in the course of which a complete understanding was reached concerning the relations between the two countries."

I assure the House I have a solid belief in the wisdom and good faith of this outstanding man, and although the news that I brought was not welcome and was not considered by them adequate, nevertheless the fact remains that we parted good friends, and, in the words which Mr. Stalin uses, a complete understanding exists between us. The Russians bore their disappointment like men. They faced the enemy, and now they have reached the winter successfully, although we were unable to give them that help which they so earnestly demanded and which we, had it been physically practicable, would so gladly have accorded them.

I have already told the House about the changes which, with the approval of the Cabinet and the advice of the Chief of the Imperial General Staff, I made in the Middle East Command and in the Command of the Eighth Army. In order that General Alexander should concentrate his whole attention upon the main object, he was relieved of all responsibility for Persia and Iraq. When you have a wild beast like Rommel in your back garden, you do not want to be worrying about things that are going on a thousand miles away. A new Command came into being there, which is now becoming a powerful force under General Maitland-Wilson. I can now read to the House the actual direction which I gave to General Alexander on 10th August, before leaving Cairo for Russia. It has at least the merit of brevity:

"1. Your prime and main duty will be to take or destroy at the earliest opportunity the German-Italian army commanded by Field-Marshal Rommel, together with all its supplies and establishments in Egypt and Libya.

2. You will discharge, or cause to be discharged, such other duties as appertain to your Command without prejudice to the task described in paragraph 1, which must be considered paramount in His Majesty's interests."

The General may very soon be sending along for further instructions.

In spite of the strain to which General Alexander had been subjected in the hard, adverse campaign in Burma, from which he had emerged with so much credit although he had nothing but retreat and misfortune, he accepted the new duties with ardour. Under him, commanding the Eighth Army, was placed that remarkable soldier, General Montgomery. These two officers set up their headquarters in the desert, and Air Vice-Marshal Coningham, who commands the air forces in the battle there, was in the same little circle of lorries, wagons and tents in which they live. In a very short time an electrifying effect was produced upon the troops, who were also reinforced by every available man and weapon. Meanwhile, in the rearward areas, the intensive training of the formations to be armed with the new American and British weapons proceeded ceaselessly. All these changes had to be made in the face of an imminent attack by Rommel's army, the preparations for which were plainly apparent. In order that the Desert Army should have the fullest freedom of manœuvre and not have to fall back if its Southward flank were turned — because the line did not extend completely to the Qattara Depression; there was an open flank — every preparation was made to defend Cairo by the assembly of a considerable force, by the mobilising of every man from the rearward Services, exactly as we should do in England in the case of invasion, by the preparation of defence works along the line of the Nile, and by the use of inundations. All this was set in train. The new Command having been installed, my work there was done, and I returned to give my report to the House.

During the night of 30th–31st August, when the moon was already on the wane, Rommel's threatened attack was delivered. Quite rightly from his point of view, he did not by-pass the army to strike at Cairo, although the road seemed open. We thought he might, but he did not. He did not care to leave behind him the Desert Army now that it was reinforced by the 44th Division, which is commanded with distinction by our Deputy Serjeant at Arms (Major-General Hughes) and which was largely reorganised and regrouped. Pivoting on the Italians in the coastal area, he therefore attacked on the Southern flank with all his armour and most of his Germans. Then followed the second Battle of Alamein, the first being General Auchinleck's which stemmed the tide in July. Rommel found himself immediately confronted with stern resistance and with artillery, used on the largest scale and abundantly supplied with ammunition. He did not press the issue to extremes, and, after about three days, he withdrew. Our losses were about 2,000. His were considerably heavier, especially a disproportionate loss in tanks.

The narrowness of the passage between us and the Qattara Depression, which had proved so serviceable to us when we were resisting Rommel's attacks in both the defensive Battles of Alamein, became of course a most serious adverse factor to our advance when we ourselves were ready in our turn to assume the offensive. Our attack had to fit in harmoniously with the great operation in French North Africa to which it was a prelude. We had to wait till our troops were trained in the use of the new weapons which were arriving. We had to have a full moon on account of the method of attack. All these conditions were satisfiable around 23rd October. Meanwhile, however, we knew that the enemy was turning the position in front of us into a veritable fortress, blasting gun-pits and trenches in the solid rock, laying enormous and elaborate minefields, and strengthening himself in every manner both by air and sea transport, in spite of the heavy toll exacted by our Air Force and our submarines. An attack by us round the enemy's Southern flank led into difficult country, with no threat to his communications. On the other hand, to blast a hole by a frontal attack in the North by the sea was a most forbidding task. However, when I spent a night on 19th August with Generals Alexander and Montgomery in their desert headquarters, General Montgomery, with General Alexander's full assent, expounded in exact detail the first stages of the plan which has since in fact been carried out. It was an anxious matter. In the last war we devised the tank to clear a way for the infantry, who were otherwise held up by the intensity of machine-gun fire. On this occasion it was the infantry who would have to clear the way for the tanks, to break through the crust and liberate the superior armour. This they could only do in the moonlight, and for this they must be supported with a concentration of artillery more powerful than any used in the present war. On a six-mile front of attack we had a 25-pounder gun, or better, every 23 yards. It is true that in the later barrages of 1918, at the Hindenburg Line, and other long-prepared positions, a concentration of one gun to every 15 yards was attained. But the field guns of those days were 18-pounders. Our 25-pounders are heavier, and we also believe they are the best field guns in the world. It was necessary to effect penetration of about 6,000 yards at the first stroke in order to get through the hostile minefields, trenches and batteries. In the last war it was nearly always possible to make this initial penetration. In those days, the artillery having blasted the gap, the next step was to gallop the cavalry through what was called the "G in Gap." But this was never done, as the horsemen were soon brought to a standstill by the machine-gun posts in the rear. Horses were shot, and the whole possibility of exploiting the breach passed away. Times have changed, however. We have a steel machine cavalry now which, once a path is cleared through the mines and anti-tank guns, can certainly go forward against machine-gun posts to encounter whatever mobile forces of the enemy may lie beyond. That is the difference in this matter between the two wars. I feel sure the House will be glad that I should put these points to them, because in all that has been written — and so much has been written — about this battle, these points which touch the sequence and articulation of events have not been made very clearly.

For the purpose of turning the breach to the fullest account, an entirely new Corps, the 10th, was formed, consisting of two British Armoured Divisions and the New Zealand Division — that "ball of fire," as it was described to me by those who had seen it at work. This very powerful force of between 40,000 and 50,000 men, including all the best tanks, the Grants and the Shermans, was withdrawn from the battle front immediately after Rommel's repulse in the second battle of Alamein, and devoted itself entirely to intensive training, exercises and preparation. It was this thunderbolt hurled through the gap which finished Rommel and his arrogant army.

The success of all these plans could not have been achieved without substantial superiority in the air. The Royal Air Force, which had a substantial proportion of American-manned squadrons with it, had first to attain ascendancy over the opposing air force. Having attained this ascendancy, it was used behind the lines to reduce the all-important supplies of fuel and ammunition without which the Germans could not effectively resist. It was also used in the battle itself to break up any threatening counter-attacks before they could develop, thus giving the troops time to consolidate the positions won. By reaching out far to the rear of the retreating army, air power completely disorganised the enemy's withdrawal, and once again by the destruction of his mechanised transport prevented the bringing of fuel and ammunition to the front. When we retreated all those hundreds of miles from Tobruk at such speed, what saved us was superior air power. What has consummated Rommel's ruin is that he has had to make this ruinous and speedy retreat with a superior air force hammering him and hampering him at every stage. In Air Marshal Tedder and Air Vice-Marshal Coningham we have two air leaders of the very highest quality, not technicians, but warriors who have worked in perfect harmony with the generals, and the manner in which in this Egyptian campaign the arrangements between the air and the military have been perfected has given a model which should be followed in all combined operations in the future.

It is true we had gathered superior forces, but all this would have been futile but for the masterly military conception of the commanders, the attention to detail which characterised their preparations, and the absolute ruthlessness with which their forces were engaged, not only at the point of rupture but in gripping the enemy along the entire battle front. This battle is in fact a very fine example of the military art as developed under modern conditions. The skill of the commanders was rivalled by the conduct of their troops. Everyone testifies to the electrifying effect which the new Command had upon the Army. This noble Desert Army, which has never doubted its power to beat the enemy, and whose pride had suffered cruelly from retreats and disasters which they could not understand, regained in a week its ardour and self-confidence. Historians may explain Tobruk. The Eighth Army has done better; it has avenged it. Very full accounts have been given of the course of the battle during the twelve days' vehement fighting by the intrepid reporters and photographers who have been given a free run over the field at the risk of their lives. I am only concerned at the moment with its sequence and articulation.

From the moment that the seaward flank of the enemy was broken and the great mass of our armour flowed forward and successfully engaged the Panzer divisions, the fate of the Axis troops to the Southward, amounting to six Italian divisions, largely motorised, was sealed. As our advance reached El Daba and later Fuka, their lines of supply and of retreat were equally severed. They were left in a waterless desert to perish or surrender. At Fuka a grim action was fought on a smaller scale, but with unexampled ardour on both sides, between the British armour and the remnants of the German Panzer Army. In this action particularly, the British and Germans had it all to themselves. The Germans were almost entirely destroyed, only remnants escaping to Mersa Matruh, where again no halting-place was found.

It is impossible to give a final estimate of the enemy's casualties. General Alexander's present estimate, which reached me late last night, is that 59,000 Germans and Italians have been killed, wounded or taken prisoner. Of these 34,000 are Germans, and 25,000 Italians. Of course there are many more Italians who may be wandering about in the desert, and every effort is being made to bring them in. The enemy also lost irretrievably about 500 tanks and not fewer than 1,000 guns of all types from 47 mm. upwards. Our losses, though severe and painful, have not been unexpectedly high having regard to the task our troops were called upon to face. They amount to 13,600 officers and men.

They were spread over the whole Army. Fifty-eight per cent of them are British troops from the United Kingdom, with a much larger proportion of officers owing to all the armoured formations being British. Australian, New Zealand and South African troops were in the forefront of the break-through. Of the three British Infantry Divisions, the 51st Division, which bore the brunt, has gained further honour for Scotland and the Highlands. The 50th and 44th Divisions also acquitted themselves with distinction. The 4th Indian Division and the Fighting French and Greek Brigades all played their part with the utmost alacrity. The pursuit has now reached far to the West, and I cannot pretend to forecast where it will stop or what will be left of the enemy at the end of it. The speed of advance of our pursuing troops exceeds anything yet seen in the several ebbs and flows of the Libyan battlefields. Egypt is already clear of the enemy; we are advancing into Cyrenaica, and we may rely upon our generals and upon the Air Force to accomplish amazing feats now that the main force of the enemy has been broken and they have before them the opportunity of regaining in a few weeks, perhaps in much less than that, ground which otherwise might have taken long campaigns to reconquer. Taken by itself, the Battle of Egypt must be regarded as an historic British victory. In order to celebrate it directions are being given to ring the bells throughout the land next Sunday morning, and I should think that many will listen to their peals with thankful hearts. The time will be notified through the agency of the B.B.C., for everyone's convenience, and also to explain that the bells are not being rung on account of invasion.

While I do not want to detain the House too long, I must say one word about the third of these elements I mentioned, a word about surprise and strategy. By a marvellous system of camouflage, complete tactical surprise was achieved in the desert. The enemy suspected, indeed knew, that an attack was impending, but where and when and how it was coming was hidden from him. The 10th Corps, which he had seen from the air exercising 50 miles in the rear, moved silently away in the night, but leaving an exact simulacrum of its tanks where it had been, and proceeded to its points of attack. The enemy suspected that the attack was impending, but did not know how, when or where, and above all he had no idea of the scale upon which he was to be assaulted.

But what was done by the Desert Army in the field was accomplished upon a far vaster scale here at home and in the United States in the gigantic Anglo-American descent upon North Africa. Here again Hitler knew that something was brewing, but what, he could not guess. He naïvely complained of "military idiots" and drunkards — he is quite uncivil from time to time — the working of whose tortuous minds he and his staffs were unable to discern. In fact, however, while he was thus wondering, the largest amphibious operation ever conceived was about to sail for a strategic area of cardinal importance, which it reached without the slightest warning, and where the ships succeeded in making their landfall.

There is a great advantage, I think, in our not publishing the shipping losses. The Germans tell their own tales, which make no difference to the mentality and steadfastness of our people, but the Germans become the victims of their own lies. They have exaggerated continuously. The losses are heavy enough in all conscience, but they have continuously exaggerated them, and consequently I do not think they believed that we had the shipping for any operation on such a scale as is now being employed. None the less, the greatest credit is due to the many hundreds of people in Britain and in the United States — hundreds, there may be more — who necessarily had to be informed because of the part they played in the preparations, or who could have inferred from the duties given to them what was in the wind. A tribute is also due to the Press for the extreme discretion which they practised, and which they were asked to practise, in avoiding all speculation upon dangerous topics. These are important matters, and will be helpful in the future. Democracies have to show that they are not incapable of keeping their war secrets. Here is a fine example.

I have completed my account of these operations. I thought it right to go into the details of them because I know the deep interest which the House takes in these matters, and also the very large number of Members who have practical experience of war. What is happening now? We, of course, foresaw the reactions which the entry of American and British Forces into North Africa would produce on the various countries affected. First of all, there was Italy, which will now come to a much fuller and better realisation of the unwisdom of entering a war when you think your antagonist is prostrate. It will bring home to the people of Italy as a whole a very much clearer realisation of the trials and horrors of war than they have had the opportunity of experiencing up to now. To-day the news reaches us that Hitler has decided to overrun all France, thus breaking the Armistice which the Vichy Government had kept with such pitiful and perverted fidelity, and at such a horrible cost, even sacrificing their ships and sailors to fire upon American rescuing troops as they arrived. Even while they were doing that for the sake of the Armistice, they have been stricken down by their German taskmasters.

This, surely, is the moment for all Frenchmen worthy of the name to stand together and to be truly united in spirit. Their trials will be many, and the difficulties into which individuals will be thrown in the circumstances which may overtake them are unimaginable. Nevertheless, here is the moment for all Frenchmen to sink personal feuds and rivalries, and to think, as General de Gaulle is thinking, only of the liberation of their native land. I must, however, confess freely to the House that I have not sufficient information at the moment about what is happening in France to add anything to the accounts which are being made public hour by hour. Only at the moment when I entered the House news reached me that in North Africa Casablanca had capitulated to the United States. Another message was that Bougie has been occupied, farther to the east of Algiers, by an amphibious expedition. Oran is already in the possession of the Allies. Algiers has been for three days in their possession. All the vital landing ports in North Africa are in Allied hands.

The House may be sure that many things are going to happen in the next few days, and I should be merely presuming if I attempted to give my own opinion upon the situation which will develop in North Africa, in France or in Italy, except that we shall shortly have far greater facilities for bombing Italy than ever existed before. That is not a matter of speculation.

I have now given to the House the best account I can, amid

the press of events, of these remarkable transactions, which, I venture to hope, have already been highly beneficial to our interests and to our cause. We are entitled to rejoice only upon the condition that we do not relax. I always liked those lines by the American poet, Walt Whitman. I have several times repeated them. They apply to-day most aptly. He said:

". . . Now understand me well — it is provided in the essence of things that from any fruition of success, no matter what, shall come forth something to make a greater struggle necessary."

The problems of victory are more agreeable than those of defeat, but they are no less difficult. In all our efforts to recapture the initiative we shall be confronted with many perplexing choices and many unavoidable hazards, and I cannot doubt that we shall meet with our full share of mistakes, vexations and disappointments. We shall need to use the stimulus of victory to increase our exertions, to perfect our systems, and to refine our processes. In that spirit, sustained by the unswerving support of the House of Commons, we shall bend again to our task.

Harrow School Songs

[*November 18, 1942*

I HAVE come down here twice before during the war to refresh myself by singing these songs with you, songs that I know so well and love so much. The first time I came, two years ago, it was rough weather — for most of you. Some of you are here to-day who had been out on the tiles putting out the incendiaries, but all were very proud of having had the honour of being under the fire of the enemy at such an early age — a very great privilege and a piece of good fortune. Many of those who were here then have now gone into the services, and some may already be fighting. If the war goes on, as go on it may, it may be that some of you who are here will also take your place in one of the various services with which we confront the enemy, and in which we defend our cause.

You have visitors here now in the shape of a sister-school — Malvern. I must say I think this is a very fine affair — to meet the needs of war, to join forces, to share alike, like two regiments that serve side by side in some famous brigade, and never forget it for a hundred years after. I was very sorry that I myself had to be responsible for giving some instructions in regard to one of our establishments which made it necessary to take over Malvern at comparatively short notice. But everyone at Harrow will, I know, make it his business to let his friends and guests carry away with them a memory which will make its mark definitely on the relationship of the two Schools — and, no doubt, to give them a beating in any of the games which you play.

Two years have passed since we stood alone. No one can doubt that we are in a better position now than we were when I came here those two years ago, when we sang many of these songs.

Certainly I think the songs are very important. I enjoy them very much. I know many of them by heart. I was telling the Head Master just now that I could pass an examination in some of them. They are a great treasure and possession of Harrow School, and keep the flame burning in a marvellous manner. Many carry them with them all their lives. You have the songs of Bowen and Howson (whom I remember well as House Masters here) with the music of John Farmer and Eaton Faning. They are wonderful; marvellous; more than could be put into bricks and mortar, or treasured in any trophies of silver or gold. They grow with the years. I treasure them and sing them with joy. When I was asked two years ago to come here, I said I would only come on one condition — "You make the boys sing to me." And if you ask me next year I will come. I hope we shall have something better to sing about; but it is not so bad. The progress we have made is very great. We were all alone, but we went on. We could not say how it was, by what means or method we should come out of our troubles. All we knew was that we should fight to the end. Now we are a great company of allied nations. We are moving forward to success and victory. As the Head Master was saying, General Alexander is a Harrow boy, and I remember him speaking to me only a short while ago with great keenness about his Harrow days.

These are very grateful thoughts, and I am entitled to bring them to your notice. We are moving forward. Far be it from me to say how long the road will be, or how great the effort will be. I cannot tell, but certainly from everything that has happened in the past we should draw encouragement and the means of keener exertion. The path leads forward; we are making our way through the dark valley. We are coming out of the wood gradually, although there are many dangers. There may be many appearances of light which turn out to be deceptive, yet nevertheless I do feel I can assure you that we are moving forward, stronger every month, and with more knowledge and confidence and power, and that the day will shortly come, through our qualities, through the qualities of the British race as much as through any other cause, when we shall reach a broader and brighter light, which when once it has shone will never be quenched.

" *Watch over Victory* "

A MESSAGE TO FREEDOM HOUSE, WASHINGTON, ON THE
FIRST ANNIVERSARY OF AN ASSOCIATION FORMED TO PRO-
MOTE THE "FOUR FREEDOMS" ENUMERATED BY PRESIDENT
ROOSEVELT: "FREEDOM FROM WANT AND FEAR AND FREE-
DOM OF EXPRESSION AND WORSHIP"
NOVEMBER 19, 1942

[November 19, 1942

ON the first anniversary of Freedom House I send you my best wishes for the success of the work you have undertaken. When this war is won, it will be our first duty to watch over the victory we have gained and to ensure that no new tyranny is again allowed to loose tragedy on the whole world. It is not too soon for those who are beating down these tyrants in war to prepare the vigilance that will defend the rights and liberties which our arms will have rescued and restored.

Victory as a Spur

A BROADCAST TO THE WORLD
NOVEMBER 29, 1942

November 12.   *As the Germans proclaimed Toulon "a free zone," Darlan asked the commanders of French warships there to bring their vessels to North Africa.*

November 13.   *Tobruk, Sollum and Bardia were recaptured by the British as Rommel's rout continued. In French North Africa, Allied forces entered Tunisia.*

Premier Stalin declared that the campaign in North Africa had turned the war in Europe radically in favour of the Allies and would relieve the pressure on Russia.

November 14.   *General Giraud, who had made a dramatic escape from the Germans, assumed command of French troops in North Africa.*

November 16.   *United States announced a naval victory off the Solomons, Japanese losses including a battleship, five cruisers, five destroyers and twelve transports.*

Allied recognition of Admiral Darlan as head of the French in North Africa emphatically denounced by General de Gaulle's party in London.

November 17.   *President Roosevelt stated that the arrangement with Darlan was a temporary expedient.*

November 18.   *Marshal Pétain gave Laval powers to make laws and sign decrees. General Weygand reported arrested by the Germans.*

November 20.   *Germans evacuated Benghazi.*

Victory as a Spur, November 29, 1942

	R.A.F. raided Turin in the war's biggest night raid on Italy.
November 22.	*Mr. Herbert Morrison (Home Secretary and Minister of Home Security) became a member of the War Cabinet in place of Sir Stafford Cripps, who was appointed Minister of Aircraft Production. Mr. Anthony Eden became Leader of the House of Commons.*
November 23.	*Admiral Darlan announced that French West Africa, including Dakar, had come under his command.*
	Australian troops captured Gona, in New Guinea.
November 26.	*The Soviet announced that in a week's offensive on the Don-Volga front they had taken 63,000 prisoners and vast quantities of arms.*
November 27.	*French warships were scuttled by their crews as the Germans entered Toulon. Three submarines, it was reported, got away.*
	Vichy announced that Pétain had signed a decree dissolving the French Army, Navy and Air Force.
November 28.	*Italy had its first experience of the R.A.F.'s 8,000-lb. bomb in a devastating raid on Turin.*

[*November 29, 1942*

Two Sundays ago all the bells rang to celebrate the victory of our desert Army at Alamein. Here was a martial episode in British history which deserved a special recognition. But the bells also carried with their clashing joyous peals our thanksgiving that, in spite of all our errors and shortcomings, we have been brought nearer to the frontiers of deliverance. We have not reached those frontiers yet, but we are becoming ever more entitled to be sure that the awful perils which might well have

blotted out our life and all that we love and cherish will be sur-
mounted, and that we shall be preserved for further service in
the vanguard of mankind.

We have to look back along the path we have trodden these
last three years of toil and strife, to value properly all that we
have escaped and all that we have achieved. No mood of
boastfulness, of vain glory, of over-confidence must cloud our
minds; but I think we have a right which history will endorse
to feel that we had the honour to play a part in saving the
freedom and the future of the world. That wonderful association
of States and races spread all over the globe called the British
Empire — or British Commonwealth if you will; I do not quarrel
about it — and above all, our small Island, stood in the gap
alone in the deadly hour. Here we stood, firm though all
was drifting; throughout the British Empire no one faltered.
All around was very dark. Here we kept the light burning
which now spreads broadly over the vast array of the United
Nations: that is why it was right to ring out the bells, and to
lift our heads for a moment in gratitude and in relief, before
we turn again to the grim and probably long ordeals which lie
before us and to the exacting tasks upon which we are engaged.

Since we rang the bells for Alamein, the good cause has prospered. The Eighth Army has advanced nearly four hundred
miles, driving before them in rout and ruin the powerful forces,
or the remnants of the powerful forces, which Rommel boasted
and Hitler and Mussolini believed would conquer Egypt. Another serious battle may be impending at the entrance to Tripolitania. I make it a rule not to prophesy about battles before they
are fought. Everyone must try to realise the immense distances
over which the North African war ranges, and the enormous
labours and self-denial of the troops who press forward relent-
lessly, twenty, thirty, forty and sometimes fifty miles in a single
day. I will say no more than that we may have the greatest confidence in Generals Alexander and Montgomery, and in our
soldiers and airmen who have at last begun to come into their
own.

At the other side of Africa, a thousand miles or more to the
westward, the tremendous joint undertaking of the United States
and Britain which was fraught with so many hazards has also

been crowned with astonishing success. To transport these large armies of several hundred thousand men, with all their intricate elaborate modern apparatus, secretly across the seas and oceans, and to strike to the hour, and almost to the minute, simultaneously at a dozen points, in spite of all the U-boats and all the chances of weather, was a feat of organisation which will long be studied with respect. It was rendered possible only by one sovereign fact — namely the perfect comradeship and understanding prevailing between the British and American staffs and troops. This majestic enterprise is under the direction and responsibility of the President of the United States, and our First British Army is serving under the orders of the American Commander-in-Chief, General Eisenhower, in whose military skill and burning energy we put our faith, and whose orders to attack we shall punctually and unflinchingly obey. Behind all lies the power of the Royal Navy, to which is joined a powerful American Fleet; the whole under the command of Admiral Cunningham, and all subordinated to the Allied Commander-in-Chief.

It was not only that the U-boats were evaded and brushed aside by the powerfully escorted British and American convoys; they were definitely beaten in the ten-days' conflict that followed the landings, both inside and outside the Mediterranean. Here was no more secrecy. We had many scores of ships continuously exposed; large numbers of U-boats were concentrated from all quarters; our destroyers and corvettes and our aircraft took up the challenge and wore them down and beat them off. For every transport or supply ship we have lost, a U-boat has been sunk or severely damaged; for every ton of Anglo-American shipping lost so far in this expedition, we have gained perhaps two tons in the shipping acquired or recovered in the French harbours of North and West Africa. Thus, in this respect, as Napoleon recommended, war has been made to support war.

General Alexander timed his battle at Alamein to suit exactly this great stroke from the West, in order that his victory should encourage friendly countries to preserve their strict neutrality, and also to rally the French Forces in North-West Africa to a full sense of their duty and of their opportunity. Now at this moment, the First British Army is striking hard at the last remaining footholds of the Germans and Italians in Tunisia.

The End of the Beginning

American, British and French troops are pressing forward side by side, vying with each other in a general rivalry and brotherhood. In this there lies the hope and the portent of the future.

I have been speaking about Africa, about the 2,000 miles of coastline fronting the underside of subjugated Europe. From all this we intend, and I will go so far as to say we expect, to expel the enemy before long. But Africa is no halting-place: it is not a seat but a springboard. We shall use Africa only to come to closer grips. Anyone can see the importance to us of re-opening the Mediterranean to military traffic and saving the long voyage round the Cape. Perhaps by this short cut and the economy of shipping resulting from it, we may strike as heavy a blow at the U-boats as has happened in the whole war; but there is another advantage to be gained by the mastery of the North African shore: we open the air battle upon a new front. In order to shorten the struggle, it is our duty to engage the enemy in the air continuously on the largest scale and at the highest intensity. To bring relief to the tortured world, there must be the maximum possible air fighting. Already, the German Air Force is a wasting asset; their new construction is not keeping pace with their losses; their front line is weakening both in numbers and, on the whole, in quality. The British, American and Russian Air Forces, already together far larger, are growing steadily and rapidly; the British and United States expansion in 1943 will be, to put it mildly, well worth watching: all we need is more frequent opportunities of contact. The new air front, from which the Americans and also the Royal Air Force are deploying along the Mediterranean shore, ought to give us these extra opportunities abundantly in 1943. Thirdly, our operations in French North Africa should enable us to bring the weight of the war home to the Italian Fascist state, in a manner not hitherto dreamed of by its guilty leaders, or still less by the unfortunate Italian people Mussolini has led, exploited and disgraced. Already the centres of war industry in Northern Italy are being subjected to harder treatment than any of our cities experienced in the winter of 1940. But if the enemy should in due course be blasted from the Tunisian tip, which is our aim, the whole of the South of Italy — all the naval bases, all the munition establishments and other military objectives

298

wherever situated — will be brought under prolonged, scientific, and shattering air attack.

It is for the Italian people, forty millions of them, to say whether they want this terrible thing to happen to their country or not. One man, and one man alone, has brought them to this pass. There was no need for them to go to war; no one was going to attack them. We tried our best to induce them to remain neutral, to enjoy peace and prosperity and exceptional profits in a world of storm. But Mussolini could not resist the temptation of stabbing prostrate France, and what he thought was helpless Britain, in the back. Mad dreams of imperial glory, the lust of conquest and of booty, the arrogance of long-unbridled tyranny, led him to his fatal, shameful act. In vain I warned him: he would not hearken. On deaf ears and a stony heart fell the wise, far-seeing appeals of the American President. The hyena in his nature broke all bounds of decency and even commonsense. To-day his Empire is gone. We have over a hundred Italian generals and nearly three hundred thousand of his soldiers in our hands as prisoners of war. Agony grips the fair land of Italy. This is only the beginning, and what have the Italians to show for it? A brief promenade by German permission along the Riviera; a flying visit to Corsica; a bloody struggle with the heroic patriots of Yugoslavia; a deed of undying shame in Greece; the ruins of Genoa, Turin, Milan; and this is only a foretaste. One man and the régime he has created have brought these measureless calamities upon the hard-working, gifted, and once happy Italian people, with whom, until the days of Mussolini, the English-speaking world had so many sympathies and never a quarrel. How long must this endure?

We may certainly be glad about what has lately happened in Africa, and we may look forward with sober confidence to the moment when we can say: one continent relieved. But these successes in Africa, swift and decisive as they have been, must not divert our attention from the prodigious blows which Russia is striking on the Eastern Front. All the world wonders at the giant strength which Russia has been able to conserve and to apply. The invincible defence of Stalingrad is matched by the commanding military leadership of Stalin. When I was leaving the Kremlin in the middle of August, I said to Premier Stalin:

The End of the Beginning

"When we have decisively defeated Rommel in Egypt, I will send you a telegram." And he replied: "When we make our counter-offensive here" (and he drew the arrow on the map), "I will send you one." Both messages have duly arrived, and both have been thankfully received.

As I speak, the immense battle, which has already yielded results of the first magnitude, is moving forward to its climax; and this, it must be remembered, is only one part of the Russian front, stretching from the White Sea to the Black Sea, along which, at many points, the Russian armies are attacking. The jaws of another Russian winter are closing on Hitler's armies — a hundred and eighty German divisions, many of them reduced to little more than brigades by the slaughters and privations they have suffered, together with a host of miserable Italians, Rumanians, and Hungarians, dragged from their homes by a maniac's fantasy: all these as they reel back from the fire and steel of the avenging Soviet Armies must prepare themselves with weakened forces and with added pangs for a second dose of what they got last year. They have, of course, the consolation of knowing that they have been commanded and led, not by the German General Staff, but by Corporal Hitler himself.

I must conduct you back to the West — to France, where another vivid scene of this strange melancholy drama has been unfolded. It was foreseen when we were planning the descent upon North Africa that this would bring about immediate reactions in France. I never had the slightest doubt myself that Hitler would break the Armistice, overrun all France, and try to capture the French fleet at Toulon; such developments were to be welcomed by the United Nations, because they entailed the extinction for all practical purposes of the sorry farce and fraud of the Vichy Government. This was a necessary prelude to that reunion of France without which French resurrection is impossible. We have taken a long step towards that unity. The artificial division between occupied and unoccupied territory has been swept away. In France all Frenchmen are equally under the German yoke, and will learn to hate it with equal intensity. Abroad all Frenchmen will fire at the common foe. We may be sure that after what has happened, the ideals and the spirit of what we have called Fighting France will exercise a dominating influence upon the whole French nation. I agree with General de Gaulle that the last scales of deception have now fallen from the eyes of the French people; indeed, it was time.

"A clever conqueror," wrote Hitler in *Mein Kampf*, "will always, if possible, impose his demands on the conquered by instalments. For a people that makes a voluntary surrender saps its own character, and with such a people you can calculate that none of those oppressions in detail will supply quite enough reason for it to resort once more to arms." How carefully, how punctiliously he lives up to his own devilish doctrines! The perfidy by which the French fleet was ensnared is the latest and most complete example. That fleet, brought by folly and by worse than folly to its melancholy end, redeemed its honour by an act of self-immolation, and from the flame and smoke of the explosions at Toulon, France will rise again.

The ceaseless flow of good news from every theatre of war, which has filled the whole month of November, confronts the British people with a new test. They have proved that they can stand defeat; they have proved that they can bear with fortitude and confidence long periods of unsatisfactory and unexplained inaction. I see no reason at all why we should not show ourselves equally resolute and active in the face of victory. I promise nothing. I predict nothing. I cannot even guarantee that more successes are not on the way. I commend to all the immortal lines of Kipling:

> If you can dream — and not make dreams your master;
>   If you can think — and not make thoughts your aim;
> If you can meet with Triumph and Disaster
>   And treat those two impostors just the same —

there is my text for this Sunday's sermon, though I have no licence to preach one. Do not let us be led away by any fair-seeming appearances of fortune; let us rather put our trust in those deep, slow-moving tides that have borne us thus far already, and will surely bear us forward, if we know how to use them, until we reach the harbour where we would be.

I know of nothing that has happened yet which justifies the hope that the war will not be long, or that bitter and bloody years do not lie ahead. Certainly the most painful experiences would lie before us if we allowed ourselves to relax our exertions, to weaken the discipline, unity and order of our array, if we fell to quarrelling about what we should do with our victory before that victory had been won. We must not build on hopes or fears, but only on the continued faithful discharge of our duty, wherein alone will be found safety and peace of mind. Remember that Hitler with his armies and his secret police holds nearly all Europe in his grip. Remember that he has millions of slaves to toil for him, a vast mass of munitions, many mighty arsenals, many fertile fields. Remember that Göring has brazenly declared that whoever starves in Europe, it will not be the Germans. Remember that these villains know their lives are at stake. Remember how small a portion of the German Army we British have yet been able to engage and to destroy. Remember that the U-boat warfare is not diminishing but growing, and that it may well be worse before it is better. Then, facing the facts, the ugly facts as well as the encouraging facts, undaunted, then we shall learn to use victory as a spur to further efforts, and make good fortune the means of gaining more.

This much only will I say about the future, and I say it with an acute consciousness of the fallibility of my own judgment. It may well be that the war in Europe will come to an end before the war in Asia. The Atlantic may be calm, while in the Pacific the hurricane rises to its full pitch. If events should take such a course, we should at once bring all our forces to the other side of the world, to the aid of the United States, to the aid of China, and above all to the aid of our kith and kin in Australia and New Zealand, in their valiant struggle against the aggressions of Japan. While we were thus engaged in the Far East, we should be sitting with the United States and with our ally Russia and those of the United Nations concerned, shaping the international instruments and national settlements which must be devised if the free life of Europe is ever to rise again, and if the fearful quarrels which have rent European civilisation are to be prevented from once more disturbing the progress of the world. It seems to me that should the war end thus, in two successive stages, there will be a far higher sense of comradeship around the council table than existed among the victors at Versailles. Then the danger had passed away. The common bond between the Allies had snapped. There was no sense of corporate re-sponsibility such as exists when victorious nations who are mas-ters of one vast scene are, most of them, still waging war side by side in another. I should hope, therefore, that we shall be able to make better solutions — more far-reaching, more lasting solutions — of the problems of Europe at the end of this war than was possible a quarter of a century ago. It is not much use pursuing these speculations farther at this time. For no one can possibly know what the state of Europe or of the world will be, when the Nazi and Fascist tyrannies have been finally broken. The dawn of 1943 will soon loom red before us, and we must brace ourselves to cope with the trials and problems of what must be a stern and terrible year. We do so with the assurance of ever-growing strength, and we do so as a nation with a strong will, a bold heart and a good conscience.

Sixty-Eighth Birthday

[*November 30, 1942*

Mr. Winston Churchill was sixty-eight on November 30, 1942, and among messages of greetings were those from the Dominion Prime Ministers. To these Mr. Churchill replied as follows: —

[TO MR. MACKENZIE KING, PRIME MINISTER OF CANADA]

I SEND to you and to all the people of Canada my warm thanks for your very kind message. The unity of purpose and the resolution for victory of our two countries remained unshaken during the dark days, and I am confident that together we shall share the final victory.

[TO MR. JOHN CURTIN, PRIME MINISTER OF AUSTRALIA]

Thank you so much for your telegram. I greatly value the good wishes you send on behalf of the Commonwealth Government and yourself, and look forward to a continuance of our friendly co-operation in the days ahead.

[TO MR. PETER FRASER, PRIME MINISTER OF NEW ZEALAND]

Thank you so much for your birthday message and for your kind words about my broadcast. It is a great comfort to us all to know that we can rely through fair days and foul on the unfailing courage and resolution of the people of New Zealand.

[TO GENERAL SMUTS, PRIME MINISTER OF SOUTH AFRICA]

Thank you so much for your birthday greetings and for all your friendship and counsel.

[TO MR. J. M. ANDREWS, PRIME MINISTER
OF NORTHERN IRELAND]
Thank you so much for the kind message from your colleagues
and yourself, which I greatly appreciated.

One Great Family

A SPEECH TO THE PEOPLE OF BRADFORD
FROM THE STEPS OF THE TOWN HALL
DECEMBER 5, 1942

---

*December 1. Sir William Beveridge's scheme for com-
pulsory social insurance for all people in
Britain between 16 and 64 was made public.*

*Admiral Darlan assumed in North Africa
Pétain's title of Chief of State "as Pétain is a
prisoner."*

*December 2. Mussolini, in a speech in Rome, said that be-
cause of R.A.F. bombing Italian cities would
have to be evacuated of all but essential personnel.*

[*December 5, 1942*

I T is a pleasure for me to come to Bradford. I have a memory
and a connection with the city which goes back a long time,
because fifty years ago my father, Lord Randolph Churchill, had
the great ambition of representing the Central Division of this
city, and he would undoubtedly have been your Member had he
not died very suddenly. I have always felt a connection with
your great city on that account.

The last time I came here I came in a time — 28 years ago — of
bitter internal struggle. We were all divided and were fiercely
ranged against one another. Parties were facing each other with
clenched teeth, and they even seemed to be drifting into violence

and broils inside the State. It was a very hard, stern time, but one which our institutions — our broad-based free, democratic institutions — enabled us to pass through and overcome and to settle our problems.

Now, I come and there is no division. All are united like one great family; all are standing together, helping each other, taking their share and doing their work, some at the front, some under the sea or on the sea in all weathers, some in the air, some in the coal mines, great numbers in the shops, some in the homes — all doing their bit, and every one of you entitled to ask himself every morning or every evening: "Am I rowing my weight in the boat?" and if you can answer that searching question "Yes, I am," then, believe me, all are bearing their part, each and every one is bearing his or her part, in one of the greatest struggles that have ever glorified, torn, and dignified the human race.

Now, we have just passed through the month of November, usually a month of fogs and gloom, but, on the whole, a month I have liked a good deal better than some other months we have seen during the course of this present unpleasantness; a month in which our affairs have prospered, in which our soldiers and sailors and airmen have been victorious, in which our gallant Russian Ally has struck redoubtable blows against the common enemy, and in which our American Allies and our kith and kin far off in the Pacific Ocean, in Australia and New Zealand, have also seen their efforts crowned with a considerable measure of success. A great month, this last month of November.

But I must tell you, and I know you will not mind my saying it, because I do not think it is wise to deal in smooth words or airy promises, that you must be on your guard not to let the good fortune that has come to us be anything else but a means of striking harder. The struggle is approaching its most tense period. The hard core of Nazi resistance and villainy is not yet broken in upon. We have to gather up all our strength.

If by any chance unexpected good tidings come to us, that would be a matter which we could rejoice at, but which we must not count upon. We count upon our strong right arms, upon our honest, hard-working hearts; we count upon our courage, which has not been found wanting either in domestic or foreign stresses during the whole course of this war. These are the simple virtues which our island race has cultured and nurtured during many generations, and these are the virtues which will bear us through all struggles and in which we must put our faith.

We have broken into North Africa, with our American Allies, and now we have, in a short time, advanced from the Atlantic Ocean almost to the centre of the Mediterranean, a distance of nearly 900 miles; but there are still twenty miles to go, and very hard fighting will take place before that small distance is overcome and the violence and military power of the enemy there has been beaten down and driven into the sea. I do not doubt of the result, but I cannot leave you to suppose that it will be easily achieved. Away on the other side of North Africa, our armies are advancing, taking thousands of prisoners and driving the enemy before them; but here again hard fighting is to be expected. But during this month, when so much fighting has been carried on by the British and Americans, there has been a feeling of gladness that we, too, are engaging the enemy closely and not leaving the entire burden to be borne by the Russians, who have carried this immense struggle through the whole of this year and a large part of last year. They are defending their own country; we are defending our own country; but we are all of us defending something which is, I won't say dearer, but greater than a country, namely, a cause. That cause is the cause of freedom and of justice; that cause is the cause of the weak against the strong; it is the cause of law against violence, of mercy and tolerance against brutality and iron-bound tyranny. That is the cause that we are fighting for. That is the cause which is moving slowly, painfully but surely, inevitably and inexorably forward to victory; and when the victory is gained you will find that you are — I will not say in a new world, but a better world; you are in a world which can be made more fair, more happy, if only all the peoples will join together to do their part, and if all classes and all parties stand together to reap the fruits of victory as they are standing together to bear, and to face, and to cast back the terrors and menaces of war.

Our enemies are very powerful; they dispose of many millions of soldiers; they have millions of prisoners whom they, in many cases, use like slaves; they have rich lands which they have conquered; they have large, gifted populations in their grip; they have a theme of their own which is the Nazi theme of tyranny, the domination of a race by the shameful idolatry of a single man, a base man, lifted almost to the stature of a god by his demented and degraded worshippers; they have this ideal of the suppression of the individual citizen, man and woman, to be a mere chattel in a State machine.

All this is, in our view, at stake, but our enemies are powerful. They consider that they will have the strength to wear us out even if they cannot beat us down. Their hope is now to prolong the struggle so that perhaps differences will arise between friends and allies, so that perhaps democracies whom they despise and whom they underrate will weary of the war.

So I say to you all here in Bradford what I said when I was here nearly thirty years ago: Let us go forward together and put the great principles we support to the proof.

Retribution for Japan

A MESSAGE TO THE BRITISH FAR EASTERN TERRITORIES ON
THE FIRST ANNIVERSARY OF JAPAN'S ASSAULT ON THE
BRITISH EMPIRE AND THE UNITED STATES OF AMERICA
DECEMBER 7, 1942

[December 7, 1942

A YEAR ago to-day we saw committed one of the most wanton acts of aggression recorded in history. Japan, made reckless by her ambitions and audacious by our difficulties, assaulted Hongkong and Malaya.

We had long been struggling — for a time alone — with two great Powers in Europe, who had carefully prepared for the war they desired. Japan coldly, greedily, treacherously calculated that we should not then have the forces available to save our British territories and the States in Malaya and Borneo for whose defence we were responsible. Those territories and states were overrun, their defenders killed or imprisoned, their inhabitants enslaved. For a year our thoughts have gone out to all of you — Malays, Indians, Burmans, Chinese, Dutch, and British — who are suffering so cruelly.

But what a change in the picture there is to-day! The years of defence, of stubborn, outnumbered, ill-equipped, almost miraculous defence, are behind us: everywhere the United Nations turn to the attack. The storm which now lowers over Germany and Italy is spreading to Japan; there will be no softness or respite for her. The growing power of the United Nations will press steadfastly on till she is stripped of her conquests, punished for her treachery, and deprived of her powers of evil. Retribution was always sure: it is now growing near.

That is the message I give you to-day: that is the message I know you want to hear. Before the Japanese invasion all of us — Malays, Indians, Burmans, Chinese, Dutch, and British — had gone far together on the road towards an ordered, civilised, and happy life. Our progress is only interrupted. When Japanese aggression is broken, as broken it will be, we shall go forward again and find together even closer comradeship, even surer paths to happiness for each and all.

Keep up your hearts, we shall not fail you.

Messages

[*December 7, 1942*

[TO PRESIDENT ROOSEVELT, SENT ON THE FIRST ANNIVERSARY OF AMERICA'S ENTRY INTO THE WAR]

OUR country no less than the United States was the object of the infamous outrage of a year ago. The injuries that we have all suffered at the hands of Japan during the past year are grievous indeed. The peoples of the British Commonwealth of Nations are deeply conscious of their duty. We look forward one and all to the day when our full strength can be joined to that of our United States, Dutch, and Chinese Allies for the utter and final destruction of Japan's aggressive power.

[REPLY TO A MESSAGE FROM GENERAL CHIANG KAI-SHEK ON THE ANNIVERSARY OF THE JAPANESE ATTACK ON PEARL HARBOUR]

PLEASE accept my thanks for your kind message on the anniversary of the day when our common enemy added to his record of unprovoked aggression by the perfidious attack at Pearl Harbour. As a result of that black deed the British people took their place with pride and determination beside your gallant countrymen. I share your conviction that the resultant comradeship will continue to be of lasting benefit to both sides, and will find expression in the ultimate construction of a new world, where free peoples shall live together in peace and amity.

Messages (Continued)

[*December 8, 1942*

[TO THE TROOPS IN INDIA AND BROADCAST BY GEN-ERAL WAVELL, THE COMMANDER-IN-CHIEF]

THE period of waiting must be irksome to all of you, eager as you must be to share in the victories our arms are winning elsewhere; but remember that the task which you are at present performing by land, sea, and air is no less vital a part of the common effort of the United Nations. Others may now be first in the field of victory, but the great forces assembling in the India Command are destined to play before the end a glorious part in achieving the downfall of our enemies.

To-day ends a year in which Japan has enjoyed the fleeting success that sometimes comes to evil-doers, but her crimes have brought mighty forces into play. What we now see portends the combined power of the British, American, Chinese, and Russian peoples. The time is surely coming when we shall be able to settle the long score we have against Japan.

The armed forces of the United Nations within the area of the India Command, drawn from the peoples of India, Britain, America, China, Burma, Nepal, Africa, and Ceylon, are the symbol of an outraged world's resistance to the forces of evil and aggression. Your task to-day is defence: the defence of India and Ceylon until the time is ripe to move forward. As Britain has been held in the west, so must India be held in the east, and all the time you, to whom this defence is entrusted, must ceaselessly prepare for the day when you will advance and drive the aggressor from the peaceful lands which he has overrun.

Fighting the U-boats

A STATEMENT TO THE HOUSE OF COMMONS
DECEMBER 15, 1942

THE prime and direct conduct of the war against the U-boats rests with the Admiralty, who have at their disposal the full assistance of the Coastal Command of the Royal Air Force. However, various other Departments are also closely involved. All this proceeds under my responsibility as Minister of Defence. In February, 1941, I formed the Battle of the Atlantic Committee and instituted meetings under my personal direction, in order to focus and emphasise the need for supreme exertions and to make sure that there was proper concert between all authorities. Meetings were held at first weekly, and later at longer intervals. Eighteen were held in 1941 and 1942. A very great alleviation of our losses occurred up till December, 1941, and I was satisfied during 1942 that the organisation was running with complete smoothness and efficiency.

In October, 1942, I felt that a new additional effort was needed on account of the ever more important part which the air had begun to play in anti-U-boat warfare, and of the consequential and complicated technical developments of air weapons of all kinds. I therefore reconstructed the Battle of the Atlantic Committee in a new form and with a somewhat different grouping of Departments, under the title of the Anti-U-boat Warfare Committee. The first meeting of this Committee was held on 4th November. I asked the Minister of Aircraft Production, who at that time was Lord Privy Seal, to act as my Deputy on the Committee on account of the special aptitudes which he possesses in forming a sound lay opinion upon these highly technical issues. I invited Field-Marshal Smuts, who rightly realised the pressing importance of the U-boat war, to attend the second and third meetings of this Committee. Although the Committee had been set up before Field-Marshal Smuts's speech, to which reference has been made, and was not in fact due to any representations on his part, several important decisions were taken at the third meeting, and this is no doubt what he had in mind in the passage in question. In order that the Field-Marshal should be thoroughly acquainted with our machinery for combating U-boats, I arranged not only that he should attend the Committee but that he should visit the Admiralty and confer with the experts there both on the technical and tactical aspects. He was impressed with what he learnt, and has authorised me to say that he was satisfied with the character and efficiency of the system.

It is not usual to give the exact composition of Cabinet Committees, but I am willing, as it is not a formal Cabinet Committee (for others who are not Ministers are on it), and provided it is not taken as a precedent, to make an exception in this case. The members of the Committee are: —

The Prime Minister (in the Chair),

Minister of Aircraft Production (Deputy Chairman),

Minister of Production,

First Lord of the Admiralty,

Secretary of State for Air,

Minister of War Transport,

The First Sea Lord,

Chief of the Air Staff,

other technical advisers being present as required. The meetings normally take place once a week; so far there have been six of them, at all of which I have presided. It must not, however, be supposed that this Committee in any way supersedes or replaces the regular and systematic control of anti-U-boat warfare by the Admiralty.

There is no question of appointing a naval super-Commander-in-Chief under the Admiralty or a special Minister to deal with the anti-U-boat campaign. The war at sea is all one, and the Admiralty organisation has been adapted by continual improvement and refinement to deal with it as a whole. It would be impossible to disentangle the anti-U-boat warfare or its control from the general organisation, and I should not recommend any attempt to do so.

The Churchill Tank

A STATEMENT TO THE HOUSE OF COMMONS
DECEMBER 15, 1942

[December 15, 1942

In reply to a Member who asked for the names of the members of the Tank Board in the Summer of 1940, when the decision to produce the Churchill tank without trial was taken, the Prime Minister said: —

ON account of persistent mischievous attempts to undermine the confidence of the troops in these weapons, which play an important part in the defence of this Island, I propose to make a statement.

On 11th June, 1940, I summoned a meeting at which the following were present: —

Sir James Grigg, Permanent Under-Secretary of State for War.

Major-General L. Carr, Assistant Chief of the Imperial General Staff.

Mr. (now Sir R.) Sinclair, Director-General of Army Requirements.

Mr. Herbert Morrison, Minister of Supply.

Mr. P. F. Bennett, Director-General of Tanks and Transport, Ministry of Supply.

Sir Walter Layton, Director-General of Programmes, Ministry of Supply.

Brigadier J. S. Crawford, Director of Mechanisation, Ministry of Supply.

The object of the meeting was to consider our tank production programme. We had at that time in the hands of the troops in the United Kingdom less than 100 tanks. These and those under production at the time were of a type which had been proved in battle in France to be too weak to stand up to the German tank guns. Invasion of this country was expected, if not in the autumn of 1940, at any rate in the spring of 1941, or even in 1942. The problem, therefore, was to produce the maximum number of tanks of a sufficiently powerful kind for Home Defence. As a result of the meeting, I called for a plan which would provide 500 or 600 such tanks if possible by March, 1941; these were to be over and above the existing programme and were not to interfere with it.

The same people met again on 20th June, and considered a specification and preliminary production programme for the new heavy tank. I gave directions that the specification should be considered by the Tank Board, but that in the meanwhile all preparations for production should proceed. The Tank Board consisted at that time of the following: —

Sir Alexander Roger (Chairman).

Mr. Durrant (Chief Mechanical Engineer [Roads] London Passenger Transport Board, later Director of Tank Design).

Mr. Moyses (Birmingham Railway Carriage and Wagon Company, Limited).

Mr. Thompson (Secretary, Union of Shipbuilding and Engineering Draughtsmen).

Mr. Geoffrey Burton (Deputy Chairman, Daimler Company, and B.S.A., then newly appointed Director-General of Tanks and Transport, Ministry of Supply).

Major-General J. S. Crawford (Director of Mechanisation, Ministry of Supply).

Major-General Pope (Director of Armoured Fighting Vehicles, War Office).

Brigadier Pratt (Commander of the First Army Tank Brigade).

Major-General Pope, who was later unhappily killed in the Middle East, had been Senior Royal Armoured Corps Adviser to the Commander-in-Chief of the British Expeditionary Force in France, and Brigadier Pratt had commanded the First Army Tank Brigade in France; thus both had up-to-date experience of the conditions of modern war. Action proceeded accordingly.

On 20th July, we met again, Major-General Pope also being present. The Tank Board had approved the specifications subject to certain modifications, and it was agreed to go forward with the utmost rapidity with the production of what became known as the A.22 Tank. The General Staff expressed themselves entirely in favour of the project. Work proceeded with the utmost enthusiasm. We could not afford the time to carry out exhaustive trials with pilot models. This would have set us back at least six months; our paramount aim was to get the maximum number we could into the hands of the troops in 1941. The pilot model was running on 12 December, 1940. Production began to flow in May, 1941, and by the autumn 400 were available for battle.

Meanwhile, the German armies had been launched against Russia and the danger of invasion had lessened. The possibility of using the A.22 tank in an overseas offensive role was therefore considered, and modifications were introduced to make the tank more suitable for extended operations abroad. That winter we began re-working these tanks, and large numbers are now in a fit condition for use in the assault of strong positions for which their armour fits them. Reports have been received from the brigades in this country now armed with these tanks, which are on the whole strongly favourable. There are between one and two thousand in the hands of troops. They are said to be the best weapons yet received by the units concerned.

It will be seen that this tank was never intended for the fast-moving long-range warfare of the desert. However, a certain number were sent to the Middle East in the autumn of 1941 for trial. It will interest the House to hear that a small number took part in the attack on Rommel's lines at Alamein, and reports show that they gave a good account of themselves, and stood up to very heavy fire.

I am glad to have had this opportunity of informing the House of the history of this tank, and of publishing the names of those who took the bold decision to introduce it. No one would go back on that decision now. The A.22 is naturally surpassed by the latest types, but the production in large numbers in less than a year of an entirely new tank of much heavier pattern than anything we had before, and thoroughly capable of going into action in Home Defence, is highly creditable to the British engineering industry and to all concerned.

In reply to a Member who asked why the tank was called "the Churchill tank," the Prime Minister replied: —

I had no part in that decision, but I can well believe that the fact that it was called by this particular name afforded a motive to various persons to endeavour to cover it with their slime.

Messages

[*December 16, 1942*

[TO MR. MACKENZIE KING, PRIME MINISTER OF
CANADA, ON THE THIRD ANNIVERSARY OF
THE BRITISH COMMONWEALTH AIR
TRAINING PLAN]

IT is now three years since the British Commonwealth Air
Training Plan was born; when I look back at the remorseless
growth of the Air Forces of the United Nations and survey the
shattering punishment we have already begun to inflict upon the
enemy, I realise how much of our success is due to the great
scheme which has been so energetically developed in Canada.

Canadians in their thousands have answered the call of the
air, and they have been joined by other thousands of young men
from Australia, New Zealand, and the United Kingdom, from
the British Colonial Empire, and from Allied nations, who have
come to Canada for air training. They have thus taken their places
as highly skilled members of the Air Forces of the United Nations,
eager to come to grips with the enemy wherever he may be
found.

A very great effort has been required to maintain this unending
flow. The factories of Britain and the United States have contributed their share, and a vast mass of training aircraft and
equipment has been produced in the arsenals of Canada. On
her broad plains the airfields and great installations have been
spread out by Canadian labour, without whose enthusiastic
efforts the plan could never have been brought so swiftly and
successfully to its present stature.

Throughout these great movements of men and material, the
instructors and ground crews, though no less eager than their
comrades for a share of the fighting, have faithfully performed

their hard and unspectacular duties. They remain far removed from the excitement of battle; but their devoted and patient work, which will not be forgotten, is playing a vital part in our victory.

Time and again the scope of the plan has been enlarged. Not once have the high hopes raised at its inception been disappointed. This great joint effort by partners of the British Commonwealth, so ably administered by Canada, has succeeded because everyone engaged in it, from the highest to the lowest, was determined that it should succeed.

Our thanks are due to the Government and people of Canada, and especially to the officers and men of the Royal Canadian Air Force, who by their wholehearted endeavours have established the plan on a sure foundation, and from it are now forging a potent instrument of victory.

[December 17, 1942

[TO MR. MACKENZIE KING]

Please accept my warm greetings for your birthday and my best wishes for a victorious future. You have been a good friend and comrade in these tremendous times.

[December 21, 1942

[TELEGRAM SENT TO PREMIER STALIN ON HIS 63RD BIRTHDAY]

Please accept my best wishes and warm personal regards on your birthday. We are watching with admiration the magnificent offensives being carried out by the Red Army.

Beware of Logic!

[December 17, 1942

Replying to a Member who asked whether the titles of Minister of Defence and Secretary of State for War were logical and fitting at the present time, and suggested that they should be changed respectively to Minister for War and Secretary of State for the Army, the Prime Minister said: —

SIR, we must beware of needless innovation, especially when guided by logic.

Bonds with America

A MESSAGE TO PRESIDENT ROOSEVELT IN REPLY TO GREET-
INGS FROM THE UNITED STATES CONGRESS TO GREAT
BRITAIN'S ARMED FORCES
DECEMBER 25, 1942

December 6.   *Port of Dakar handed over for the use of the United Nations' Fleets.*

December 10.   *It was announced that the German prisoners in Britain and Canada, who had been manacled since October 10th, were to be unchained.*

December 11.   *President Roosevelt revealed that by the end of the year a million Americans would be fighting overseas.*

December 13.   *The Germans retired from their strong position at El Agheila and resumed their rapid retreat towards Tripolitania.*

December 15.   *Russians encircled large German forces in the Stalingrad sector.*

December 19.   *Russians in Voronezh area gained from 30 to 50 miles of territory and recaptured over 200 towns and villages.*

   British troops advanced into Burma from India.

December 24.   *Admiral Darlan was assassinated in Algiers.*

[*December 25, 1942*

I HAVE received the stirring message sent by you, Mr. President, at this season from Congress and on behalf of the people of the United States, and have arranged for its transmission to the armed forces of Great Britain on land and sea and in the air, in all parts of the Empire or in enemy territory. I know it would be their wish that I should cordially reciprocate these greetings.

During the past year we have welcomed ever growing forces from America in our ports and camps and on our airfields. In all theatres of operations men of America and men of Britain have fought side by side under each other's command as circumstances required. Bonds of respect, comprehension and comradeship have been forged which will, I pray, far outlive this war, and be a lasting support in the labours of peace, when, after we have won the victory, we strive to build together a better and a happier world.

378